Window Shopping with Helen Keller

∴

Window Shopping with Helen Keller

∴

ARCHITECTURE AND DISABILITY
IN MODERN CULTURE

David Serlin

THE UNIVERSITY OF CHICAGO PRESS

CHICAGO AND LONDON

The University of Chicago Press, Chicago 60637
The University of Chicago Press, Ltd., London
© 2025 by The University of Chicago
Published 2025
Printed in the United States of America

34 33 32 31 30 29 28 27 26 25   1 2 3 4 5

ISBN-13: 978-0-226-74896-2 (cloth)
ISBN-13: 978-0-226-74897-9 (paper)
ISBN-13: 978-0-226-83458-0 (e-book)
DOI: https://doi.org/10.7208/chicago/9780226834580.001.0001

Library of Congress Cataloging-in-Publication Data

Names: Serlin, David, author.
Title: Window shopping with Helen Keller : architecture and disability in modern culture / David Serlin.
Other titles: Architecture and disability in modern culture
Description: Chicago : The University of Chicago Press, 2025. | Includes bibliographical references and index.
Identifiers: LCCN 2024032684 | ISBN 9780226748962 (cloth) | ISBN 9780226748979 (paperback) | ISBN 9780226834580 (ebook)
Subjects: LCSH: Merrick, Joseph Carey, 1862–1890. | Keller, Helen, 1880–1968. | United States. Work Projects Administration. | Illinois Regional Library for the Blind and Physically Handicapped. | Architecture—Human factors—History. | Architecture—Human factors—Case studies. | People with disabilities—History—19th century. | People with disabilities—History—20th century.
Classification: LCC NA2545.A1 S47 2025 | DDC 306.4/7—dc23/eng/20240821
LC record available at https://lccn.loc.gov/2024032684

for Brian Selznick
casa mia e cuore mio

and

for Doug Mitchell (1943–2019)
friend, editor, bon vivant

I'm troubled that a society which so greedily consumes the posters of charity forgets to ask itself questions about its consequences, its uses, and its limits. And I begin to wonder if the lovely and touching iconography . . . is not the alibi by which a sizable part of the nation authorizes itself, once again, to substitute the signs of charity for the reality of justice.

—Roland Barthes, "Iconography of Abbé Pierre" (1955)

Contents

Introduction

In the October 1931 issue of *La Construction moderne*, a biweekly French architectural journal, readers were treated to a glimpse of a new house built in Paris's 14th arrondissement by Jean-Julien Lemordant, a celebrated painter and decorated veteran who had been blinded during the Great War (see figure I.1). Lemordant built the house for himself and his family on a jagged and impossibly narrow shard of property he purchased in 1927 on the avenue Parc de Montsouris (now the avenue René Coty). Supervised and executed over several years in collaboration with local architect Henri Jean Launay, the project as conceived by Lemordant was a four-story concrete and steel structure giving the appearance of an Art Deco ocean liner, intended to invoke the waterfronts of his seaside hometown of Saint-Malo in the Brittany region of northern France. In one extended passage, journalist Antony Goissaud described the process by which the painter used his sense of touch to translate his understanding of the site's specifications into the material design of the building:

> Thanks to the knowledge [Lemordant] had about the very irregular ground soil and the shape and size of each one of the many designed floors . . . [he] was able to approximately outline the drawing plans of all the house floors, including the ground. On the basis of Lemordant's data [Launay] drew the plans, which were later completed with some wooden strips glued on the lay-out of all the house walls, including the partition ones. By simply touching these strips, Lemordant was able to assess his work and change it accordingly, understanding which parts could work and which had to change in order to better fulfill the purposes he had in mind, be they aesthetic or functional. In the final version of the approved plans, Lemordant illustrated how he wanted the projection of the façades, the openings, and the balconies to be simple and modern. . . . [and] some [models] were also made especially for this. Lemordant analyzed the dummies by touching them and then modified them accordingly.[1]

Chevojon, Phot.

HÔTEL PARTICULIER POUR UN ARTISTE PEINTRE, 58, AVENUE DE MONTSOURIS, A PARIS.
FAÇADE SUR L'AVENUE : JEAN-JULIEN LEMORDANT, Architecte.

(Constructions particulières.)   La Construction Moderne N° 1 (Page 8).

FIGURE I.1. Photograph of a clean, white building with multiple floors, each of which has distinctive windows that are either square or rectangular. The façade of the building looks like that of a modern steamship; the perspective of the photograph is that of a pedestrian or automobile passenger who is moving by it. This is the house designed by the blind painter Jean-Julien Lemordant and architect Henri Jean Launay, which still stands at 50, avenue René Coty, Paris. Photograph by Studio Chevojon and published in the French architecture journal *La Construction moderne* 47, no. 1 (October 4, 1931): 8. Reprinted with permission of Bernard Chevojon.

In addition to translating Lemordant's drawings and tactile "dummies" of walls into "aesthetic" and "functional" layouts, Launay also fulfilled Lemordant's requests for modern conveniences, including two elevators (one for passengers, one for freight), central heating, a functional garage for two automobiles, and an internal telephone system that allowed family members to communicate across its multiple floors. He also helped Lemordant realize the house's most distinguished physical feature: a two-story artist's atelier that gave Lemordant complete privacy since it would be connected by a staircase to his bedroom one floor above and so would not disturb any other members of the household.

A little more than twenty miles northwest of chez Lemordant stands another modern house with a far more famous pedigree. The Villa Savoye, built between 1928 and 1931 and co-designed by famed French architect Le Corbusier (Charles Jeanneret) and his brother, Pierre Jeanneret, in the leafy suburb of Poissy on the outskirts of Paris, is usually regarded as one of the most influential works of Western architecture of the first half of the twentieth century (see figure I.2). Le Corbusier and Jeanneret were inspired by the aesthetic of industrial buildings, which manifested in unusual choices such as an unbroken band of windows emulating those of factories, or metal balustrades emulating ship railings. The structure's multiple layers are connected vertically by way of an undulating central staircase and a narrow ramp that moves inside and outside the house to facilitate what Le Corbusier famously called the *promenade architecturale*. This was his philosophy that in experiencing the "itinerary" of a building, a visitor should move through different levels of spatial and aesthetic awareness that are mediated by vistas that continually surprise and uplift the architectural experience. A *promenade architecturale* through a building is not exclusively visual, of course.[2] But for Le Corbusier and his aesthetic adherents, the villa's ramp is the unfolding drama of space through mobility as organized around the visual, enabling a slow and controlled set of encounters revealing the different spaces through which the wholeness of Le Corbusier's architectural vision can become evident (see figure I.3).

Why do we know so much about the Villa Savoye while we know virtually nothing about chez Lemordant? The short answer may be that the Villa Savoye, which helped crystallize Le Corbusier's international reputation, has been part of the canon of modern architecture for nearly a century, whereas Lemordant's house is remembered—if it is remembered at all—as a footnote to his painting career. Of course, Lemordant's wealth made it possible for him, working with Launay, to achieve his aesthetic ambitions in the same way that Le Corbusier and Jeanneret were able to achieve theirs for *la famille Savoye*. When Lemordant's architectural achievement was

FIGURE I.2. Photograph of a clean, white, horizontally square building on an open plot of land surrounded by trees. The second floor, which has large, thin rectangular windows around the perimeter of the building, creates a portico on the first floor that is supported by thin columns. This is the Villa Savoye, designed by famed French architect Le Corbusier (Charles Jeanneret) and his brother, Pierre Jeanneret, between 1928 and 1931, for the Savoye family, in Poissy, a suburb of Paris. Photograph c. 2015 by Adaptor-Plug and reprinted with permission CC BY-NC 2.0. https://creativecommons.org/licenses/by-nc/2.0/.

discussed the following year in the high-end Belgian design journal *La Cité & tekhne* (1932), however, images of the house and its atelier were inserted into an issue on the theme of hospital architecture, a reminder that the private lives of people with disabilities were routinely associated with modern medical care rather than with modern aesthetics.[3]

For some readers of *La Construction moderne*, Lemordant's extravagant atelier may have come across as an ironic feature of the house since it juxtaposed soaring ceilings and abundant light—the ingredients of an ideal artist's studio—with the perceived limitations of the "blind artist" who would not be able to use or appreciate them. But there was nothing ironic or arch about the presentation of the house. This may be because news of Lemordant's house arrived during a moment when both state-run veterans' agencies and private charities were distributing other technology-oriented forms of support to blind veterans that included radios, telephones, record players, and Braille books and newspapers.[4] In the hierarchy of disability, blind veterans were often privileged over other people with disabilities, in-

FIGURE I.3. Photograph of a ramp inclining upward with a dark handrail on the left side and a blank white wall on the right side. The continuation of the ramp can be seen at the upper left above the dark handrail. This is the ramp built for the Villa Savoye, which functions like a staircase and enables a user to move between levels of the house (see figure I.2). Le Corbusier called this ramp a *promenade architecturale*, designed to give users an experience of movement and discovery that was central to his idea of a new type of architecture: a "machine for living in." Photograph c. 2015 by Adaptor-Plug and reprinted with permission CC BY-NC 2.0. https://creativecommons.org/licenses/by-nc/2.0/.

cluding disabled veterans, since they were regarded as capable of learning trades and becoming productive economic agents.[5] They occupied a status distinct from their counterparts with physical or psychological disabilities, many of whom had difficulty securing employment after the war and were considered a burden on the state, a concern shared by France and other European nations following the global economic depression of the early 1930s. No matter how it was framed, Lemordant's atelier was as central to his understanding of what a house could be for a person with disabilities as any other feature of the architectural type that the French call a *hôtel particulier*.

Lemordant's house and the Villa Savoye were equally revolutionary for the ways that their architects imagined the user, how they imagined the concept of home, how they used modern elements, how they presented architecture as the medium through which the sensuous body moves. What makes Lemordant's house distinct, though, is not just its design per se; rather, it is that its creator used a design process proportionate to how a person with visual impairments—and, not insignificantly, with ample resources—fashioned a space that centered his own subjective needs as a blind person. Whereas the Villa Savoye is a magnificent example of Le Corbusier's *promenade architecturale* that facilitates new ways of experiencing domestic spaces by sighted users, Lemordant's house makes possible recognizable arrangements of domestic space that are not oriented primarily around a *promenade architecturale*. Instead, the house is spatially oriented in ways that extend and enhance the experiences of a user who does not depend on sight as their primary mode of engaging with the world. Yet the Villa Savoye is the one that is remembered or taught—a status that continues to be replicated across the curricula of architecture schools and the pages of coffee-table books alike. How much more instructive and powerful would it be if chez Lemordant were taught alongside the Villa Savoye as an example of the capacity of early twentieth-century architects to change the ways we think about the effect of modern design on modern forms of domestic life?

Jean-Julien Lemordant's house is one of the many examples I use in this book to examine how people with visual, hearing, and/or mobility impairments engaged proactively with architecture and urban spaces in the decades before the disability rights movement of the late 1960s mandated the earliest and now familiar accommodations for people with disabilities. The chapters in this book do not trace the histories of wheelchair ramps, lift bars in bathroom stalls, vibrating crosswalk buttons, teletype machines, or chirping elevators—tools of access that made accommodations for differential bodily experiences a mainstream legal and social concern.[6] Perhaps you are reading this book on a tablet with adjustable font sizes, or you are listening to it through voice-activated software—tools of access that were galvanized by the legal and commercial successes of the disability rights movement.[7] The chapters in this book ask historical, political, and aesthetic questions about the experiences of people with disabilities—some like Lemordant, others completely unlike him—in the built environment in the century before the disability rights movement, deploying the tools of critical disability studies, sensory studies, media archaeology, and urban anthropology to do so. In unearthing new stories or reexamining familiar ones, my goal is to put people like Jean-Julien Lemordant at the generative center of modern culture rather than assuming (as far too many do) that their sensory or physical or cognitive disabilities precluded them from navigating the multimodal machinations of modern culture. *Window Shopping with Helen Keller* is not intended as a historical "recovery" project per se that seeks to insert people with disabilities into preexisting histories of modernity. Rather, it is intended to reassess those preexisting histories of modernity by reckoning with those physical, sensory, or cognitive modalities that do not depend on sight, hearing, or mobility, the conventional and nondisabled[8] signposts for what it has meant to be urban and modern in historical perspective and in the contemporary world.

∵

Architecture designed for or by people with disabilities often gets short shrift from academics, practitioners, and the public—not because such works of architecture are deemed uninteresting or unimportant but because they often carry an implicit message: *Those* buildings are about *those* people, not about *us*. Even when historically significant works of architecture designed for people with chronic health issues are discussed—Josef Hoffmann's Purkersdorf Sanatorium (Vienna, Austria, 1904), for instance, or Alvar Aalto's Paimio Sanatorium (Paimio, Finland, 1930)—they are invariably treated as "specific" (or, worse, "special") when compared to putatively "universal" masterpieces such as the Villa Savoye.[9] In *Civic Training* (1936), a social studies textbook used in US junior high school classrooms through the 1950s, a photograph depicting young, cheerful white boys and girls in wheelchairs or in beds on casters posed on a sun porch at the Pennsylvania State Hospital for Crippled Children in Elizabethtown offers the following caption: "You wouldn't want to be one of these children; nevertheless, they are getting the benefit of sunshine and the best of care."[10] The assumption that no child at the hospital could be one of the book's readers—indeed, that no one reading such a textbook could themselves have a disability— captures how notions of inclusion and exclusion were imparted in previous generations: not only through paternalistic declarations of pity but through the spatial distinctions associated with civic institutions like hospitals (for *those* children) and public schools (for children *like us*).

For design historians like Margaret Campbell, there was a direct line of influence from designing hospitals for patients to designing houses for non-disabled consumers in the cities and suburbs; as Campbell writes, hospital architecture "was the forerunner for an important modernist design solution to make [a] small house or flat appear larger . . . By the 1930s, these external features of modernism were commonplace in low and high rise blocks of flats . . . in social housing . . . and [in] municipal housing schemes."[11] The directional emphasis of these designs is revealing; rather than disability being honored as constitutive of modernism, it was regarded as evidence of modernism's ever-unfolding and always adaptable capacities. Aalto's designs for tuberculosis patients, which included wood-and-steel chairs that can be found in many modern design collections around the world, may be beautiful, but they were always about *those* people, not about *us*. Such a division between *us* and *them* prevents nondisabled historians and practitioners of architecture from stepping back and thinking about *those* buildings not as special needs or tangents but as central to definitions of modern architecture and, indeed, modern culture. The late, great Bruno Latour had it right as usual: we are methodologically hamstrung by historical categories that replicate the same narratives over and over again.

In this book, I argue that there is empirical and representational evidence of an adjacent universe in which architects and designers in the nineteenth and twentieth centuries took a keen interest in the embodied experiences of people with disabilities. Some, like Jean-Julien Lemordant, had the opportunity to parlay their experience directly into a form that met their own needs. Others became increasingly sensitive to experiences like Lemordant's and used them to manifest new ways of thinking about architecture and space. These were not merely accommodative or inclusive designs created to meet legal benchmarks, because such benchmarks did not exist until 1968.[12] Rather, they were benchmarks of design experimentation that were motivated by the desire to help people with disabilities begin to imagine ways of living in a world that so clearly was not designed with them in mind.

If one measures successful architecture only by the intentions of the designer and not by the experiences of the user, then one is willfully and brazenly ignoring what a user's perspective can lend not only to the *utility* of the design but also to its *meaning*. The empathic US architect Louis Kahn once famously anthropomorphized common building materials and declared that "ordinary brick . . . wants to be something better than it is," a wry way of reminding architects that, as with the materials they choose, they also have the capacity to make buildings better for the people who use them.[13] In 2019, students using the new addition to the Fine Arts Library at Cornell University protested the design by the architect Wolfgang Tschapeller, an open-stack structure of bookshelves folded into a scaffolding of slotted steel platforms in an enormous, hangar-like space. Tschapeller had already declared that in his design "everything is scaled to the book. As a human, you are not the main character, you are a guest between the books."[14] But human students using the library quickly discovered that the platforms, which enabled air and light to circulate in between levels, had also inadvertently enabled some patrons to stare up the dresses and skirts of users standing above them, while those wearing high heels or using mobility devices feared getting stuck between the slots. What was Tschapeller's response to the platforms' spatially sanctioned voyeurism? He declared that any alterations to his design would "literally destroy the project" and urged library patrons "to respect each other and not look up."[15]

Sadly, the case of the Fine Arts Library is far from unique. As disability scholar and theorist Aimi Hamraie has shown, when architects and designers do try to anticipate user experiences, they frequently do so by imagining uncritically, using nondisabled generic "types" rather a range of bodies.[16] The anthropometric measurements of the body for creating design standards, put forward by twentieth-century designers like Le Corbusier and Henry Dreyfus, were themselves drawn from normative standards, such as those developed by the US military during the two world wars. Seventy years later, as architectural historian Wanda Liebermann has shown, such design standards are treated as inviolable within design curricula in architecture schools throughout the world.[17] It does not have to be this way. As geographer Rob Imrie has observed:

> What I find frustrating is that there are data available about the interrelationships between senses, spaces, and practice, yet much of it is ignored, sidelined, or rendered as irrelevant by design practitioners. [The] need to "mainstream" knowledge of/about the body as a precursor to non-ableist practices emerging . . . will involve professionals' exposure to a range of learning environments.[18]

Having faith in the existence of normative body types may give off the comforting feel of objectivity, but it is only an affirmation of the status quo. Its power lay in its capacity to be rhetorically loaded while masquerading as commonsensical and noncontroversial. It is so much easier to design if one is committed to the presumptive ideal of a normative user—designing for nondisabled white cisgender men and women of average height and weight, for instance—rather than being committed to challenging such ideals or exploring the experiences of users whose bodies do not comply with or which are statistically or institutionally illegible to mainstream design practices.[19]

Recognizing that people with disabilities already carry a priori knowledge in their bodies shifts the focus away from thinking about architecture as a tool of managing or leveling difference and toward thinking about how architecture can be aligned with, rather than in opposition to, embodied subjectivities. Architectural historian Catherine Ingraham has asserted that "while historically our dwelling places have appeared to serve as the static ground for the variability of our biocultural lives—our 'permanent address,' so to speak—it may be that this stasis or constancy actually has been supplied by *a biological homeostasis*, not an architectural one."[20] The consequences of this recognition for architectural practice are enormous and demand a recalibration of the presumptions about the body that architects and urban planners take for granted. As architectural historian and disability theorist David Gissen has observed, "The 'failures' of the body/space interaction . . . always fall back either on the 'disabled' person or the 'larger social' milieu in which disability appears rather than calling into question the failures of the architect or of particular theories of architecture"—an observation that captures fully the discrepancy between Wolfgang Tschapeller's ambitions for the Fine Arts Library at Cornell University and how users of that library actually experienced it.[21]

One of the grand narratives of disability history written since the 1970s is that architecture has been transformed from being an oppressive enemy of people with disabilities to being an empowering tool of people with disabilities. This narrative shares many features, both explicitly and implicitly, with those deployed by the civil rights movement of the 1950s and 1960s as well as movements for postcolonial independence and human liberation after World War Two. In all cases, architecture, as a material and political medium used to segregate, discipline, and control bodies, became a medium that could be used to provide access, enfranchisement, and equality. The seductiveness of this narrative is that architecture itself becomes, in effect, a medium of accessing civil protections and achieving personhood in the modern era. Rights, access, and enfranchisement are all operationalized through the medium of architecture. For activists in the 1960s and 1970s who fought for disability rights alongside other civil protections, changes to laws regarding architectural accommodation in public and commercial spaces were evidence that the social model of disability—the concept that obstacles to access were located in the environment and not in the body of the individual—was not an abstract social or legal concept but one that could be made material. Overcoming environmental and technological obstacles was the common struggle, not subjecting people with disabilities to the earnest fantasies of nondisabled wholeness in which they were rescued or rehabilitated by well-meaning experts. In these ways, the emphasis on social and structural change over individual and bodily change conferred a power upon architecture as a singular medium of change that treats the pre–disability rights "past" and the post–disability rights "future" with a reductive simplicity in which the prefixes *pre-* and *post-* signify a distinction brought about by new spatial and legal authorities given to the built environment.

Yet such neat bifurcations hardly begin to capture the complex, and arguably uneven, relationships to architecture that people with disabilities have had, which go way beyond its status as either a medium of physical and aesthetic liberation or a medium of physical and aesthetic control. For every story about how modern architecture's innovative use of materials and forms introduced abundant light and space, or transformed urban scale and density, or was compared with other aesthetic innovations in photography, cinema, sculpture, or choreography there is a parallel story of how those same materials and forms were put to tyrannical ends by the controlling machinations of physicians, therapists, fascist dictators, and colonial administrators seeking to shape the minds and bodies of those over whom they wielded professional authority and, in many cases, the power of life and death (see figure I.4). Which stories about architecture should we tell? Which stories should we teach? Some believe that we should separate these stories, distinguishing aesthetic form from political function (or its lack thereof), while others believe we should tell these stories together. Admitting that there is more than one texture in the fabric does not make the dominant textures any less present or the experience of feeling it any less significant.

While I was working on this book, sometimes I would refer to it as "an architectural prehistory of the Americans with Disabilities Act"; not only was it a convenient shorthand phrase (as one often seeks out while working on a project that is difficult to explain) but also it was the most immediate way to convey what I was trying to explore, even though the historical scope and thematic content of these chapters are much broader than the United States. Many of my colleagues, friends, and former students in disability history, architectural history, and design history—a coterie of like-minded souls including Jos Boys, Ignacio Galán, David Gissen, Elizabeth Guffey, Aimi Hamraie, Sara Hendren, Louise Hickman, Rob Imrie, Wanda Katja Liebermann, Laura Mauldin, Katherine Ott, Barbara Penner, Graham Pullin, Jaipreet Vardi, and Bess Williamson—have devoted their careers to plumbing these depths across a number of domains and disciplines. In this book, however, I focus less on legal or technological innovations related to accessibility and more on the subjective experiences of individuals whose needs were spatially and affectively considered outside any immediate framework for creating accessibility. Turning from questions of access to questions of subjectivity is in no way intended to diminish the life-changing work of disability rights activists both in the United States and around the world who have fought for, and won, enforcement of spatial accommodations and helped to create opportunities for people with disabilities—the basis for creating a just world that can be, and should be, equitably designed. It is to suggest there are ways of historicizing architecture and design that do not follow the watershed achievements of accessibility. The distinction I make in this book is not between accessible and inaccessible or equitable and inequitable uses of architecture or space. Rather, I engage

FIGURE 1.4. Diagram c. 1922 of a long rectangular building organized around a central communal area and broken up into smaller rooms that are all labeled by their intended diagnostic use. This is the examination building used by the administrators and judges of "Fitter Families" contests, which operated at the Kansas Free Fair in Topeka throughout the 1920s. Buildings like this one, which were designed and built for similar contests around the country, were a critical part of the US eugenics movement since the staff not only examined and measured adults and children who competed in the contests but also compiled statistical data and photographic studies. Reprinted with permission of the American Philosophical Society.

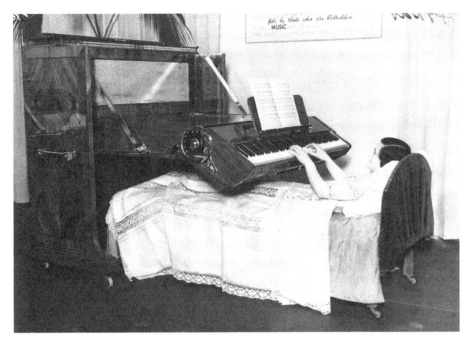

FIGURE I.5. Photograph of a large upright piano on casters with its front and top cabinet doors open exposing a piano keyboard that is extended out as if it were a convertible desktop. The weight of the keyboard is supported by two long steel arms and a round axle mechanism that allows the keyboard to be tilted at a downward angle. A young white woman with a sleek short haircut is in a bed that has been slid underneath the extended part of the piano. The woman's head and neck are propped on pillows, which allows her to extend her hands out in front of her so she can reach the piano keys and read sheet music. Above her is a sign that says, by using this piano, music can be "felt by those who are Bedridden." Photograph taken at a trade show in England, c. 1935. Reprinted with permission of Album / Alamy Stock Photo.

with historical examples of architecture and design that addressed the potential for disabled subjectivities to transform how people imagined architecture and design in the first place.

In the mid-1930s, for example, a female model working at a trade show in London gave a public demonstration of how to play a piano in bed while sitting up in bed (see figure I.5). Although we know next to nothing about the designer or manufacturer of the piano, it was being promoted as a convertible piano for users who were "bedridden." The design intervention here is not a formal reinvention of the piano; instead, it takes the frame of the piano, an otherwise horizontal object, and tilts it forty-five degrees in order to make it accessible to someone with a limited range of vertical movement. The design does build upon the user's desire for physical access to an object, but it also aligns it with a user's sensuous relationship to an object, a potent reminder that not all inventions or design experiments were focused on facilitating access for the purposes of communication or transportation. Of course, pianos are not common objects, and were typically the provenance of a middle-class household. But for those who could afford a piano, it provided a new way of imagining leisure activity that did not require learning an instrument with normative expectations of use already embedded in its design.

As with many of the buildings and objects that will be discussed throughout this book, the piano belongs to a list of improvised alternatives to conventional designs that were created to hold the subjective experience of the user in mind. Such designs start from the proposition that a user may have needs outside of their identity as a patient. It is an object drawn from the history of disability, but it is not an object of medical care. It is an object of self-realization, forged in the crucible of the early twentieth century when the multisensory and multimodal experiences of people with disabilities were activated in order to transform their own relationships to architecture and space. They may have lived in a broader world that was decidedly not designed for them, but, as I will demonstrate, many lived in and among people who acknowledged their capacities more often than the extant historical record has led us to believe.

∴

In his epic work of modernist literature, *À la recherche du temps perdu* (1922), the French queer author Marcel Proust asserts that the invention of the novel is what, finally, enables us to know people in a way that empirical experience cannot offer.

> None of the feelings which the joys or misfortunes of a 'real' person awaken in us can be awakened except through a mental picture [provided by the novel] of those joys or misfortunes ... A 'real' person, profoundly as we may sympathise with him, is in a great measure perceptible only through our senses, that is to say, he remains opaque, offers a dead weight which our sensibilities have not the strength to lift.[22]

The idea that "knowing" a person through narrative form might be preferable to "knowing" a person empirically through human encounters—someone whose "real" life will always be "opaque" or a "dead weight"—may be characteristic of Proust's particular elevation of art as a substitute for the real, particularly his interest in how narrative transforms questions of time and memory and reflection. But Proust's observation is not just an aesthetic claim. It is in fact an epistemological claim, one that privileges a structured narrative over unstructured sensory experience. *How* one claims to know or understand a person in the world—or how one believes that one *can* know and, by extension, master knowledge of a person or the world—is entirely dependent on *how* we engage with other people and the world on our respective epistemological journeys.

Nearly thirty years ago, the pioneering disability activist and theorist Simi Linton observed that "one research domain that is yet to be fully explored from the perspective of disabled people is the kinesthetic, proprioceptive, sensory, and cognitive experiences of people with an array of disabilities."[23] This is because, until the efforts of activists like Linton, the identities of people with disabilities were routinely hitched to a medical model of disability that was forged in a dualistic epistemology—a binary formulation in which there was, on the one side, a medical *authority*, and a medical *beneficiary* on the other side. Medical doctors, rehabilitation experts, and clinical administrators—as well as family members, some with the best of intentions—not only held legal authority over people with disabilities but made life decisions for them. The disability rights movement's insistence on legal recognition and social autonomy, as illustrated by activists' phrase "nothing about us without us," challenged the presumptive inevitability of this binary formulation.

Yet this dualistic approach does not begin to characterize the multiple and often asymmetrical relationships that people with disabilities have had with the architectural or spatial contexts they use or encounter, whether on their own or in tandem with others. An example: one can't talk about an urban subject (for instance, a pedestrian) without also talking about the type of mobility or navigation (for instance, walking or seeing) that has been presumptively embedded into the built environment (for instance, the sidewalk) as a spatial object. A sidewalk is not a neutral piece of urban infrastructure; as Susan Schweik has shown, it is an object that emerged historically from the creation of municipal governments that sought to maintain public spaces as efficient zones of transit and consumption unsullied by prostitutes, vagrants, and the "unsightly" people with disabilities.[24] The controlling interests of urban planners may have wanted to limit who gets to access the sidewalk; in terms of its design, however, a sidewalk has never structurally precluded a person with physical or sensory impairments from using it if their preferred type of movement or navigation substitutes one modality (a wheelchair, a white cane) for its normative counterpart (legs, roller skates).

The sidewalk as a spatial object may play a significant role in the story of exclusionary city planning, but the fact of its existence is only one part of the story of urban modernity. Indeed, the sidewalk is a good object for Linton's call for a more engaged, multimodal research practice. The sidewalk became ground zero for disability rights activists in cities like Berkeley and Denver who used sledgehammers to introduce the curb cut as a new type of spatial object for navigating the urban environment before accessible sidewalks were mandated by law.[25] The subjective experience of the sidewalk by the urban subject who uses a wheelchair or white cane, or who descends from the sidewalk at the curb cut, is not a "degraded" version of mobility or navigation any more than reading Proust in Braille is not a degraded version of the experience of that modernist work of art. Here the sidewalk offers a disability-oriented widening and deepening of feminist historian of science Donna Haraway's concept of "situated knowledges," which considers the "partial perspectives" and discrepant subjectivities of all of the entities— including not only the humans but the sidewalk and the wheelchair and the sledgehammer and legal apparatus—involved in an encounter or form of practice.[26]

Thinking about urban subjects and spatial objects and multimodal encounters has had a profound effect on the theoretical and methodological approaches to disability and architecture deployed in this book. Architectural theorists attuned to the empathic dimensions of spatial experience such as Kimberley Dovey, Karen Franck, Juhani Pallasmaa, and Peter Zumthor have advocated for many years an "architecture from the inside out" (to quote the title of one of Franck's books) that begins with the belief that *all* bodies are nonmodal, neither "special" nor "different" as our language tends to be oriented.[27] But disability does in fact expose the ways which the urban subject—presumptively pristine, unblemished, in full control of their abilities—is as much a social fantasy as that of universal humanism or whiteness or heterosexuality, themselves culpable fantasies of a seemingly natural, coherent, and unchanging urbanity. Such insights, and many others in the pages to follow, have helped me conceptualize histories of disability, architecture, and urban culture in more expansive ways than I could have ever anticipated.

Twenty years ago, for instance, when I first encountered a photograph (see figure I.6) of Helen Keller and her secretary, Polly Thomson, window shopping on the Champs-Élysées in January 1937—yet another scene of Parisian consumption from the 1930s not too far removed from those of chez Lemordant or the Villa Savoye—my impulse was to treat it as an object of visual culture.[28] As a historian trained to analyze and interpret media objects, I examined the photograph in the context of when it first appeared, relating it to other forms of media consumption of the era—how

FIGURE I.6. Photograph of two elegantly dressed white women wearing hats and heavy winter coats who are facing toward a shop window displaying women's dresses, blouses, and hats. This is Helen Keller, on the left, and Polly Thomson, on the right, window shopping on the avenue des Champs-Élysées in Paris. Keller is smiling and using her right hand to finger-spell a message into Thomson's right hand. Photograph taken January 30, 1937, for the French evening newspaper *Le Soir*. Reprinted with permission of Bettmann / Getty Images.

it compares to similar images, for instance, or how readers may have responded to it, or how news agencies might have picked it up and circulated it around the world. It hadn't yet occurred to me to try to discern what was actually happening *in* the photograph beyond the ways that it confirmed or challenged taxonomies or practices of disability representation. When I encounter the photograph now, I believe that I am bearing witness to numerous complex modalities revealing a triangular set of relationships involving Helen Keller, Polly Thomson, and a display made for window shopping on a busy street in Paris. Thomson may serve as a recognizable facilitator between the external world and the inner subjectivity of her companion, just as the window facilitates Thomson's gaze and Keller's affective response to it. But Keller is not passively receiving information here; with a broad smile on her face, she is proactively signing into Thomson's hand. Thus, the photograph is not merely a document of two American women traipsing down the Champs-Élysées on a cold January afternoon, or a moment of conspicuous consumption by the world's most famous deafblind woman. Rather, it is a document of multimodal communication frozen in time, a co-created multisensory experience between two people in situ. Indeed, it is more than a multimodal triangle. It is also a rectangular conversation between Keller, Thomson, a window display, and me: a queer middle-aged academic who identifies as neuro-atypical, whose brain processes information in a specific way.

Coordinating her experiences with a sighted companion like Polly Thomson—or Anne Sullivan Macy, her famous mentor and companion before Sullivan's untimely death in 1936—was not the only means by which Keller moved through the world, of course. Keller reveled in her time alone and used the written word to characterize her sensual impressions of people and places in the urban environment. Touching her hand to the plate-glass windows of the Empire State Building, or stroking the face of a world leader, or feeling the bodies of professional dancers in the company of choreographer Martha Graham, were mainstays in the media's repertoire of representing a person for whom there was no celebrity equal. In images like figure I.7, taken from footage shot for the 1954 documentary *The Unconquered: Helen Keller in Her Story*, the camera bears witness to Keller's subjective experience taking shape at a particular juncture of space and in time—drinking coffee with friends at a café on the Île de la Cité, the central island in the Seine, while touring the city. Whether in the 1930s or the 1950s or even today, Paris remains a place where the effects of modernity (economic, industrial, political, architectural) have dramatically shaped the built environment. But it has also served as a seedbed for billions of subjective encounters and autonomous choices that are responses to those same effects of modernity. And in the middle of it all is Helen Keller, whose sensory experiences enabled her own version of urban modernity on a sunny day in Paris in late June 1952.

To identify Keller as "deafblind" is not an inaccurate statement. At the same time, to say she was "a person with disabilities" is not to describe what *she* experienced but to use the word "disability" as a boundary object that prevents a nondisabled person from understanding Keller's subjective experience of the world on her own terms. Keller had faint memories of vision and hearing from "before" she contracted scarlet fever at the age of two, and these hovered in her consciousness like a dream. But rather than tantalizing her with examples of a nondisabled life "before," those memories became a kind of reverse translational device for people who are sighted and/or hearing. Memories drawn from experience (the color of the sky, the sound of the rain) and empirical evidence experienced in the moment (the feel of the humidity in the atmosphere surrounding her, the taste of rain in her

FIGURE I.7. Film still of a white man (left) and two white women at a restaurant table drinking coffee. The woman in the center is Helen Keller; the unknown male guest is to her right, and Polly Thomson is to her left. The friends are sitting at L'Auberge du Vert Galant, a restaurant formerly located at 42, Quai des Orfèvres on the Île de la Cité, the ancient island in the center of Paris. Outtake c. late June 1952 shot by Jacques Letellier for *The Unconquered: Helen Keller in Her Story*, the documentary film directed by Nancy Hamilton (1954), and for which Hamilton won the 1956 Academy Award for Best Documentary Film. Reprinted courtesy of the Helen Keller Archives, American Foundation for the Blind, and the Nancy Hamilton Papers, Sophia Smith Collection, Smith College.

mouth) were twin vectors of her understanding. For Keller, such modalities were not "compensatory," a word that, like "disability," often centers the experience of a nondisabled person who can understand the world only through the comparative metaphor of compensation. They were simply the available tools she used to navigate the world. Access to the modalities of sight, hearing, and mobility may preserve the illusion that autonomy depends on a state of nondisability. Keller's activities challenge that illusion by foregrounding modalities like touch and smell that call into question the boundaries between autonomy and dependence, between self and other, between subject and object.[29]

Clearly, any attempt to historicize the self is never a project about its isolated singularity but about its relational encounters with people and things in the world. As anthropologist François Laplantine has written, when we talk about "people and things," we are not just talking about a subject and "an *object* (be it sonorous, tasteful, colored)"; we are talking about "the necessarily unstable *relationship* a subject entertains with objects (as well as other subjects), in an experience that is itself singular and rarely reproducible."[30] This is why concepts with great currency in critical disability studies—the ideas of "Deaf gain" and "disability conservation" put forward by scholars such as H-Dirksen L. Bauman and Joseph J. Murray and Rosemarie Garland-Thomson—are such needed correctives.[31] Projects like Bauman's DeafSpace, which advocates for an architecture based on how D/deaf people subjectively experience space, is not merely an abstract call to insert people with hearing impairments into existing structures that leave the rest of the built environment intact. Rather, it is a call to reimagine (and, in some cases, raze) existing structures (spatial, social, communicative) in order to move beyond models of compliance and accommodation and, instead, hold architects and designers to a higher standard of social and ethical accountability. They ask why and in what ways we—not just *those* people, but all of us—gain collectively when our subjective differences are not only honored but conserved. They inform and renew the ethical claims with which we co-construct the worlds we inhabit. When we affirm that each person does indeed experience their own version of modernity differently, we are all intimately changed. "Our relation to others," Michel de Certeau plaintively asserted more than a half-century ago, "modified by our realization of this process of cultural leveling, transforms our relation to ourselves."[32]

∵

Each of the chapters as well as the epilogue in this book explores a different way of thinking about the multimodal relationships that some people with disabilities have had with architectural or urban spaces that, as I will show, shaped them as much as their experiences shaped the meaning of those spaces in the nineteenth and twentieth centuries.

Chapter 1, "The Church of the Elephant Man," focuses on the sensory and architectural *entanglements*—to borrow a phrase from anthropologist Ian Hodder—of Joseph Merrick, better known within British medical and social history as The Elephant Man. While many studies, including a wildly successful play and film, have focused on Merrick's rescue from a cruel and exploitative freak-show circuit by doctors and administrators at the London Hospital, this chapter situates Merrick as a figure within late Victorian industrial society whose experiences were shaped through two particular institutions: the workhouse and the hospital. Neither of these institutional forms, architectural or social, was invented in the late nineteenth century, but by the 1870s, both were so embedded within networks of poverty and/or disability that they serve as useful sites for working through the triangulation between urban subjects, spatial objects, and modalities of physical, sensory, and cognitive experience.

Most of what we know about Merrick comes from the time he spent in London, particularly at the London Hospital in the Whitechapel district of London, even though that period only occupied the last six years of his life until his death in April 1890 at the age of twenty-seven. The majority of Merrick's life, however, was spent in his hometown of Leicester, which in the 1870s was an industrial generator of wealth for the Midlands region and the nation. The streets and other urban spaces of the city of Leicester were instrumental in shaping his earliest experiences, until 1879 when at the age of seventeen he was forced to enter the Leicester Union Workhouse; four years later, he would be exhibited at a theater in the entertainment district of Leicester that was about two hundred feet from the house where he was born. I depart from mythological retellings of Merrick's life—especially as mediated through such well-known cultural productions as cinema and theater, and, in recent years, graphic novels and television series where he is presented as both a comic and tragic character—by examining how intersections of sensory experience and spatial context played a perpetually dynamic and influential role in his life. Using a wide range of source materials including photographs, maps, engravings, material objects used or made by him, and existing architectural spaces in both Leicester and London, I argue that mythologies surrounding Merrick, however sensitively presented, typically result in an objectification of him that is devoid of dimensionality, reducing him to caricature, a specimen under glass. I try to present Merrick as a compelling example of a historical figure whose sui generis bodily subjectivity continuously shaped, and was continuously shaped by, his entanglements with architecture and within urban spaces.

Chapter 2, "Helen Keller and the Urban Archive," returns to the person whose photograph inspired the research arc of this entire book. Like Merrick, Keller was a complex figure born in the late Victorian era who has been treated dramatically and cinematically (and also comically) through a host of textual and visual objects, though as an international author Keller had more precise control over her self-presentation than Merrick ever did. And Keller, like Merrick, was someone shaped by the urban environments in which she traveled and lived. Unlike Merrick, however, she was not born into impoverished conditions in an industrial city; rather, she was born into a life of middle-class comfort in Tuscumbia, Alabama. But Keller's sensorium was shaped dramatically by the urban environments within which she circulated. Between 1888 and 1917, Keller lived in either Boston or its suburbs: first at the Perkins School for the Blind when it was located in South Boston; then at a series of boardinghouses in Cambridge while she attended the Cambridge School for Young Ladies and, later, Radcliffe; and finally in a house she purchased in Wrentham, about thirty miles southwest of Boston. In 1917, Keller and Sullivan Macy moved to Forest Hills, Queens, where she became a full-fledged New Yorker and world-class traveler. In the early 1920s she had a short-lived career performing on the East Coast vaudeville circuit, during which she would verbally recite her life story, with live translation by Sullivan Macy, to packed houses from Buffalo to Philadelphia and points between. For decades she wrote, as often as she entertained interviews by a perpetually beguiled news media, about her experiences on the streets, on public transportation, and in commercial spaces in cities across the globe.

Among those who have written about Keller's sensory experiences with and through architecture, Diana Fuss has examined in depth the example of Keller's house, Arcan Ridge, that was designed for her in 1937 in Easton, Connecticut, according to her own specifications by Cameron Clark, a New York City–based architect. Shifting away from Fuss's focus on Keller's domestic life in the suburbs, this chapter examines Keller's multimodal engagements with urban space, using maps, advertisements, newsreel footage, and photographs as well as outtakes from Nancy Hamilton's documentary, *The Unconquered: Helen Keller in Her Story* (1954), which won the 1956 Academy Award for Best Documentary. Covering a thirty-year span, from the early 1920s to the early 1950s, I investigate a wide range of Keller's urban experiences: from her visit to the Empire State Building in 1931 to her return voyage to Paris in 1952, when she was made a Chevalier of the Ordre National de la Légion d'Honneur by the French government and invited to participate in the centenary memorial of the death of Louis Braille, which included the interment of his bones in the Panthéon. I also reconsider Keller's multimodal urban encounters as unfairly neglected historical precedents for the development of the field of psychogeography as an urban research method, one that has deeply influenced generations of sociologists, ethnographers, artists, and urban activists since the 1950s. There is a genealogical line—from Charles Baudelaire's characterization of the *flâneur* in the 1860s, to Walter Benjamin's theorizing of sensory encounters in the urban environment in the 1930s, to the writings and inspired activities of the Marxist urban research group known as the Situationist International in the 1950s—that has completely skipped over Keller. Yet all of them, I argue, are indebted to Keller as a pioneering cosmopolitan whose subjectivity as a deafblind woman needs to be centered, not footnoted, in histories and counter-histories of urban modernity.

Following these first two chapters, which focus on well-known individuals, the next two chapters focus less on individuals per se than on state and local institutions and agencies that enabled deeply empathic relationships with populations of adults and children with disabilities whose subjective experiences were the basis for a design approach and ethos decades ahead of their time.

In chapter 3, "Disabling the WPA," I look at the mid-twentieth-century phenomenon of the Works Progress Administration (hereafter WPA), one of the many agencies active during President Franklin Delano Roosevelt's New Deal administration, and the little-known but important services it provided for people with disabilities both as employer and as producer of useful objects. The presence of people with disabilities in historical narratives about work during the WPA era has been limited at best. In this chapter, I argue that the WPA was not a discriminatory agency across the board, given evidence of the number of people with disabilities who were employed by it as well as the number of architectural and design projects for which children and young adults with disabilities were its beneficiaries. Using a host of sources including documents, blueprints, film footage, and objects drawn from federal and state archives, museum collections, and local historical societies, I show how the WPA's capacity to think about disability as a potentially generative economic, social, and educational opportunity was the last gasp of a kind of democratic pluralism that blossomed in the mid-1930s but which had all but evaporated by the end of World War II and the beginning of the Cold War.

There is a neglected and altogether forgotten body of work made in the 1930s by architects and educators who endeavored to meet the needs of schoolchildren with disabilities in cities across the United States. Some architects and educators were aligned with the progressive social values of their European and Scandinavian counterparts; their radical rethinking of space and design were used to address and improve housing and laboring conditions for working-class people as well as learning conditions for students and educators. These values translated easily for some architects employed by the WPA who designed schools that encouraged social bonding and pleasure in seeing and being seen—virtues rarely attached to schools for children with disabilities that tended to be paternalistic (or worse). Chapter 3 also examines a little-known branch of the WPA called the Museum Extension Project (hereafter MEP), which has received scant attention from scholars of the New Deal era. Supported financially and programmatically by twenty-four states between 1936 and 1943, state-run MEPs produced audiovisual technologies such as lantern slides, record players, and overhead projectors along with tactile objects, embossed maps, and books printed in Braille for use in classrooms all over the country to better serve multiple learning styles and modalities. The vast majority of the schools and objects were ignored even in their own time; the preeminent compendium of modernist architecture built at the height of the WPA era, Elizabeth Mock's *Built in USA 1932–1944*, an accompaniment to an exhibition at the Museum of Modern Art, does not feature even one such school.[33] Yet these schools not only improved the lives of thousands of young people; they also permanently changed ideas about what civic care through design might look like.

Much of chapter 3 is concerned with charting a genealogy of disability's relationship to building typologies or design forms associated with architectural modernism in the early decades of the twentieth century. During and after World War II, architectural modernism sustained a pronounced critique when many began to associate it with the stylized monumental projects of Nazi architect Albert Speer and Italian fascist architect Marcello Piacentini. But as Elizabeth Guffey and Bess Williamson have discussed in their important collection *Making Disability Modern*, some of architectural modernism's most recognizable supporters, such as US architect Philip Johnson, were sympathetic to Hitler, and embraced a technological utopianism explicitly circumscribed by eugenics and racial hygiene.[34] As Anne Anlin Cheng and Adrienne Brown have pointed out, architectural modernism's claims of ideological neutrality were in fact a ploy to make a white supremacist cultural aesthetic seem innocent of its relationship to settler colonialism and legalized segregation.[35] Some architectural historians, such as Beatriz Colomina, have added nuance to this critique, suggesting, for instance, that architectural modernism's association with racial politics faded over time: as the design aesthetic spread to ranch houses and consumer goods (and was rechristened as "midcentury modern" or "Danish modern") it became less associated with any particular ideology or politics besides capitalism. Many scholars, however, remain unconvinced; in *Eugenic Design*, for instance, Christina Cogdell argued two decades ago that even the most banal midcentury modernist objects remain tainted with prewar aspirations of social engineering.[36] "There are those who say that it is not Modernism but the perversion of its principles that are to blame," write Joy Monice Malnar and Frank Vodvarka. "Yet these were principles so rooted in the belief that humans were flawed, that offered so little recognition of human attributes, that such perversion must have been easy."[37]

Architectural modernism lingered well into the 1950s and 1960s, and debates surrounding its relevance form the backdrop for chapter 4, "Overdue at the Library," which examines the work of Stanley Tigerman and in particular his Illinois Regional Library for the Blind and Physically Handicapped (1978), a public library sited on the west side of Chicago adjacent to the Little Italy neighborhood and the Brutalist campus of the University of Illinois at Chicago. For Tigerman, the visual and physical impairments of its intended users were opportunities for him to return to some of the social values associated with architectural modernism and use them as the basis for his design. It is true that many elements of the library show off Tigerman's reputation as a provocateur who delighted in treating architecture as a series of playful semiotic games. For Tigerman, however, thinking about the disabled subjectivity of a user—not what their disabilities prevented them from doing but what they made possible—gave him license to imagine types of semiotic play that might engage a library patron with disabilities: from the use of rubber flooring, curving walls, and bright primary colors to allow people with visual impairments and/or who use wheelchairs to navigate interior spaces more easily, to the creation of an entire play area for blind children featuring dark tunnels and recessed sitting areas for reading Braille books, which Tigerman believed would give children an important experience of autonomy even if it made their teachers and parents nervous. Sadly, most of these features were destroyed in 2012 after the library was sold to and refurbished by a local bank.

For Tigerman, the Illinois Regional Library for the Blind and Physically Handicapped was a kind of pivot from the self-righteousness associated with certain forms of architectural modernism to the playfulness associated with certain forms of postmodernism. No one in the 1970s was designing postmodern architecture with disability in mind. Yet one could argue that Tigerman's engagement with architectural modernism is not in the building itself but rather in the histories, both individual and collective, of the people served by the building. This is a different way of thinking about historicism beyond aesthetic form and more about what is produced in the triangulation between a user, a building, and the physical and sensory modalities through which the user experiences it. It is an archaeology of the sensual rather than a taxonomy for only the mind or for the disciplines. It is a type of historicism based not simply on the materiality of forms but on how both successes and failures of those forms have the potential to inspire what design could be—not just for people with disabilities, but for all people who encounter architecture in urban spaces.

The book concludes with an epilogue, "1968," a meditation on a year in the twentieth century when it felt as if life might end with a bang and not a whimper. During a summer when all corners of the globe seemed to be on fire, in August 1968 the US Congress passed the Architectural Barriers Act (ABA), the first piece of disability-oriented architectural legislation anywhere in the world and arguably the most significant affirmation of architecture as a medium of social justice since the Supreme Court's decision in *Brown v. Board of Education of Topeka* fourteen years earlier in 1954. The ABA did not magically transform the built environment overnight, of course, but it was instrumental, as architectural theorist Kenny Cuppers argues, in beginning the process of lifting the modernist spell and turning "subjects" back into "people."[38] It was the kind of massive shift in federal policy as well as social consciousness that changed the way that public architecture would be conceived, and the kinds of expectations it generated, by architects as well as by members of the public, especially members an increasingly visible community of people with disabilities and their allies and advocates.

The civil rights revolutions of the 1950s and 1960s that culminated in legislation like the ABA are often credited as the backdrop against which architects, beginning in the 1970s, directly addressed the needs of people with disabilities. Working in tandem with disability rights activists, they collectively sought to challenge the one-size-fits-all spatial logics of modernism as they were conceived and implemented during the nineteenth and twentieth centuries. In the chapters that follow, I argue there were many moments before the mid-twentieth century when the spell of modernism was not an impenetrable dark cloud but a brief glimpse of a silver lining. Indeed, many of the stories in this book reveal the seeds that were planted for contemporary conversations about accessible design, universal design, and, more recently, user-centered design, or what some disability activists and theorists have called crip design. Aimi Hamraie has written that crip design "is not a synonym for disability, nor is it simply a political orientation. Rather, *it is a specific commitment to shifting material arrangements*."[39] For the architects, designers, and users in this book, Hamraie's phrase "shifting material arrangements" captures something of the flavor of experimentation and the attunement to difference that enabled some people with disabilities to have experiences with architecture and space on their own terms—experiences like building your own house or visiting a library or using your skill set in a workshop or going window shopping with a friend—that are all the more remarkable for having taken place during historical moments when we are accustomed to thinking about people with disabilities as having little if any control over the material arrangements that structure their lives.

A Note on Methodology: Re-Touching Photographs

In her award-winning book, *An Archive of Skin, An Archive of Kin*, the historian Adria Imada dives deep into the photographic collections of physicians, hospital administrators, and government agencies in order to show how Native Hawaiian people with Hansen's disease (better known by its more familiar name, leprosy) were visually represented during the late nineteenth and early twentieth centuries. In the book's introduction, Imada is careful to explain not only what is depicted in the photographs printed in her book, most of which have never been published before, but also how she intends to use them. "Each photograph of a person is analyzed, rather than treated as a mere illustration or clinical condition," Imada writes. "I also attempt to provide biographical and genealogical information about imaged subjects in order to convey lifeworlds . . . Family members seeking to learn more about exiled relatives may find these biographies and sources elaborated in the notes."[40]

Statements like Imada's come from recognition of the hotly contested status of such images within academic and activist circles. In fields like history and anthropology as well as in LGBTQ+ studies, postcolonial studies, and disability studies, many argue that publishing photographs taken in clinical settings, or which operate from a position of medical or juridical authority, can never be a neutral activity. The publication or republication of such photographs, from this perspective, re-enacts the violence perpetrated against people in the first place. For this reason, some scholars have chosen to forgo publishing historical images of people with disabilities as a matter of practicing a transhistorical ethics of care for people photographed, often against their will, who cannot speak for themselves.[41]

Like Imada's book, this book contains many archival photographs of people with physical or sensory disabilities. And, like those in Imada's book, many of the images in my book originated in contexts considerably less empathic than a modern sensibility might prefer. When such images appear, I never share them for "mere illustration." They appear in these pages to glean some insight into the lifeworlds of the people depicted in them rather than using them only as objects of the gaze of a photographer or clinician. Even within recognizable conventions of looking or staring, I try to present the photos as examples of engaged sensory action and reaction, modes of moving through and encountering the world, that are frozen in time and waiting to be recovered. In all cases, I have written extended captions that I believe make these images not only accessible in terms of their content descriptions but also in terms of what people are doing, how they are being, how they are using their bodies. For some readers, nothing can justify publishing archival photographs that were ethically compromised from the moment of their conception. In this book, however, I try to show how, methodologically speaking, there may be ways for modern viewers to reckon with what is happening in the photographs that does not ignore the original contexts that brought them into being.

The ethics of using photographs in a book or any other medium will undoubtedly continue to be fraught. To this end, I find Imada's self-reflective approach to the topic to be among the most thoughtful of anyone writing on the subject:

> I recognize these images may trouble and upset some viewers, but I hold to an ethical and political commitment to contextualize and analyze them as best I can . . . I include some difficult and problematic images in an obscured colonial history of disability and medicine for constituencies like my students, in hopes that we will craft better and more ethical practices of looking at contingent bodies going forward.[42]

It is my hope that, in seeing how I present photographs in this book, the reader might come away from presumptions that their meanings are locked into place simply because they exist and instead consider how meanings can result from more ethical practices of looking. I believe that images deserve the same dignified approach to interpretive complexity that we accord to people when we trace their biographical complexity.

CHAPTER ONE

The Church of the Elephant Man

The doll-sized cardboard model of the Mainz Cathedral, part of the collections of the Royal London Hospital Archives and held by the Barts Health NHS Trust in central London, is not an especially remarkable object (see figure 1.1). Measuring 17 inches (43 cm) long and 19 inches (49 cm) high, and sitting on a rough bed of sandpaper, the cathedral model is permanently frozen in a glass vitrine, its edges held together by thin layers of black masking tape. The model is composed of parts taken from a prefabricated kit of lithographed four-color cardboard pieces individually numbered for ease of construction. Fancifully stylized details, such as Romanesque towers and a central dome and soaring roof spires, are held in place with streaks of glue still shiny from their original application in the late nineteenth century. Alphabetical and numerical guide tabs for putting the structure together, exposed on various pieces of the body of the building, suggest that the model might be a souvenir from Germany, perhaps even purchased on the streets of Mainz, or else a parlor entertainment purchased from any urban street vendor or toy store specializing in rainy-day leisure activities.

What one ultimately makes of this model is shaped as much by the visitor's own subjective experience with it as it is by the visitor's knowledge about the person who built it—Joseph Carey Merrick, the person otherwise known to history as "The Elephant Man." Merrick was a resident of the London Hospital from 1886 until his death in 1890, and spent countless hours engaged in building the Mainz Cathedral model before offering it as a gift to the popular Victorian actress, Madge Kendal, in gratitude for her warm support. In 1917, nearly thirty years after Merrick's death, Kendal donated the model to the hospital's Medical College, after which it was promptly installed in a clear vitrine, like a laboratory specimen, in order to protect its fragile state from any further damage.[1] The vitrine offers no descriptive label to explain to the viewer what they are looking at—assuming,

FIGURE 1.1. Photograph of a model of a cathedral enclosed in a clear vitrine. This is the cardboard model of Mainz Cathedral, Germany, made from a kit of prefabricated parts and put together by Joseph Merrick during his residence at the London Hospital (1886– 90). The model is one of the few surviving objects made or owned by Merrick held in the collections of the Barts Health NHS Trust. Photograph c. 2012 by the author.

of course, that the visitor is not visually impaired, in which case they will have to find another way to encounter the model.

Versions of Merrick's story have been told multiple times and in multiple formats, both scholarly and popular, including a Tony Award–winning play (*The Elephant Man*, written by Bernard Pomerance, 1978) and an Oscar-winning film (*The Elephant Man*, directed by David Lynch, 1980). Merrick was born in 1862, and his bodily difference, which began to manifest visibly after the age of twelve, is now believed to have been a rare form of neuro-fibromatosis identified as Proteus Syndrome. Reactions to his outside appearance encouraged him to wear items such as a bespoke cap and attached mask cut with a single horizontal rectangular opening so that he could see out but not have people see in, allowing him to move anonymously through the physical world. He was treated as an extraordinary spectacle by theatrical promoters and medical professionals alike whose interest in Merrick was neither wholly exploitative nor wholly empathic. But in terms of his relationship to disability, Merrick was imagined more as an economic liability than as a person with a disability. He was not regarded as "crippled" in the way that the Victorians used the word to characterize people with physical impairments; rather, he moved through the world with physical impairments that made it difficult for him to secure or maintain employment.[2]

The Mainz Cathedral model is one of a small number of surviving objects owned or created by Merrick during his lifetime.[3] Almost all of the medical records, personal correspondence, and pathological specimens generated during Merrick's residency were destroyed when Nazi planes bombed the hospital during air raids over East London in World War II. Until 2016, when the hospital's historical collections were transferred offsite, the model was on display with a handful of other objects owned by or related to Merrick, all of them positioned among displays pertaining to the many other patients, surgeons, nurses, and administrators who have been connected to the hospital over the span of its nearly three hundred-year history. For decades, visitors wishing to see the model were required to descend a set of steep stone steps unaffected by accessibility requirements down to the crypt of St. Philips's Church on Newark Street, where the Royal London Hospital Archives were formerly located, so that they might observe the miniature cathedral languishing in its clear vitrine. The model was presented visually (and not through any other means, such as audio description) within a constellation of related objects, such as Merrick's hat and mask, a photographic carte de visite, and the only piece of surviving correspondence written in his own hand, a thank-you note to a benefactor, a wealthy widow named Leila Maturin. The display even included a replica of Merrick's own skeleton—created after the notoriety the original gained in the 1980s when Michael Jackson offered to purchase it for more than £1 million.

In the existing scholarship about the significance of Merrick's life within late nineteenth-century Victorian culture, the Mainz Cathedral model plays little more than a symbolic role, when it is mentioned at all. It gets short shrift in the two canonical tomes about Merrick's life, Michael Howell and Peter Ford's *The True History of the Elephant Man* (1980) and Peter W. Graham and Fritz H. Oehlschlaeger's *Articulating the Elephant Man* (1992).[4] By contrast, cultural productions of Merrick's life have taken an entirely different attitude toward the model. Both Bernard Pomerance's play and David Lynch's film seize upon the church model eagerly as a metonym for its creator's unbroken spirit and spiritual grace in the face of adversity.[5] Scenes that depict Merrick making the church model and presenting it to Madge Kendal function as pivotal moments in the emotional arc of their two respective narratives. In both the play and the film, Merrick does not simply put together the Mainz Cathedral from a prefabricated kit. Instead, he is shown building *from scratch a* small church, St. Philip's—the very church where objects from the real Merrick's life will be displayed in decades hence—that he observes from the window of his hospital room. The model Merrick designs and builds is an exquisite white neo-Gothic church that is both angelic and anglophilic, meant dramaturgically to affirm the intrinsic aesthetic and spiritual order submerged beneath his chaotic exterior. But Merrick never observed anything quite so majestic as a Gothic church from his hospital window. In reality, he occupied a basement room toward the back of the northeast wing of the London Hospital that faced an interior courtyard, the remains of which were obliterated following a particularly savage Nazi air blitz over the East End in January 1945. Given the violence, both interpersonal and ontological, suffered by Merrick at the hands of his contemporaries, establishing a distinction between Merrick-as-subject (the person who makes the model) and Merrick-as-object (the person scrutinized by the gaze of theatrical patrons and doctors) is a key aspect of the humanitarian ethos at the heart of both the play and the film. But the material objects the real Merrick used, and the physical spaces he occupied, were not separate. One can see, for instance, some visible streaks of glue on the tower of the cathedral model, while small indentations made during the assembly process seem to be the result of the unique interactions that Merrick had with the object through the use of his right hand and the types of tools he must have used in order to construct it.

If we treat the Mainz Cathedral model only as one of the few surviving artifacts of Merrick's time in residence at the hospital, does it mean that the model does not have its own history, or that its meaning resides only in how or in what ways it illuminates the history of its human creator? Anthropologist Ian Hodder has written that "things have lives, vibrant lives and temporalities, and they depend on each other and on humans. . . . The social world of humans and the material world of things are entangled together by dependences and dependencies that create potentials, further investments and entrapments."[6] Although Hodder does not discuss disability, his ideas are similar to those of disability studies scholar Katherine Ott, who encourages us to think about "disability objects" as technologies that enable an intimate interdependence between people with disabilities and the objects they make or use.[7] Hodder argues that, rather than isolate objects as distinguished from the social world of humans, so-called "inanimate" objects and human actors are entangled in the process of meaning-making on a shared scale of importance. Hodder does not subordinate objects to human agency, nor does he believe that human agency is subordinate to the status of things; rather, he argues for the ways they co-create each other, so that what we think of as ownership and control might be better described as shared coexistence in which all entities contribute to a shared sense of meaning.

In this chapter I make a deliberate break from the aforementioned scholarly works and cultural productions by thinking about the Mainz Cathedral model as an example of the kinds of architectural and spatial entanglements that formed a central though neglected element of Merrick's biography. As literary scholar William Cohen has written, bodies like Merrick's, "through their porousness and lack of containment, open a range of possibilities for engagement with, and belonging in, the world."[8] Using the concept of entanglements as a methodology encourages us to try to grasp something about Merrick's experience as a person whose physical impairments shaped his subjective experiences of space and whose subjective experiences of space shaped his experience of his physical impairments. Situating Merrick in relation to the Mainz Cathedral model within, or in the absence of, a sensory-oriented field allows us to view Merrick as an active agent of meaning-making rather than a passive subject who is acted upon.

The critical disability studies scholars Aimi Hamraie and Kelly Fritsch have proposed that we think about the entanglements between people with disabilities and the technologies they use or invent or improvise as examples of an emergent crip sensibility, one that positions subjects and objects in a shared co-production of meaning anchored by a disabled subjectivity.[9] So is Merrick's model of Mainz Cathedral a disability object, a crip object, both, or neither? Perhaps one way to think about disability objects and crip objects is that while the former enables function and compensation for lack of accessibility, the latter is an intervention into accessibility as a process, form, or genre of normative design. The crip object, akin to a queer object, exposes a way of doing something and not doing something at the same time, the turning of something upside down. A crip object is not only a relational object in terms of its user; it is relational to the concept of disability itself.

The Elephant Man arrived in the public imagination in the mid-1880s as a medieval leper, a misunderstood Romantic, and a Victorian charity case all fused together.[10] Nearly 150 years later, the Elephant Man remains, to some degree, locked in that same airless sepulchre. Merrick's model, like the larger story of the Elephant Man, seems to defy relationality, and thus it remains virtually unchanged from when Kendal donated it to the London Hospital over a century ago. As I hope to show, approaching Merrick's entanglements with and through the built environment breaks the glass of the case, enabling us to observe a complex urban subject intertwined inextricably with the new worlds he co-created: from Leicester, where he first became the Elephant Man, to London, the place where he became Joseph Merrick again.

From the Workhouse to the Hospital

We have very little material evidence about what Merrick's daily life was like in Leicester prior to 1881, when he was nineteen years old. If one were to plot significant points on a map of Leicester, one would find an area of roughly one square mile within which Merrick moved: sites of home or lodging, education, work, and worship embedded into the tiny eighteenth-century streets of St. George's Ward in the northeast section of Leicester's historic center (see figure 1.2). Some locations on the map—such as Russell Square, where Merrick lived briefly with an uncle who operated a men's haberdashery—still exist but in an abbreviated form that is little more than a block-long intersection of several surviving streets. Other locations—from his birthplace at 50 Lee Street, now gone, to the Baptist church where his family worshipped (Christ Church of Bow Street, bulldozed in 1958 to make way for a fly-over perimeter road), to the school he attended on Syston Street before new family arrangements forced him to drop out and earn a living—have been destroyed or are now unrecognizable.

In 2004, Ramnik Kavia, the first person of South Asian descent elected to the position of Lord Mayor in Leicester, unveiled one of Britain's famous blue plaques at a building on the corner of South Wharf Street and Gladstone Street as a public acknowledgment of Joseph Merrick's importance to the history of the neighborhood. Because Merrick's family home on Lee Street had been destroyed, the blue plaque was affixed to the exterior wall of the former New Empire Theatre of Varieties that once stood at this intersection, where, in 1883, Merrick accepted showman Sam Torr's offer for him to be presented to the public as the Elephant Man. The building and its adjacent hotel opened in 1862, the year of Merrick's birth. By the 1970s, the theater had been gutted and turned into a spare parts shop for a car mechanic. Unfortunately, the plaque did not last very long; after being stolen twice by local Elephant Man aficionados, the plaque was returned and permanently relocated to the wall of a conference room at Moat Community College, the school built on the former grounds of the Leicester Union Workhouse where Merrick lived for four years.

For nearly a decade, the smudgy residue of the plaque's original placement could be observed on the brick wall, an even more haunting reminder of Merrick's presence in the neighborhood than any blue marker could ever hope to capture. In 2012, the building was torn down to make way for

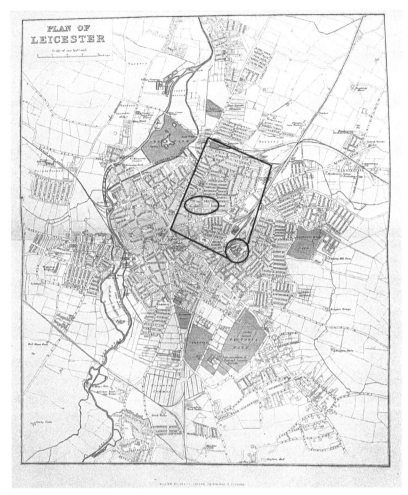

FIGURE 1.2. Close-up view of a map, published c. 1900, showing St. George's Ward, part of the historic center of Leicester, England. Thick black lines mark the square mile within which Joseph Merrick lived and worked during his formative years (1862–83) in Leicester. The black oval on the left side of the marked area shows the location of Lee Street (now the site of Lee Circle Car Park), where Merrick was born in 1862. The black circle at the bottom right corner of the marked area shows the former site of the Leicester Union Workhouse (now the site of Moat Community College), where Merrick stayed from 1879 to 1883. Author's collection.

the construction of a modest apartment building that, a dozen years later, has yet to materialize. Behind thin, graffitied prop plywood walls, the remains of the original theater building sit in an empty lot strewn with castoff bricks, rusty oil drums, bare wires, and the material and psychic detritus of its many former occupants. One wonders if the bones of the building that lie beneath the dirt are waiting patiently to tell their stories about this tiny pocket of Leicester, not unlike the bones of King Richard III excavated from beneath a car park a half-mile away.

Beginning in the mid-1950s, regional planners in the Midlands identified Leicester as a test case for practicing a new kind of urbanism, one that would bring more consumers from the outer rings of cities to newly configured and tourist-friendly versions of historic city centers. Leicester developed two different historical trajectories for its national profile: first, to clean up the central historic district in order to create an influx of new businesses; and second, to undertake urban renewal projects that would gut whole sections of the central historic district in favor of apartment complexes, shopping zones, and parking structures that would lure people downtown before they made their escape back to the suburbs. In 1962, the "Auto-Magic Car Park," the first automated self-parking garage in Europe, opened to exuberant media fanfare in Lee Circle, a new circular structure made up of tiny eighteenth-century streets—including the site of Merrick's birthplace. In the short BBC documentary *Two Town Mad* (1964), journalist Ray Gosling takes the viewer on a first-person drive up the ramp at the car park before heading out to two other sites of enthusiastic innovation: the drive-in post office, where he mails a letter, and the drive-in bank, where he attempts to charm a female teller out of extra cash.[11] Unsurprisingly, the urban renewal schemes changed the overall character of this pocket of Leicester. By the 1970s, Leicester's overall industrial decline made it even easier for playwrights, directors, and biographers to equate Merrick's suffering with urban images of Victorian Leicester, thus failing to recognize that the city's spectacular burst of postwar prosperity depended on the isolation of St. George's Ward in the first place. Not unexpectedly, the march of gentrification across many pockets of inner-city Leicester, as embodied in a 2016 "action plan" for developing a "St. George's Cultural Quarter," cuts off most of the area including Lee Circle, thereby leaving much of the northern ward's historical isolation and attendant poverty intact.[12] In 2019, a local public health study ranked the area as one of the most neglected in the entire Midlands region.[13]

Shortly after appearing at the New Empire Theatre of Varieties, Merrick signed with important theatrical promoter Tom Norman, who gave him the opportunity to leave Leicester to tour England and parts of Europe.[14] Before he shifted into the phase where he earned a solid living by exhibiting himself, however, Merrick lived as an "inmate" of the Leicester Union Workhouse between the ages of seventeen and twenty-three. Merrick was a second-generation beneficiary of the Poor Law Amendment Act of 1834, the legislation responsible for creating hundreds of workhouse institutions across England, Wales, Scotland, and Ireland, and spatially organizing the "deserving" and "undeserving" poor into discrete social units. The physical spaces of the workhouse made it possible for individuals like Merrick to find some semblance of domestic security after being shuttled between the homes of relatives and experiencing poverty due to the difficulty of finding work that made use of his limited repertoire of employable skills. Some of Merrick's jobs revolved around bodily capacities, such as hand-rolling cigars, which he did until he was fifteen, and hawking merchandise on the streets, which he did until he was seventeen.

In 1836, the city of Leicester selected local architect William Flint to design its first workhouse—a hexagonal building with an internal Y-shaped structure that separated men and women into different yards of the institution, fronted by a gatehouse entrance that borrowed its fanciful structure from the Gothic Revival style brought into fashion by Charles Barry and Augustus Pugin, the architects of the Palace of Westminster in London.[15] At its core, however, Flint's design borrowed from the penal architecture of Jeremy Bentham, whose prison designs in the 1790s had influenced at least two generations of architects who wanted to show how architecture could not only control but also reform those who had been sentenced to prison time. This was not an extreme position; according to British Poor Laws, people who could work but chose not to were perceived as more or less criminals in the sense that they chose, for whatever reason, to withhold their labor from the local and national economy. While adults and children with disabilities may have been cared for by religious and charitable organizations, and the elderly and infirm were cared for by local caregiving institutions, anyone else, particularly young men and women above the age of fifteen, were regarded as parasites who should be housed in lodgings that were but a crumb away from prison time.[16]

Merrick fit this last category. Workhouse administrators did not exempt him from being economically productive even if they recognized (and perhaps even empathized with) his bodily difference. In his 1881 entry in workhouse records, for instance, Merrick identified his age ("19"), his profession ("Hawker"), and his place of origin ("Leicester"), but provided no other information about himself.[17] Scanning the logbooks, one frequently sees people who identify in the parlance of the time as "disfigured" and "lame," though no explanation is given for why they are not receiving care in another institutional setting. The 1881 roll also records five blind inmates, one "deaf and dumb," one idiot, and seventeen "imbeciles." These were pre-workhouse categories that were recognizable according to centuries-old criteria for organizing bodily difference in the public sphere. Meanwhile, Merrick belonged to the category of "able-bodied males" rather than "the aged and really impotent."[18] Merrick grew up in an economic and political milieu in which he would have understood intimately the inherent tradeoff of the workhouse arrangement: to maintain a modest amount of domestic comfort, he would have to forfeit his freedom as well as his ability to earn a private wage in exchange for the benevolent care of the workhouse wardens and their administrators of the City of Leicester's Board of Directors.[19]

Despite its lack of comfort and privacy, within a decade the Leicester Union Workhouse was filled to capacity, prompting town commissioners to build a new workhouse that could accommodate as many as a thousand potential inmates. In 1851, the town contracted with architects William Parsons and M. J. Dain; Parsons had been responsible for the designs of local institutions such as Leicester Prison (1825–28), still in use, and the Leicester and Rutland Lunatic Asylum (1837), the original buildings of which are now part of the campus of the University of Leicester. Parsons and Dain leveled Flint's design but kept its Gothic Revival entrance; in place of the hexagon, they delivered a massive H-shaped structure that separated men's and women's sleeping, eating, work, and recreational spaces into yards interspersed in and around the layout (see figure 1.3). The seventeen-year-old Merrick would have encountered both the original Gothic Revival entrance and the later Victorian H-shaped structure as a synthetic amalgam of styles that were intended to produce a particular kind of subject: one who was at the mercy of an institution that would rather he and his fellow inmates not be there but tolerated them all the same. It seems to be no accident, then, that the word "inmate" was used interchangeably in mid-nineteenth-century Britain to characterize prisoners, workhouse residents, and asylum patients. This is because workhouse architecture, like prison architecture, had more than a common moral or social vision; each borrowed from the other because the forms of spatial organization employed in their construction best expressed the larger political goals that both had for reforming their residents.

In *Power and Pauperism*, his classic account of the moral and ideological origins of the British workhouse system, geographer Felix Driver argues that the Poor Laws inaugurated an active distinction between two different types of institutional reform.[20] Under the new Poor Laws, reformers made a deliberate break from *associational functionalism*, which emphasized the relationships between sensation, perception, and behavior, and replaced it with *spatial functionalism*, which stressed that moral improvement and social control could be achieved through the manipulation of space. Associational functionalism had its roots in the seventeenth- and eighteenth-century moral philosophy of groups like the Quakers, who built institutions designed to provide "moral treatment" that, ideally, uplifted those who vol-

FIGURE 1.3. Aerial photograph, taken August 7, 1959, of a small section of central Leicester showing railroad lines (center right) parallel to the second Leicester Union Workhouse (1851), where Joseph Merrick stayed between 1879 and 1883. In the dead center of the photograph are two small buildings with a path between them; this is the original gatehouse designed for the first iteration of the Leicester Union Workhouse (1839). In the 1930s, the whole workhouse was converted into a hospital; in 1977, the entire site was demolished to make way for the campus of Moat Community College, which opened in 1982. Photograph © Historic England (Aerofilms Collection) and reprinted with permission.

untarily or involuntarily entered them.[21] "With a separate apparatus [for washing] in each room," Driver observes, "every tenant becomes directly responsible for his own acts . . . [T]he dirty and disorderly may by teaching and warning be brought to a higher order of feeling of appreciation of cleanliness and order which, once attained, will never desert him."[22] The open-ended and sensuously rigorous humanistic principles deployed in associational functionalism never had a chance against the cold instrumental logic deployed in the spatial functionalism approach. The control of inmates through spatial segregation became the institutional norm in workhouse architecture. Yet, as we will see, the appeal of associational functionalism did not entirely disappear, and its relationship to character and order became a moral component of Merrick's new life following his transition from Leicester to London.

In the 1930s, the Leicester Union Workhouse was finally closed and converted to a hospital; in 1977, when the hospital was closed, a local news-paper published photographs of the demolition in which one could see remnants of William Flint's first design and the second design by William Parsons and M. J. Dain, the late Regency and the early Victorian fighting tooth and claw over the influence of the Gothic and the needs of town ad-ministrators to exercise control over its citizens. On the campus of Moat Community College, a secondary school opened in 1982 on the site of the former Leicester Union Workhouse, a lone black iron fence and rusty gate are the only surviving elements of Flint's 1836 iteration, though the town has not marked them with a plaque. For more than a century, the fence demar-cated autonomy and voluntary servitude, with Merrick and thousands of other workhouse inmates passing through its gates during the active years of the institution, which only closed its doors in the 1930s. One can still see it where Sparkenhoe Street meets Swain Street, the latter suggesting a young shepherd on bended knee playing his lute to woo an apple-cheeked maiden.

In 1884, Tom Norman brought Merrick back to London after a short tour across the country and chose, as the site for exhibiting the Elephant Man for public audiences, a dark storefront space at 259 Whitechapel Road, di-rectly across the street from the London Hospital, the central institution of care in the East End. It was here that Dr. Frederick Treves, the physician who would come to play an instrumental part in Merrick's biography, first saw Merrick on display and, after promising him compensation for his time away from the storefront, invited him to participate in a session of medical photography, using the technology of a glass-plate camera, at the Patholog-ical Society of London, a short distance from Whitechapel Road. Treves published engravings based on the photographs in the *Transactions of the Pathological Society of London* in 1885, but the original photographs—which were not published at the time and did not surface publicly until many years later—are far more illuminating about Merrick's physical relationship to the camera, and to the physical site of the studio space itself, than the engrav-ings illustrate.[23]

In two of the surviving photographs from that session, Merrick is seen standing, leaning forward and balancing his hand on a Windsor chair (see figures 1.4 and 1.5).[24] In both photographs, Merrick's affective gesture is one of exhaustion; the tilt of the head suggests a form of orientation toward the chair and toward the assignment itself held by someone whose phys-ically demanding labor does not use a chair for sitting, a mark of leisure, but instead uses it as a prop or even a tool with which to exhibit the body and to be able to move around it so as to add dimensionality to the expe-rience of display. One thinks, for instance, of the collection of anthropological daguerreotypes of enslaved men and women taken in 1850 by W. T. Zealy in Charleston, South Carolina, commissioned by Harvard zoologist Louis Agassiz to support his research into racial typologies.[25] When random articles of furniture appear in the Zealy daguerreotypes, it is not for the purpose of set dressing; like the presence of stirrups or shackles, such domestic objects were used instrumentally as orientation devices to force the photographic object to stretch their body if necessary—to be able to stand still—especially given the requirements of the daguerreotype, which might have taken as much as ten minutes to fix onto a silver plate. Surrounding Merrick are walls that have been covered in leather or silk or some other fabric, exposing brass or silver buttons that suggest a room divider or a modesty screen to separate the person being examined from their examiner. The photographer has gone on the other side of the screen to photograph Merrick, abandoning the affective ritual of dressing and undressing, thus combining all activities on one side of an otherwise reliable divide. If, however, we push against the photograph as a form of visual representation and examine it as a document of Merrick's sensory experience as captured by the photograph, we are able to discern something that an emphasis on the visual point of view—that of the medical gaze—cannot, because, while he is being directed, one can see his comportment and his orientation toward the objects against which he is leaning. At high resolution one can see aspects of Merrick's body that have been activated differently in the space of the examination room or private office than they would have been in the space of the workhouse or the storefront sideshow.

If we are going to historicize disability or its adjacent bodily experiences, we need to be mindful of the various and discrepant relationships between spaces and objects (such as those arrested in a photograph) and the bodies involved in the production of that object. After all, what makes the Mainz Cathedral model significant is less the facticity of its existence than how a life experience shaped or was shaped by its use. The sociologist Kevin Hetherington has argued that there is knowledge to be gained from how we understand the *proximal* (what Merrick is doing with his body in the photograph) that challenges and even repudiates what we understand as the *distal* (the sense that what is primary is visual, both historically, as in the camera's gaze, and in terms of our contemporary relationship to such a media object).[26] Merrick's experiences with proximal objects seem to have given him an understanding of what a different kind of life might offer him: not so much a life of luxurious fabrics or carved furniture in the posh offices of medical professionals, but, rather, one where he was taken out of the scripted performances of the freak-show aesthetic to which he'd become accustomed and introduced to other ways of orienting his body and,

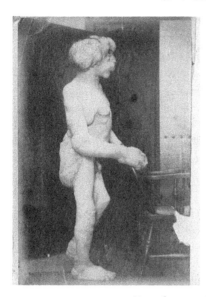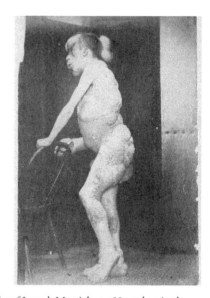

FIGURES 1.4 AND 1.5. Two photographs of Joseph Merrick, c. 1884, taken in the offices of the Pathological Society of London at 6 Alie Street, less than a mile from the storefront at 259 Whitechapel Road where Tom Norman exhibited Merrick. In both photographs Merrick exposes his body to the camera and steadies himself by holding the back of a rounded Windsor chair. He has also shifted his weight onto his right foot since his left foot, which is raised off the ground, caused him discomfort and made it difficult for him to walk. Neither photograph was published during Merrick's lifetime but both were used as the basis for engravings published in Frederick Treves, "A Case of Congenital Deformity," *Transactions of the Pathological Society of London* 36 (March 1885), 494–98. Published courtesy of Barts Health NHS Trust.

in particular, his hands. The sensual qualities of such objects—a woven rug on the floor, fabric next to the body, the fine curve of a painted wooden chair, a jet of gaslight bright enough to light a room with blinds or curtains drawn—are just as entangled and embedded within architectural spaces like the Pathological Society of London as they are within the workhouse, the public hospital, or the private home.

Several years later, after Merrick had left the Leicester Union Workhouse behind, his capacity to use his hands in a recognizably productive manner would be one of the ways in which he would be introduced to a curious Victorian reading public. In one of the London Hospital's first appeals to solicit funds for Merrick, in the form of a letter written to the editors of the London *Times* in December 1886, an administrator characterized the pathetic fate of its charge by describing how Merrick "occupies his time in the hospital by making with his own available hand little cardboard models, which he sends to the matron, doctor, and those who have been kind to him."[27] In many ways, the model brought Merrick closer to the experiences of men, women, and children with disabilities than the Leicester Workhouse ever could, especially given the ways in which contemporary discourses of rehabilitation emphasized handicrafts and handiwork as a way for people to channel their energies into aesthetic (and often commercial) avenues of productive expression. In the rehabilitative milieux of late nineteenth-century charitable institutions, and public and private schools for the blind, deaf, crippled, and infirm, hand-oriented vocational skills, such as working a loom, stuffing mattresses, doing laundry, sewing textiles, or honing small crafts in collective workshops, were endorsed as methods for giving people practical skills while also promoting the kind of individualized focus that would de-emphasize their perceived physical or sensory difference—though, ironically, such labor-intensive projects often served to reinforce those differences or at least mark them as capable of certain routinized forms of domestic or workshop labor.[28] Under the right conditions, model-making could be a tactile, independent activity into which one could pour one's own initiative and develop one's own skills and sense of self-worth that confirmed the rhetoric of self-sufficiency. Perhaps in the end the Mainz Cathedral model reminded Merrick of the Gothic Revival style deployed by architects like William Flint at the gatehouse to the Leicester Union Workhouse—a style that tapped a rich vein of nostalgia for Britons born in the second half of the nineteenth century.

Making a New London Hospital

The London Hospital (rededicated in 1990 as the Royal London Hospital) itself is embedded in a broader history of institutions in London that relate both to the history of the city and to the history of people with disabilities or chronic illnesses, or victims of accidents, and the care they received as members of often marginal populations. Almshouses and wards constructed to care for poor, elderly, and chronically infirm people stretch back a thousand years in London as a function of Christian duty by nuns and monks to dispense care for the relief of suffering. Such institutions were located on church-owned lands or else in the "liberties" that contained publicly held enclosures, such as farmland, and free spaces for dissident religious communities. In London, these operated outside the formal walls of the City's boundaries (following the pattern of the old Roman city) in areas that still bear their names: Spitalfields, Westminster, St. Giles. As Carole Rawcliffe has argued, these were as much institutions of segregation and isolation as they were civic institutions for demonstrating charity and care in a world organized around religious devotion.[29] The idea of segregating those with contagious illnesses or chronic conditions to the peripheral zones of the outer city remained a central principle in urban planning well into the nineteenth and twentieth centuries, and was a fundamental component of architect Ebenezer Howard's plan for spatial hierarchies of ability and disability as mapped out in his *Garden Cities of To-morrow: A Peaceful Path to Real Reform* (1898).

The London Hospital's origins go back to the 1740s, when a group of local businessmen established the London Infirmary to help provide care to the growing population of the East End, especially with the growth of waterfront industries that brought sailors, prostitutes, orphans, itinerant workers, and immigrants from across Europe who began filling the parishes of Wapping, St. Katherine's, and Shadwell on the northern shore of the Thames.[30] The first location for the infirmary was a townhouse on Prescott Street in Goodman's Fields, a district just outside the boundaries of the medieval city, organized around a small parcel of land attached to an ancient abbey that had been seized by Henry VIII in the sixteenth century. A century later, the area had developed a reputation for artisanal work in metal and wood, and for small inventors of what we think of today as prosthetic and orthotic instruments. A mid-eighteenth-century advertisement for "steel trusses" and other assistive devices, preserved in the collections of the Bishopsgate Institute in Spitalfields, indicates that Goodman's Fields was known throughout the city, and perhaps beyond, for these kinds of appliances. At the same time, Goodman's Fields served the underground as a rookery where petty thieves and criminals could easily disappear into its intricate maze of ancient alleys and yards. By the early 1750s, the trustees of the London Infirmary recognized that they needed larger quarters that would offer a less dangerous setting, even if it meant uprooting from an area known for its medical and surgical device production. After negotiating with several landowners, the trustees purchased land on Whitechapel High Street, which in the first half of the eighteenth century was a wide dirt road from the east into the city, with visible rolling hills and medieval hamlets within its purview.

The plans for the new hospital were drawn up by a nonarchitect, Boulton Mainwaring, who had come to the role as a land surveyor who had in his early professional career apprenticed under a draftsman.[31] Mainwaring was one of a large number of young men whose architectural training came not through formal education but through the study of architectural drawings and engravings of Andrea Palladio (1508–80), the Italian architect and designer whose revisiting of ancient Greek and Roman forms imparted a new aesthetic across the continent.[32] Mainwaring had numerous local examples of the Palladian style on which to draw, both by reputation and by personal experience: the hospitals at Chelsea and Greenwich, for example, designed by Christopher Wren in the 1680s, were the first attempts by a British architect influenced by Palladio to create institutions for the chronically ill and for retired sailors who had no place of residence after serving in the Royal Navy—a nod to the importance of veterans in seventeenth-century social and political life not unlike Louis XIV's royal edict to build the Hôpital des Invalides in Paris. Similarly, Mainwaring may have also been influenced by the use of the Palladian style in the building of asylums like the notorious Bethlem Hospital, which was only a short distance from Whitechapel (on the site where Liverpool Street Station now stands), as well as almshouses for the poor and other purpose-built institutions for the care of vulnerable populations.

For Palladio, the classical proportions of Greek and Roman grandeur found their way into both private homes and public buildings that were erected in Italian city-states like Padua, Mantua, Vicenza, and Venice, where princes and dukes with more money than the popes erected their own *palazzi*. As Michael Baxandall has described it, this patronage system between wealthy noblemen and architects like Palladio shaped a sophisticated visual urbanity that transformed medieval city-states, coaxing them toward styles associated with Renaissance Italy.[33] Within a generation, Palladio's influence spread throughout cities in Europe, ushering in the tradition of the Grand Tour for wealthy gentlemen (and, later, ladies) who would travel around Italy absorbing Palladio's vision and filling sketchbooks and trunks with memories and objects unmoored from their original sites.

Palladio's influence was especially pronounced in global centers of commerce like London. Elites recognized in the hallmarks of the Palladian style—pediments atop columns both supportive and decorative, colonnades, high ceilings, tiled floors with checkerboards of black and white tile or terrazzo, raised parlor floors (the *piano nobile*), and perfectly symmetrical wings—a stylistic counterpart to their own global ascendance. Palladian styles, as architectural historian Dana Arnold has argued, helped them to build estates organized around formal elements like courtyards, gardens, fountains, croquet lawns, and other places for celebration and ritual.[34] Yet the proportions and refinements associated with Palladian architecture were themselves a kind of masquerade: most of Britain was still predominantly rural, while in cities like London or even Leicester, urban institutions could play with the Palladian form to invoke ancient Rome as well as those Italian city-states that held both allure and sophistication for British aristocrats. Meanwhile, architects like Wren—and, later, Wren's apprentice, Nicholas Hawksmoor—believed that buildings should match a nation's ambitions as well as its global importance, which in the seventeenth and eighteenth centuries meant an architecture with a recognizable "brand" that could support activities as diverse and yet structurally interdependent as Christian worship and banking and investing, with their gains made possible by the absorption of lands, resources, and peoples across the Southern Hemisphere. For Arnold, the Palladian style represented an "ordered physical structure that acted as a metonym for other inherited structures—this encompasses the makeup of a society as a whole, a code of morality, a body of manners, a system of language and the way in which an individual relates to their cultural inheritance" that reveals "much about the period's dominant culture and ideology."[35]

Mainwaring's initial plan called for a U-shaped structure that would present on the south side of what is now Whitechapel Road as a long country house, an exaggerated single pediment above a small but eloquent street entrance, with smaller perpendicular buildings forming a central courtyard in the back that opened onto acres of open land.[36] The central building was composed of three stories, with service rooms and examination rooms, toward the central core, with long corridors running in either direction from the center that opened up into patient wards, all of which were lit by large windows that infused the corridors with light while also endeavoring to protect them from dust and smell. A commercial print from 1752 (see figure 1.6), now in the collection of the Wellcome Library, illustrates how the hospital, after all, was still rural even by mid-eighteenth-century London standards; the land purchased for the hospital was right next to a gigantic hill of dirt and detritus known locally as "The Mount," which had been an infamous attraction and even the site of mystery plays before its removal to make room for the expansion of the hospital. In this sense, the London Hospital was a kind of urban gentrification instrument claiming a space that was best known for its wide dirt highway that enabled farmers from the east to bring goods to market. With its classical proportions and its position in the center of an emerging neighborhood, the London Hospital communicated for its local population something akin to how those symmetrical and well-proportioned buildings functioned in different parts of the city where they underscored commercial interests, such as banks and commodity exchanges, as well as the kind of townhouses purchased by the newly rich in an age of expansive economic and social transformation.

In cities like Leicester and London, the Palladian style became synonymous with civic architecture and civic values: the importance of municipal benevolence, the contributions of academic institutions and scientific societies, the role of fundraising and recruitment of the rich and powerful to local projects, the value of professional societies for the distribution of

FIGURE 1.6. Engraving of the London Hospital, designed by surveyor Boulton
Mainwaring in 1751, showing its relative isolation on what is now Whitechapel Road
as well as its proximity to parishes to the south that the hospital sought to serve.
Historically the road was a main artery for bringing animals, shown in the lower
right of the engraving, and other goods to market from east of the city. The ancient
earthen mound called "The Mount" is shown directly to the right of the hospital
building and is memorialized by the name given to a small street, East Mount Street,
which marks the eastern boundary of the Royal London Hospital site. Engraving
dated 1752 by William Bellers and published by J. B. C. Chatelain and W. H. Toms,
London, 1753. Public domain image reprinted courtesy of the Wellcome Collection.

knowledge, and medical care as delivered by the industrious medical staffs
of urban institutions like the London Hospital. The Palladian style also
became synonymous with the emergent urban institution known as the
museum—the British Museum, for instance, opened in 1751—suggesting
ways that one can see symmetrical relationships between the hospital,
the museum, the court of law, and the bourse; all forms that harnessed architectural style in order to communicate form and content as rationally
synthetic. By the early eighteenth century, classically-inspired forms were
adapted with great enthusiasm by the landed gentry and municipal elites in
cities like London and across Britain and its centers of commerce and political power, a kind of aestheticized soft power that established an aesthetic
rationale for using Palladian architecture that filtered down as Georgian
(and, in the United States, Federal) styles throughout the nineteenth and

early twentieth centuries. In the case of museums and hospitals, however, there is an even more significant alignment. The spirit of amateur scientific exploration that one finds in the earliest museums settings in Britain—the Ashmolean (1680) at the University of Oxford, for instance—derives from the collections of wealthy collectors who furnished their homes with cabinets of curiosities that included everything from animal and human relics to pottery and statues from classical Athens and Rome. The creation of museums and the creation of hospitals therefore tap into a certain presumption about what kind of architectural container best serves the mission of the institution whose stewardship (of plundered objects, of living human bodies) is based on an urban ideal metaphorized by the architecture itself. The neoclassical style, which would be even further streamlined as the Georgian style of the early nineteenth century, would expand beyond Palladio's wildest dreams in places like Leicester, a city granted a royal charter in the seventeenth century, and one that soon would be filled with Palladian- and Georgian-inspired buildings and streets full of new types of institutions like museums and literary societies as well as churches.

Architectural historians such as Irene Cheng, Mabel Wilson, and Charles Davis have written about the role that Palladian-inspired architecture played across the Atlantic in the creation of the Federal style in the emerging British colonies and, later, plantation and university architecture as well as designs for postrevolutionary federal and state institutions.[37] Indeed, Davis shows how seemingly "neutral" styles can contribute to white supremacy; by the 1930s, historicism was weaponized through its revival of the "colonial" in the era of Jim Crow segregation. In the 1820s the English-born architect John Haviland designed two Palladian-inspired buildings at approximately the same time: the Pennsylvania Institution for the Deaf and Dumb (1825), which still stands in majestic splendor on Broad Street in downtown Philadelphia, and the Eastern Penitentiary (1829), a prison that combines neoclassical elements with Jeremy Bentham's ideas of the panopticon that still stands as a tourist destination. The association cemented between style (neoclassical) and content (civic), in which buildings are outward-facing and draped in white marble, are for Cheng, Wilson, and Davis fundamental examples of how power is both explicitly and implicitly exerted through style and content. This is why Mainwaring adopted the same style for the London Hospital nearly a century earlier: in the 1750s, it was understood to be the only viable architectural language for public buildings, especially those aimed at the vulnerable and destitute in need of some kind of paternalistic uplift that only the state or its institutions could provide.

The impulse by political leaders and economic elites on both sides of the

Atlantic to try to contain illness and ameliorate suffering was embedded in the entire enterprise of building hospitals, asylums, almshouses, and prisons outside the boundaries of the city, leaving the west side of London as a commercial and political center while maintaining those who were poor or ill or disabled on the opposite end of the city. The street that forms the western boundary of the East End—Bishopsgate, which moving north turns into Norton Folgate and then into Shoreditch Road—marked for centuries the boundary between the financial and political center of London and those lands where, prior to the reign of Henry the VIII, monastic orders had built spaces for the chronically and terminal ill, such as St. Mary Spital. In an era marked by the spread of contagious disease, spanning everything from plague to leprosy to medical conditions caused by invisible viruses, sites like St. Mary Spital acquired enormous power as symbols of urban care and compassion, even if their existence relied entirely on their exclusion from the city center.

In 2012, while conducting research for this book at the Bishopsgate Institute in Spitalfields, I traveled east along Whitechapel Road to witness the refurbishment of the Royal London Hospital's buildings when it was being converted to Tower Hamlets Town Hall. For the first time in more than two and a half centuries, one could easily see the exposed eighteenth-century bones of Boulton Mainwaring's original design, as well as nineteenth-century spaces and inner courtyards obscured since the rebuilding of the hospital after World War II. Some of these can be seen on an 1893 map of the London Hospital (see figure 1.7) that indicates the open-air work area known to hospital staff as "Bedstead Square," where custodians repaired, cleaned, and painted bed frames and other pieces of furniture and equipment, and the addition of a nurses' residence to the south. These additions completed a safe quadrangle of sorts within which Merrick could take short perambulations late at night, relatively unnoticed by all but late-night hospital staff accustomed to the sight of the hooded figure. Merrick did not move past the interior boundaries of the square but one can imagine him taking it all in: smelling the tang of cleaning agents and new paint, feeling the rain or the thickness of humidity in the air, hearing the activity of horses' hooves and people's conversations echoing off the surfaces of brick walls and cobblestone courtyards, and then seeing the origins of those sounds emerge from darkness into the light of gas lamps and take material form. This was a completely different sensory environment than that of the two basement rooms he occupied in the London Hospital, both of which were deliberately engineered by Treves and staff to provide Merrick with domestic spaces that were as far removed as possible from the world of storefronts, workhouses, and common lodging houses.

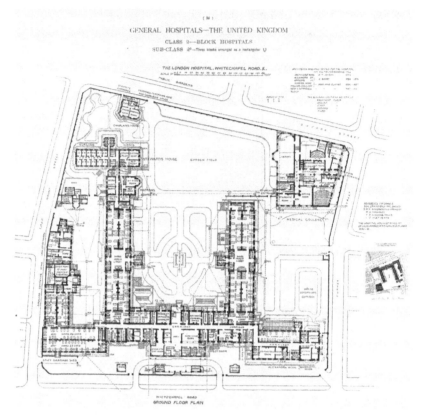

FIGURE 1.7. A line-drawing map of the scale of the campus of the London Hospital at the time when Joseph Merrick lived there, c. 1890. Mainwaring's original 1751 design extends horizontally across the bottom of the map. On the far left side of the map are two vertical lines marking East Mount Street that intersect with an unmarked street (Ravens Row on a contemporary map). The courtyard space to the right of this intersection was known as "Bedstead Square" since it was used for repairing and painting bed frames and other furniture used by the hospital. Administrators built a private basement-level apartment for Joseph Merrick in one of the buildings facing the square. Many of these buildings suffered extensive bomb damage during World War II and were torn down. Map originally published in Henry C. Burdett, *Hospitals and Asylums of the World*, vol. 4 (London: J. & A. Churchill / The Scientific Press, 1893), 36.

All the Comforts of Home

"I have a nice bright room," Merrick wrote in December 1888, "made cheerful with flowers, books, and pictures. I am very *comfortable*, and I may say as happy as my condition will allow me to be."[38] Two and a half years earlier, in June 1886, Merrick had been rescued from Liverpool Street Station and admitted as a short-term patient to the London Hospital in Whitechapel under the care of Frederic Treves, who would famously become Merrick's principal physician and champion. But after Merrick had received the hospital's care for six months, administrators actively sought out a way to make him a permanent resident of the hospital. As a voluntary institution dedicated to serving emergency cases among the East End's poor, the London Hospital was not permitted to accept long-term patients who might use up the limited resources of the staff beyond immediate medical attention. At first the hospital's various boards of governance explored several different options, including the transfer of Merrick to the Royal Hospital for Incurables and the British Home for Incurables. A public appeal to the readers of the London *Times* in December 1886, however, brought in £230, in an era when a comfortable middle-class Victorian family could rent a detached three-story terraced house for £50 a year. A further pledge of £50 per annum from a wealthy London businessman thus ensured that Merrick could remain as a ward of the hospital for as long as he wanted.

In early 1887, a team of carpenters, masons, and plumbers began the process of converting an underutilized storeroom in the basement of the hospital's Northeast Wing into what today we might call a studio apartment for Merrick, complete with a small fireplace and decorative mantelpiece, a small table and chairs for taking meals, and an armchair specially designed to support his body and head for sleeping. The basement-level room had one large casement window and a windowpane door that looked out onto a small square that could be accessed by walking up a narrow flight of stairs from the apartment. The hospital architects also carved out space to install a separate room with a flush toilet and bathtub, the latter of which Treves stipulated was necessary for the patient's daily ablutions. The *British Medical Journal* explained that, for Merrick, "a bath is not merely a luxury but, from the nature of his affliction, a daily necessity."[39]

Literary historian Martha Stoddard Holmes has argued that "few Victorians of any class had a family member or close associate whose body approximated Joseph Merrick's . . . [but it] was very common to know someone with mobility impairment or chronic illness, or to have a relative who was deaf or blind."[40] The way that such persons were known to visitors was through the spatial medium of the "sickroom," common enough in nineteenth and twentieth century domestic spaces to have its own recognizable architectural features. According to literary scholar Maria Frawley, many self-identified invalids in nineteenth-century Britain embraced their relationship to the sickroom, a space specifically transformed for someone living with chronic illness or bouts of infection within a middle-class home, especially "its extreme domestic sphere rhetoric of the home as a haven . . .

that was in sharp contrast to the flux associated with both the market and social life and that mimicked the activity associated with household management."[41] Frawley argues that the sickroom's segregation from the rest of the home mirrored Victorian virtues of stoicism, interiority, and restraint. Merrick's room, by contrast, was not a sickroom, nor a hospital room nor an isolation ward—it was more like an apartment than any of those typologies of medical space, and one with a decidedly performative dimension since Merrick received visitors there on a regular basis after becoming a cause célèbre. Authors Howell and Ford describe a pre-Christmas holiday conversation between Treves and Merrick held in 1887, which is worth quoting at length:

> Treves asked Joseph what he felt he would like, for several donations of money had been handed in for his benefit. Joseph showed no hesitation. He had seen an advertisement for a gentleman's dressing case with silver fittings that appealed to him so much he had kept the cuttings from the newspaper. The set consisted of silver-backed hairbrushes and comb, a silver shoehorn, and a hat brush as well as ivory-handled razors and toothbrushes. It seemed an incongruous choice, but Treves understood the feelings behind it and purchased the set at once. He intervened only to prepare the gift by removing the mirror and carefully filling the cigarette case with cigarettes, though he knew Joseph never smoked and never could with his deformed lips; but then every item in the case was equally useless to him in any utilitarian sense.
>
> The dressing case turned out to be the perfect prop for Joseph's imagination. In the privacy of his small room, sitting quietly as he arranged its contents, opening and closing the cigarette case, he became an elegant, sophisticated man-about-town, preparing in his dressing-room for some formal dinner or glittering occasion.[42]

Focusing their attention on these luxurious commodities in the dressing case, Howell and Ford offer familiar and recognizable entanglements between Merrick and the elite social codes he desired to participate in or at least emulate in his own privately concocted fantasies.[43] But Howell and Ford present the normative codes of Victorian masculinity to which Merrick aspired as a given—they treat masculinity as a single-story building with only one address rather than as a neighborhood with multiple addresses and many ways to arrive there—without suggesting that Merrick had the capacity to reframe those objects in new ways, not only for himself but for those who believe that such codes of masculinity are inviolable. Thus, the authors seem perfectly settled with Treves's decision to remove the hand mirror from the dressing case, a paternalistic act of protection intended to safeguard Merrick after a lifetime of abuse. It was also an act of control, one that denied Merrick the opportunity to reframe his visual experience of his own body on his own terms. Merrick's subjective sense of self, after all, developed *because of* his relationship to his physical body, not *despite* it. The dressing case and its implements were, for Merrick, totems of social aspiration as much as other body-oriented objects that resituated his subjectivity in relation to pleasure, not pain; to abundance, not deprivation; to agency, not exploitation.

Merrick was not the only public figure whose bodily experiences resituated or reframed objects perceived to be locked in a singular context. For example, among the aristocrats, dignitaries, medical professionals, and society figures who visited Merrick in his rooms during his nearly four years at London Hospital, none was more remarked upon than Alexandra, Princess of Wales, one of Queen Victoria's daughters, with whom Merrick met in 1887. A much beloved figure and the eponymous designee of the "People's Palace" built in north London in 1863 (just a year after Merrick's birth), Alexandra would later become queen after her husband Albert ascended to the throne as King-Emperor Edward VII in 1901. A romanticized retelling of the meeting between the Elephant Man and the People's Princess might offer an allegory of power dynamics working in both directions: Alexandra's embrace of her "inferior" despite his social standing; Merrick's transfiguration from medical object to social subject who teaches his "better" the meaning of humility. Yet both Merrick and Alexandra were scrutinized as medical subjects who employed objects as part of their somatic repertoire. In 1867, as part of her recovery from a case of rheumatic fever, Alexandra began to use a walking cane, inspiring a short-lived fashion—"the Alexandra limp"—in which nondisabled society women wielded decorative canes, wore shoes with uneven heels, and affected a sympathetic (if exaggerated) physical gait that emulated that of their fashionable heroine. As one chronicler of Alexandra's life wrote, "canes became the rage . . . for three months all Society cultivated the 'Alexandra limp.'"[44] The "limp" may not have lasted past the fashionable season in 1867, but Alexandra later took to wearing veils and heavy face makeup as she grew older. By the time she and Merrick met two decades later, their experiences of the world outside of their respective bubbles may have encouraged the same kinds of protective face gear and mobility devices, motivated by the same desire to pass without eliciting commentary from the social worlds to which they belonged.

For Merrick, being "very *comfortable*" was not merely aesthetic or psychic; rather, it was a fully embodied experience that emerged from a confluence of spatial security and physical intimacy that was felt in the sensations of the body. Descending into a bath full of hot water and scented soap, enjoying a warm meal, sitting before a well-stoked fire, wearing clean clothes, admiring a vase full of fresh-cut flowers gave him pleasure as well as comfort. Beginning in the eighteenth century, John E. Crowley has argued, "Anglo-American political economists, moral philosophers, scientists, humanitarian reformers, even novelists" transformed the term *comfort* from "its centuries-old reference to moral, emotional, spiritual, and political support in difficult circumstances" to mean a "self-conscious satisfaction with the relationship between one's body and its immediate physical comfort."[45] Experiencing comfort in one's domestic sphere was the opposite of, or a respite from, whatever discomfort one experienced in the public sphere, and as such became a component of being a modern person in the world that George R. Sims described in his 1883 investigation, *How the Poor Live*. Sims described an East End lodging house in which "men, women, and children are lolling about, though it is midday, apparently with nothing to do but make themselves *comfortable*," giving a contemporary indication of how the conditions of material deprivation did not obliterate the possibility of moments of physical or psychic self-satisfaction.[46]

There are other, more immediately relevant reasons why the focus on Merrick's physical comfort within his new apartment setting is so vital to recovering the varied dimensions of his subjective experience. According to biographers who characterized Merrick's body, the large masses of pendulous skin and cauliflower-like growths on his back, buttocks, legs, and underarms, if left unwashed, were alleged to have emitted a "well-remembered stench" much commented upon by Treves and the other physicians who attended Merrick.[47] Surely, however, Merrick experienced his own smell differently than this, in the way that humans become aware of their own subjective corona of body odor prior to subduing it with soap and water or dousing it with fragrance. This would not have been unknown olfactory territory for someone who had spent years in a workhouse. In addition to the compromises to personal privacy that characteristically attend group living, institutional living required workhouse inmates to become intimately acquainted with the body's needs, rhythms, and involuntary expulsions, not only their own but those of the other members of their cohort. In 1885, one prison inmate described the olfactory experience of another prisoner's morning toilet use as a "nasal telegram," a sharp reference to contemporary communication technology to characterize the immediacy with which private bodily smells, typically concealed within middle-class domestic environments, were so ubiquitous as to permeate "the already over-tainted atmosphere" of the prison ward.[48]

Beneath his characteristic cloak, hood, and enormous hat that he wore when he traveled, all of which were constructed of a heavy black velour-like material to protect him from cold weather, Merrick's bodily aromas would have circulated internally and mingled with the environmental smells that entered through the folds in his clothing and the narrow horizontal aperture in his mask used for peering out. This would have enabled Merrick to distinguish and acclimate to his own bodily smells; distinct from, for instance, the smell of gas lamps in city streets, the smell of decomposing vegetable refuse and butchered meat in the commercial market stalls, or the smell of public lavatories before they were obliterated by cleaning agents, in much the same way that he would have distinguished himself from the hospital odors that wafted down to the basement from the London Hospital's various offices, hallways, and kitchens. In the corridors and waiting rooms of late nineteenth-century public hospitals, these distinctive smells included the metallic odor of iodine and ammonia, the sweet smell of ether, and the chlorine smell of commercial detergents that emerged after Louis Pasteur's discovery of germ theory in the 1870s and from which soon followed Joseph Lister's invention of disinfectants to promote personal hygiene through the cleansing of both architectural and bodily spaces. Thus, while Treves insisted to the London Hospital's nursing staff that his charge take a daily bath, we have no reason to believe that the baths were for the benefit of anyone other than Treves himself. And despite, or perhaps because of, his constant circulation through different institutional spaces, the time Merrick spent alone before his admission to the London Hospital may have attuned him to olfactory experiences that were neither horrific nor alluring but that simply signaled personal identification, an immediate recognition of where his body ended and another body began.

The degree of domestic comfort—a bathtub of one's own—to which Merrick quickly became acclimated in his new room was more than a marker of his access to modern hygiene and personal comfort. Amenities like flush toilets and hot water taps, both of which were fairly new household commodities in the last quarter of the nineteenth century, became political artifacts of debates about urban infrastructure from which the poor had been characteristically excluded. Toilets were components of a privileged built environment that effectively segregated the poor from the privileged urban grid of technological modernity as well as the social, political, and aesthetic codes of civility. It is no wonder that, among the British Empire's many legacies in its colonial excursions abroad, the building of latrines, irrigation canals, and clean water cisterns were, along with the development of roads and bridges and postal networks, among the central infrastructural commitments mandated as methods of upgrading perceived unhealthy social practices among native populations and fighting outbreaks of infectious disease. While such commitments were used as evidence of the benevolent rule of empire, reformers and advocates back home in Britain, such as Charles Booth, Edwin Chadwick, and Henry Mayhew, pointed to widespread disease and unsanitary living conditions arising from a failed plumbing infrastructure as evidence of a breakdown of the social contract between government and citizen, a breakdown that could only be addressed through municipal works created through acts of Parliament as well as through those of Victorian philanthropy. In 1885, for instance, a group of British Jewish businessmen organized the Four Percent Industrial Dwellings Company, the name a reference to the amount of net return that investors could expect from their initial outlay on architectural projects designed for the poor. For its first undertaking, the company proposed "a block of Model Dwellings affording accommodation for 186 families, each tenement having two or three rooms, with separate w.c. and scullery" on a "freehold site of about three quarters of an acre" near Brady Street in Whitechapel, about a hundred yards from the London Hospital."[49] In December 1886, at approximately the same moment when the hospital was beginning to construct Merrick's pied-à-terre, the same company announced that the new dwellings under construction "in Thrawl Street, Flower and Dean Street, and George Street," a densely packed area in Spitalfields about a quarter of a mile from the London Hospital, "will afford accommodation for upwards of 150 families."[50] The significance of the Four Percent houses, however, rested not only on high construction values relative to the period and the local environment but also on the requisite, almost casual, emphasis on toilet access for which only two families would be required to share a water supply that included a toilet.

Britain's middle-class population already had enjoyed these material dignities for several decades in the revolutionary form of hot water heaters installed in the 1860s and modern siphon flush toilets developed in the 1870s. But well into the early twentieth century, great swaths of the poor and working class were excluded from these standard elements of domestic comfort.[51] East Enders were not entirely cut off from the urban geometries of hygiene, of course, having learned to rely on commercial and semi-public spaces such as Liverpool Street Station and public urinals, known colloquially as cottages, as well as chamber pots and hip baths, outdoor privies, and the streets themselves. The Goulston Street Baths in Aldgate, for instance, about a quarter of a mile from Merrick's rooms at the London Hospital, reportedly saw attendance rates for 1888 in excess of 110,000 paying customers, with almost 30,000 first-class users who took warm baths and almost 90,000 second-class users who took cold baths even on cold days.[52] But it was not until the Jack the Ripper murders that took place in the autumn of 1888, at precisely the same moment that Merrick was writing about the comforts of his new domestic space , that Queen Victoria demanded that gas lighting be installed in the pitch-black streets, alleys, and rookeries of the East End as a potential deterrent against violent criminal acts.[53] The lack of urban infrastructure was such that the distribution of police officers to the East End only occurred in 1894, a full six years after the Ripper's last known murders already had taken place.

The lack of adequate toilet facilities was part of the requisite denigration of the poor, but it also demonstrated the enduring gendered character imposed on architectural spaces, with the assumption being that even in dire circumstances women and men had essentially distinct bodily needs that required a modicum of dignity. One investigative report published in the late 1880s, for instance, described a sleeping house "situated at 59 Mile End Road, a few doors from Cleveland Street" in Whitechapel and about an eighth of a mile from the London Hospital, as "two compartments which are separated by a curtain. In the front portion which measures 80ft long, 12ft wide and 9ft high, were huddled together about 100 men; in the rear portion which measures about 20ft square, were about 60 women in the same condition as the men; the rooms are badly ventilated and there is only one WC which the women alone are allowed to use."[54] Clearly, poor men were expected to find public facilities, such as those located in "cottages" or train stations, or simply use a side alley or back lot, which were created specifically for working men and those who used public conveyances, such as omnibuses, tubes, and trains, to conduct their business in the public sphere. By contrast, as late as the 1890s, public provisions for women's toilets were still considered "German abominations," a xenophobic remark that imagined public toilets as mechanisms for drawing in sex workers and loose women of dubious reputation.

Department stores, restaurants, and other commercial businesses were among the few spaces developed to provide toilet access in the public sphere for both genders. But poor women "huddled together" in rank shelters nightly for a few pence were unlikely to patronize such places, let alone travel across town to use them, which made the accommodation of women's toilet needs, along with a low price, a significant factor in the shelter's appeal. As Erika Rappaport has argued, "Public toilets were thus at the very center of the debate about women and the city, public space, and the public sphere."[55] Merrick, therefore, had a lavatory experience that was qualitatively different from that of the typical East Ender of either gender, as well as from that of those constituencies with whom he had previously identified: the urban poor, the workhouse inmate, and the struggling working-class family for whom the lack of a stable domestic space, let alone stable access to a toilet or bathtub, was a social and economic obstacle to any sense of personal comfort. The private domestic bathroom, as interpreted through modern codes of privacy and autonomy, represented a sense of self-empowerment, often coded as narcissistic self-indulgence, that poor urban men like Merrick previously would never have been able to take for granted.

Sitting with the Elephant Man

In 2014, Bonhams put up for auction the armchair custom-built for Merrick during his time at the London Hospital (see figure 1.8). Merrick bequeathed the chair to Edward Taylor, a young hospital worker who had spent many an afternoon playing the violin for Merrick and filling his rooms with the sounds of classical music. The armchair quickly became a family heirloom and was passed down internally within the Taylor family until it was displayed for a brief time in the early 1990s at the Royal London Hospital Museum, where it shared pride of place with a host of other objects associated with Merrick. On the back of the chair someone had affixed a gray leather strap on which the words "The Elephant Man's Chair" were painted in yellow capital letters. The chair ultimately sold for £6,000 to an anonymous buyer, thereby keeping in private hands one of the few objects either used by or associated with Merrick that survives to the present day.

At a cursory glance, Merrick's armchair looks like any number of tufted armchairs from the Victorian era, covered with a pleasant but bland patterned fabric and framed in ebonized wood that would have been familiar to nearly any consumer in London in the last quarter of the nineteenth century. The chair is significantly larger than a regular armchair; although not as large as a loveseat, it is about one and a half times the size of a conventional armchair, a piece of furniture that could conceivably serve multiple functions including that of a vertical bed. Each of the chair's legs sports a wheel that rotates a full 360 degrees, and which can be positioned or manipulated by the person while they are already sitting in the chair. What makes the armchair specific to Merrick's subjective experience is the addition of height to the two front legs, thereby putting the sitter in a fixed, backward-leaning orientation. The expectation for Merrick and his allies at the hospital was that he would feel more comfortable sitting in a chair that had a certain degree of spatial flexibility, one that could accommodate his size while also offering him options for either relaxing or, as many speculate, sleeping, since conventional horizontal sleep was not feasible for him as his head was too large to allow for a more recognizable sleeping practice.

FIGURE 1.8. Photograph of a large-size armchair covered in an elaborate floral pattern, resting on dark wood legs with wheel attachments that can rotate in multiple directions. This is the custom-made armchair constructed c. 1886 and bequeathed to Edward Taylor, a worker at the London Hospital who befriended Joseph Merrick during his three and a half years in residence. The chair's back and seat were built to accommodate Merrick comfortably, while the legs with wheels allowed him to lean back since he could not sleep in a horizontal position on a conventional bed. The chair was auctioned by Bonhams and sold in 2014 for £6,000. Photograph reprinted with permission of Bonhams.

Disability studies scholars such as Aimi Hamraie, Kelly Fritsch, and Bess Williamson have discussed the significance of disability objects and crip objects made for bodies that do not conform to standardization or expectations of normative use; such objects are deliberately intended to mark a type of intervention that characterizes many design projects of the post–disability rights era. One thinks of, for instance, the radical interventions of disability rights activists in cities like Berkeley, California, and Denver, Colorado, who took a sledgehammer to sidewalks to create what we now think of as curb cuts. In other contexts, carpenters, metal workers, and other skilled artisans have taken existing materials and, through a process of improvisation or tinkering or both, helped to create prototypes for what would become familiar objects, such as ramps on wheels for people who use wheelchairs, extended metal hooks or hands to reach items on shelves, and even the humble can opener, reinvented for people with arthritis or other types of flexibility impairments in their hands. These innovations are part of a lineage of technological interventions that scholars like Williamson and Elizabeth Guffey have characterized as part of what makes disability a modern experience; after all, these are interventions or improvisations that require a motivation by a maker or manufacturer to meet a particular need. The armchair created for Merrick could be seen as an example of design-ing *for* disability nearly a century before commercial and activist initiatives promulgated by the disability rights and universal design movements came into being.

In one sense, Merrick's armchair is not unique; custom-made assistive objects existed long before the twentieth century. But it is important for us to recognize and illuminate when an object that originates outside of a disability context is customized or reinvented in a way that puts the object into a dialectical relationship with the subjective experience of a user. In many ways, there is resonance between the armchair and the Mainz Ca-thedral model with which this chapter began. Neither was technologically deterministic, but both were materially expressive of Merrick's subjective experience embedded within multiple layers of physical sediment. Mer-rick's armchair could be characterized as a disability object for the ways that it exposes a process for honoring disabled subjectivity and material-izing in the form of an empathic design. The Mainz Cathedral model also could be characterized as a crip object—not for its use-value or its design, but for the ways in which it is an artifact of Merrick's distinctly subjective physical encounter with the built environment, and in this case, one that he fashioned with his own hands. Meanwhile, the current disposition of the model, inertly occupying its translucent sepulchre for perpetuity, tells us something about the flatness of an archival object that is knowable only through its visual appearance.

Sociologist Kevin Hetherington has described the different forms of knowledge that emerge from apprehending an object through discrepant sensory modalities—what it means, for example, to experience an object or a person through a distal relationship as opposed to a proximal rela-tionship.[56] Hetherington argues that, in the former, an object comes to be known by a person visually, usually at a distance, which clarifies and main-tains a divide between the subject and object. The distal is gained through looking, but the kind of looking that firmly puts the object at an empirical distance; even when a microscope or magnifying glass is used, the distance between the looking subject and the looked-at object is insuperable. By contrast, in the proximal, a person or object comes to be known through intimate tactile and/or olfactory means, sometimes in opposition to or in contrast with visual means. For Hetherington, the proximal is not an objectively superior form of knowledge but one that has the capacity to dissolve the difference between subject and object, intermingling their respective differences and merging them together.

Objects like the Mainz Cathedral model provide evidence of the proximal relationship produced through Merrick's tactile interaction with an object. One can see parapets tweaked to adhere to exterior walls, and eaves that are glossy with glue from the pressure exerted by the fingers of Merrick's "available hand" trying to hold the cardboard edges together, giving the appearance of a physical technique of enormous delicacy while also self-conscious about the intended result (see figure 1.9). One can also see the central Gothic tower with crenellations and ornamental figures that are slightly askew and tilted. As with all handmade objects, however, further examination reveals the keen distinction between a product-oriented shape stipulated by artistic design or vocational training and a process-oriented shape defined by subjective choice that follows the contours of *how* one relates to an object, not merely the expectation of what something should putatively look like when it's finished. Indeed, one could argue that Merrick's engagement with the Mainz Cathedral model was both a physical and a virtual space through which we might savor the material evidence of his spatial relationship to an external object constructed through his sense of bodily inhabitation. Sara Ahmed has argued that physical objects "are not only material: they may be values, capital, aspirations, projects, and styles . . . [but] we also inherit orientations, that is, we inherit the nearness of certain objects more than others, which means we inherit *ways of inhabiting and extending into space*."[57] Perhaps this explains the historical silence that has accumulated around the model, because it does not seem to have anything "meaningful" to say to the visitor about the social or political or medical circumstances in which Merrick lived.[58] The present and future disposition of the model seems to confirm Merrick's own premonition, as literary scholar Jon McKenzie has written, that Merrick knew was destined to survive for posterity as a spectacle under glass, both highly visible and deceptively invisible at the same time.[59]

The desire to protect the Mainz Cathedral model from damage as well as from the aging process is understandable given its fragility and its historical significance as one of the few surviving objects of Merrick's life. As Fernando Domínguez Rubio has written, an object like the Mainz Cathedral

FIGURE 1.9. Close-up photograph of the roof of the model of Mainz
Cathedral made by Joseph Merrick, showing shiny streaks of glue
and indentations that are evidence of Merrick's intimate physical
interactions with the object. Photograph c. 2012 by the author.

model is not so much protected as it is embalmed forever within a controlled infrastructure that prevents its decay, an intensive care unit for material objects.[60] Like Merrick himself, the model is a kind of patient arrested
in a hospital bed that is clocked out by sympathetic passersby but inevita-
bly is one that cannot be known without some physical contact that allows
a sensory engagement with it as opposed to looking at it from afar. The
cathedral model in this sense also serves as a kind of metonym for the experience of the person who has the desire to know Merrick and his illness,
though this knowledge is locked in a medical model that regards his identity
through his illness rather than through his experience.

∴

In 2019, author and historian Joanne Vigor-Mungovin initiated a campaign to raise £130,000 for the design, construction, and installation of
a statue of Merrick in adulthood in the pedestrian shopping district in
Leicester's city center, next to the city's famous Clock Tower. In an appeal

to would-be investors through a GoFundMe campaign, Vigor-Mungovin declared, "In Leicester itself, we have over twenty statues around the city, including Thomas Cooke, John Manners, The Leicester Seamstress, John Biggs, The Statue of Liberty, and of course our own King in the Car Park— Richard III. But how many of those do you stand and gaze at, contemplate on, think about their lives, what they did? who they were? Probably not many."[61] Initial sketches for the proposed statue by well-regarded Leicester sculptor Sean Hedges-Quinn depict Merrick realistically in a theatrical pose, balanced on a cane and surrounded by a cape, the inner swoop of which gives his body dimension like a sturdy mast beneath the billow of a sail. Importantly, Merrick's head is not hooded, its dimensionality visible to sighted viewers from all sides. To anchor Merrick through an honorific object in the city's best known commercial district would, in theory, serve as a significant marker of disability history, one that would be seen by locals and tourists in a rapidly gentrifying quarter of Leicester. And in terms of supporting disability visibility, Vigor-Mungovin became an active challenger to critics of the project who compared Merrick's physical difference to Leicester's physical decline; one resident of Leicester objected to the statue being placed in a prominent public space by declaring that "our poor city has become ugly enough without a statue of this poor man being displayed."[62]

Yet however earnestly conceived, sensitively executed, and politically assertive, one could argue that the design for the Merrick statue is deeply normative in terms of its reliance on visual and spatial distance from a prospective visitor. To "stand and gaze at" a representation of Merrick under the Clock Tower in the middle of the city of his birth is an urban fantasy that relies upon sight and objectifies him in precisely the same ways that theatrical and scientific eyes scrutinized him, the dependencies of a so-called enlightened age. In certain ways, the realistic bronze sculpture of Merrick atop a tall plinth recalls Marc Quin's provocative and highly controversial *Alison Lapper Pregnant* (2005), which, rendered in classical white marble, was both subversive and transformative when placed in the same space alongside bronze statues of male military heroes on plinths in London's Trafalgar Square.[63] But the singular and isolated Merrick sculpture replicates and sustains the visual scrutiny by which Merrick came to be known to the public—from his first exhibition at the New Empire Theatre of Varieties in Leicester in 1883, to his photo session at the Pathological Society of London in 1884, to the contemporary theatrical, film, and television representations by which he continues to be known. It freezes Merrick's life story as that of the looked-upon, the object of the gaze, since ultimately the statue is a representation of his appearance but not of his experience. As Fiona Candlin reminds us, *all* sculptures start out as multisensorial objects, but in their move to the gallery or museum or town square they become isolated behind velvet ropes or atop a plinth, their distance communicating to us that they can only be appreciated by those without any kind of visual impairments.[64]

In June 2023, Vigor-Mungovin announced that due to lack of support she had decided to abandon the statue project; after four years she had raised only £3,000.[65] "No-one is interested," she claimed somewhat bitterly before describing her two alternate plans: to install yet another plaque, this time on the tiny sliver of what remains of Lee Street, in recognition of Merrick's relationship to St George's Ward where he spent his formative years; and the creation of "Joseph's Garden" in the vicinity of the Royal London Hospital, now the Tower Hamlets Town Hall. What Vigor-Mungovin has expressed as disappointed resignation, however, might be an opportunity to create a monument to Merrick that is founded on principles of the proximal—that is, in the contemporary urban design approaches that are inspired by thinking about how disability can engage visitors or users beyond the conventions of designing for a normative public sphere. A garden design does not a have to be a second-best plan; rather, it can be a plan that is not exclusively visual or even representational but instead one that is *experiential*. It could foreground the vicissitudes of Merrick's sensory experiences as an urban subject. More than what a statue, let alone a plaque, could ever do, a garden would promote Merrick's life and legacy through a deliberate attunement to sensory experience in an urban environment.

Of course, what that attunement would look and sound and smell and feel and taste like would be entirely up to Vigor-Mungovin and her collaborators. And, fortunately for her, she need not look very far. Since the 1990s, Leicester has been an incubator of projects that think differently and creatively about disability as a historical topic and mode of encounter for visitors. The School of Museum Studies at the University of Leicester, for instance, under the leadership of Richard Sandell, initiated an innovative series of curatorial interventions at local museums around Britain using disability objects from its collections to challenge visitors' expectations about what constitutes local history. In 2005, the University of Leicester partnered with the Richard Attenborough estate to create the Attenborough Arts Center, which for nearly twenty years has programmed events and performances rooted in a disability arts approach. And 2010 saw the opening of the Sense Atelier, a multisensory education program in Leicester for children with special needs and young people on the autism spectrum that engages them through sensory encounters in ways that a static object in a conventional medium and spatial position never will. Whatever its final orientation, a garden devoted to the life and memory of Joseph Merrick would be superior in every way to a statue that can only preserve Merrick as an object to be scrutinized, a church model trapped under glass and not as a fully embodied subject in the world.

CHAPTER TWO

Helen Keller and the Urban Archive

In 2014, French artist Silvia Radelli debuted her work *Métroféminin*, a re-imagined map of the Paris Métro that rechristens existing stations with the names of important (and often neglected) historical or contemporary women (see figure 2.1).[1] A cartographic counterpart to US artist Judy Chicago's famed installation piece *The Dinner Party* (1974–79)—a masterpiece of second-wave feminist art in which Chicago created an enormous triangular table with genitalia-inspired place settings for thirty-nine women and embroidered references to 999 more—*Métroféminin* transmutes women's historical significance into the spatial scale of public transportation.[2] Eschewing the dinner table for the subway platform, Radelli subverts the masculine space of the Métro in order to celebrate the biographies of the women through whose names the stations are transformed. The Étienne Marcel station, for instance, a station near the Louvre Museum named for a medieval royal official, is renamed for Helen Keller. Unknown to Radelli at the time, this was an uncannily accurate choice, since its privileged location was among those tourist-friendly spaces that Keller routinely visited during her many trips to Paris. Across the Seine, in a calm if rather nondescript residential section near the Jardin des Plantes and the Gare d'Austerlitz, Radelli rechristened the Saint-Marcel stop for Anne Sullivan Macy, Keller's famed teacher and companion.

In 2016, US authors Rebecca Solnit and Joshua Jelly-Schapiro published *Nonstop Metropolis*, an atlas project somewhat comparable to Radelli's, of New York City neighborhoods where prominent women in the arts, sciences, and politics grew up or lived during their time as New Yorkers.[3] Solnit and Jelly-Schapiro marked the neighborhood of Forest Hills, Queens, where Keller lived from 1917 to 1938, when she moved to Easton, Connecticut, her home base for the rest of her life. But whereas Solnit and Jelly-Schapiro use the atlas format to recollect forgotten or marginalized histories of women, Radelli's Métro map is made up not of existing histories but of possible counter-histories of infrastructure. Radelli's map engages

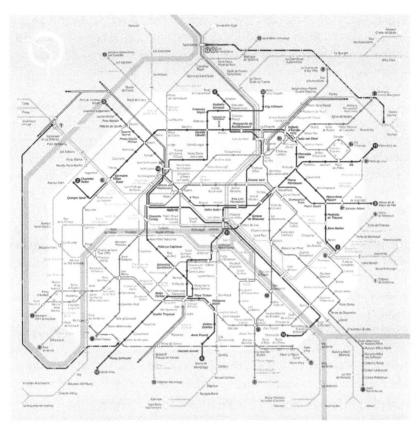

FIGURE 2.1. Photograph of a map with multiple lines going horizontally, vertically, and diagonally over a large rectangular area. Although it looks like a map of the Paris underground subway system (or Métro), it is the art project *Métroféminin* (2014) made by French artist Silvia Radelli. Radelli has renamed all of the Métro stations for women of historical significance, including Helen Keller and Anne Sullivan Macy. Radelli's project anticipated by nearly a decade the naming of two new stations on Line 4 for World War II resistance fighter Lucie Aubrac and singer-songwriter Barbara, both of which opened in 2022. Before this, only four of Métro's 308 stations were named for women. Map reprinted with permission of Silvia Radelli.

in what some feminist, queer, and critical disability studies scholars have called alternative modes of knowledge-making, an epistemological project that transforms what we think we already know—about public transportation, about the people who use it, about cities as forms of symbolic capital—through a deliberate spatial reorientation that has the capacity to produce new forms of urban knowledge as well as modes of inhabiting urban space.[4] Move through any city, and you quickly understand that there is no single "city" but instead a palimpsest of adjacent, coexisting forms and experiences of the same city that are as varied and discrepant as the people who occupy it. Each and every urban encounter is in fact a wholly subjective experience for each person, despite the best efforts of planners to give those encounters the appearance of a neat, Jenga-like nest of interlocking pieces.[5]

Architectural theorist David Gissen has observed that calls for an accessible city leave dominant urban forms intact rather than asking what kinds of transformations would need to take place in order to make cities accessible from their conception.[6] What, then, is the value of an atlas designation or renamed Métro station if it is not also a call to make neighborhoods or stations more accessible for people with mobility, sensory, or cognitive disabilities? Of course, making art projects, however ambitious or clarifying, is not the same as making structural interventions into subway design or urban policy. Keller adored New York and Paris, and waxed rhapsodic about their feel and smell and taste. Knowing them sensorially was central to her broader understanding of what it meant to be a citizen of the world. As she wrote in 1929, "I like any mode of transit—subway, elevated or the bus—that brings me into closer contact with people. Polly describes their faces and their talk. Through the sense of smell impressions tell me much—powder, perfume, tobacco, shoe polish . . . In an automobile I miss these intimate revelations of how my fellow creatures live."[7] So is the logical extension of the potent histories (and counter-histories) offered by *Nonstop Metropolis* and *Métroféminin* that each station will reflect in some way the subjective experiences of the person for whom it is named? Will a station renamed for Keller get a structural makeover so that its entry, its tunnels and walkways, its platform, and its exit are all organized around the modalities she used as a deafblind white middle-class woman?

In their respective ways, the aforementioned cartographic projects challenge collective histories of how cities remember those who have lived there; but they also challenge presumptions about Keller's own biography. In the final years of her life, Keller had to live with distorted characterizations that reduced her to her famous language-learning epiphany at the water pump (her "wawa" moment) at her family home in Tuscumbia, Alabama, as a result of the vigilant work of her teacher, Anne Sullivan Macy (1866–1936). As historians like Kim Nielsen and literary scholars like Georgina Kleege have argued, Keller's "wawa" moment was a kind of biographical albatross that burdened Keller with an association, both symbolic and empirical, of the rurality of her southern heritage and domestic spaces of home as sources of the synthetic sensory miracle that brought her, as was often said, "out of the darkness."[8] This association was not entirely a historical fabrication; Keller frequently invoked the pastoral within the urban as a southern girl who was not a "city girl." From 1894 to 1896, for example, Keller attended the Wright-Humason School for the Deaf in New York City; writing a decade later, she reminisced, "I remember especially the walks [Sullivan and I] took together every day in Central Park, the only part of the city that was congenial to me. I never lost a jot of my delight in this great park. I loved to have it described every time I entered it; for it was beautiful in all its aspects."[9] Yet Keller's popular image was *inextricable* from urban culture, not just urban parks that offered visitors a bucolic retreat. Readers during the first half of the twentieth century were far more familiar with a version of Keller who was deeply intertwined with the streets and sidewalks and buildings and other sites of urban encounter one has in cities like New York and Paris. She visited Paris on numerous occasions, well into the 1950s, as part of the international travel she did as a global ambassador for the American Foundation for the Blind, the organization she helped to establish in 1921.

For historians like Nielsen, Keller's occasional presentation of self as nonurban was strategic. Nielsen argues that Keller was willing to perform "civic fitness"—that is, she presented an image of herself as a deafblind person in the world who was self-sufficient, noncontroversial, productive, and nonthreatening—in an era when sterilization and segregation were typical responses to many people with physical or sensory or intellectual disabilities who were framed within the racialized language of the eugenics movement, for which "fitness" was a measure not of athletic ability but of reproductive value.[10] Keller's sustained connection to urban life and its various architectural and spatial configurations may have been deliberately sidelined or outright ignored as a way to downplay Keller's activism not directly related to her advocacy for the American Foundation for the Blind. Keller's commitments to some of the most significant social and political movements of the first half of the twentieth century—including support for women's suffrage, educational opportunities for African Americans, the right to unionize, political candidates for the Socialist Party of America, and organizations like the American Civil Liberties Union, which she co-founded in 1920—were oriented around the potency of her physical presence in urban spaces.[11] As literary scholar Marie Dominique Garnier has written, Keller's "actual motion down city streets . . . involved taking steps, marching in public view as a way of making manifest the urge for another 'destiny' for the United States [that] involved bodies in motion."[12] Over time, the absence of these spatialized forms of urban dissent from Keller's biography served to preserve her in her earliest incarnation as the miraculous little girl, the southern girl who was intellectually precocious yet socially immature and politically naive. This is why, by the time of Keller's biographical "third act" in the 1950s, her celebrity had calcified around that primary scene of language acquisition through playwright William Gibson's wildly successful television production *The Miracle Worker* (1957), the Rosetta Stone of the Helen Keller story, when it was transferred to Broadway and became a Tony Award–winning play (1959), and later was transformed into a screenplay and an Academy Award–winning film (1962).

In the first chapter of this book, we looked at the embodied entanglements across the span of Joseph Merrick's remarkable but short life. By contrast, this chapter will look at two selected periods in the remarkable and very long life of Helen Keller in order to think about her sensory engagements with urban environments and, by extension, the ways that such periods highlight her vexed relationship to urban modernity in historical perspective. I discuss Keller in the "midstream" of her life: her two decades spent in New York City, from 1917 to 1938, before she moved to suburban Connecticut; and her 1937 and 1952 trips to Paris, the latter of which she took when she was made a Chevalier of the Ordre National de la Légion d'Honneur, the highest award of merit bestowed by the French government. I dip into Keller's vast archive of textual and visual objects, many of which are available digitally through the American Foundation for the Blind (www.afb.org). I also closely examine footage, some of it unreleased, from the 1954 documentary, *The Unconquered: Helen Keller in Her Story*, sometimes known by just its subtitle. The film, which garnered international praise and won for its director, Nancy Hamilton, the 1956 Academy Award for Best Documentary, does a superb job of capturing and preserving those moments when Keller's position as a deafblind white woman of economic and social privilege shaped her multimodal entanglements with the kinds of urban experiences—moving through the streets, encountering buildings, drinking coffee in cafés, and of course window shopping—that, as I will argue, were not exceptions to what we have come to understand as conventional nondisabled experiences of urban modernity. Rather, these moments capture and preserve entanglements that constitute urban modernity either alongside or in opposition to those conventional nondisabled experiences.

Historians and theorists of urbanism who regard cities as either nodes of wealth creation or mechanisms of social control (or as the nefarious intertwining of both) have defined "urban modernity" in ways that generalize and genericize the subjective experiences of city dwellers. Part of the inherent contradiction of the phrase, however, is that in order for it to maintain its authority, it has to presume that all people will react to "the urban" and "the modern" in a fundamentally similar way. The specificity of an individual's bodily or social difference in such a formulation is utterly absent from such broad claims. During the mid-1980s, for instance, literary historians Peter Stallybrass and Allon White wrote that nineteenth-century public spaces in Britain, such as "the tram, the railway station, the ice rink, above all the streets themselves were shockingly promiscuous. And the fear of that promiscuity was encoded above all in terms of the fear of being touched. 'Contagion' and 'contamination' became the tropes through which city life was apprehended."[13] But from whose point of view did Stallybrass and White make such pronouncements? Such formulations may well capture bourgeois fantasies of the contaminating physicality of public spaces. But who, exactly, was *imagined* by such invocations of the Victorian epidemiological-cum-moralistic gaze, to say nothing about those for whom "promiscuous" tactility was a form of physical and social engagement with the external world?

Some urban historians, such as Patrick Joyce, have argued that new forms of civic architecture and urban planning during the nineteenth century in cities like Vienna, Manchester, and Paris created spaces that perpetuated fantasies of freedom for all citizens even as individual bodies (and fortunes) were subjugated, disciplined, and controlled by government officials, financial elites, urban planners, and the vagaries of the free market.[14] This was itself not a new phenomenon; as scholars such as Chandra Mukerji and Dale Upton have argued in their respective works, seventeenth- and eighteenth-century cities in Europe were sites of power exercised by political and commercial entities—from ancient aristocratic landowners to the latest upstart nouveaux riches.[15] Yet despite the fact that the dual experiences of freedom and control in these new urban configurations produced many new experiences of architecture that shaped generations of urban subjectivities—one thinks of, for instance, the installation of public baths for working-class, poor, and immigrant communities in London's East End that we examined in chapter 1—historical attention to "the urban subject" has remained largely focused on people without physical or sensory or cognitive impairments. As anthropologists Carol A. Breckenridge and Candace Vogler observed over two decades ago, "the 'person' at the center of the traditional liberal theory is not simply an individual locus of subjectivity (however psychologically fragmented, incoherent, or troubled). He is an *able-bodied* locus of subjectivity, one whose unskilled labor may be substituted freely for the labor of other such individuals, who can imagine himself largely self-sufficient because almost everything conspires to help him take his enabling body for granted (even when he is scrambling for the means of subsistence)."[16]

In her classic book of urban media studies, *Window Shopping* (1994), Anne Friedberg deployed her book's titular phrase to characterize a whole set of technological and spatial transformations during the late nineteenth and early twentieth centuries that catapulted the act of seeing to the vanguard of modern urban culture.[17] Building upon the media archaeology of art historians like Jonathan Crary, Friedberg argues that experiences of urban space and advanced capitalism were mutually reinforced through the emergence of department stores, museum dioramas, parlor entertainments like zoetropes and stereoscopes, and, ultimately, the rise of cinema. Although she does not acknowledge it in her writings, Friedberg's description of visual media like the department store window display as a communication device par excellence relies on the nondisabled urban subject that can look, wander, eavesdrop, and even occasionally purchase, though that final act of consumer consummation was never foregrounded in Friedberg's scholarship. This is why the fantasies of liberty attributed to (male) figures like the *flâneur*—an archetype of nineteenth-century urban modernity described by Charles Baudelaire and subsequently taken up by German philosopher Walter Benjamin in the 1930s and the French Marxist urban collective Situationist International in the 1950s—require a presumptive belief in certain bodily orientations toward the built environment that make those orientations seem inevitable rather than habituations to urban culture that have accumulated through routine and repetition.[18]

In this chapter, I will argue that any seemingly radical moves to think about sensory approaches to the city as a form of counter-urbanism, and, later, as a revolutionary movement, were pioneered by Keller. In her time, however, her movement through the world became an object of fascination and epistemic exoticism despite attempts to domesticate her or infantilize her. She was publicly discussed as the exemplary "super crip" who could navigate the world to the paternalistic amazement of nondisabled passersby. But Keller was not building a counter-modernity or practice. Only when your senses are already organized around binaries does the effort to challenge or subvert those binaries hold any meaning for you. Her urbanity was constituted through her subjectivity, not as compensation for her subjectivity. *All* of it was her experience of modernity. If anything, these moments from Keller's life highlight the ways that the urban is not, and never was, a pregiven set of environmental or technological or even ideological forms. The urban is made through action.

Keenly Conscious of Curves

Keller's celebrity was fashioned not only around her status as a deafblind woman, but also around her relationship to geographical mobility. After the age of eight, Keller shifted from a comfortable, middle-class rural life in the small southern town of Tuscumbia, Alabama, to an urban-oriented life centered on the East Coast, specifically the corridor between Boston and New York City. From 1888 until 1917, she made her home in either South Boston, Manhattan, Cambridge, or the town of Wrentham, Massachusetts, about thirty miles southwest of Boston (see figure 2.2). After 1917, she lived full time in New York, setting up house in the upscale outer borough of Forest Hills, Queens. In 1938, she left Queens for Connecticut, moving into a house custom-designed for her by architect Cameron Clark in the historic village of Aspetuck, near Easton. Having these home bases anchored in or near large cities gave Keller the freedom to voyage out to the cities of the world, reveling in the kinds of urban experiences for which her well-lubricated sensory modalities of tactility and olfaction were endlessly curious and endlessly epicurean.

Around the same the time Silvia Radelli debuted her *Métroféminin* project, disability studies scholars Robert McRuer and Lisa Merri Johnson co-edited an important issue of the *Journal of Literary and Cultural Disability Studies* on the topic of "cripistemology."[19] The word is a portmanteau that combines the philosophical tradition of epistemology with the activist inversion of "crip" from a term of condemnation into one of positive, albeit ironic, identification. Cripistemology represents a kind of rapprochement with the medical model of disability: it recognizes and honors physical, sensory, and cognitive difference as central to how people with disabilities make meaning in the world. Embodied differences, such as having a chronic condition or being neuroatypical, are not problems to solve or states of being to manage; they are emphasized as critical features in the making of a disabled subjectivity. This is why, over the past two decades, scholars and activists in critical disability studies have sought to foreground individual embodied experiences rather than downplay them, paying attention to the specific ways in which disabled subjectivities offer a more compelling starting point than treating access and accommodation as universally applicable to bodies and all situations. This marks a profound break from the social model of disability that downplayed physical difference in order to emphasize the role of the environment in producing limitations and boundaries.[20]

This is not to say that a cripistemological approach considers the social model of disability outmoded or irrelevant; rather, it prioritizes subjective experience—and even the idea that people with disabilities have a subjectivity in the first place—in the design and creation of a better world, whether through law or design or social policy.[21] For McRuer and Johnson, cripistemology repositions the person with physical, sensory, or cognitive impairments not as a passive object but as an active subject whose subjectivity is shaped by their sensory encounters. Much of this work is in direct

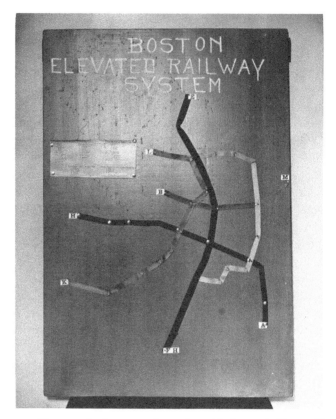

FIGURE 2.2. Photograph of a rectangular surface with the words "Boston Elevated Railway System" handwritten at the top. The map was produced c. 1925 for students at the Perkins School for the Blind in Watertown, Massachusetts, who, as Helen Keller had done in the 1890s and early 1900s, made or used tactile objects like this one to know and navigate the urban environment. The different rail lines are indicated by multicolored pieces of satin ribbon that have been fixed to the surface with pushpins that designate the stations on each rail line as they would have existed in the mid-1920s. At center left is a handwritten key with the corresponding names and originating and terminating stations of the different rail lines. Photograph c. 1930. Reprinted with permission of the Perkins School for the Blind Archives.

response to disability studies as a field. Since the 1970s, when researchers in the social sciences began to write about how urban designs have impacted people with disabilities, the focus has been on inaccessibility stemming from real-world obstacles as well as on larger trends that have reflected goals associated with postwar urbanism, such as maximizing efficiency and utility. While the social model of disability encouraged researchers and policy makers to break down actual barriers and reconfigure architectural and urban spaces in order to promote equity and inclusion, it was also deliberately disembodied and somatically abstracted. The lack of ramp or elevator, or the omission of sign-language interpretation or Braille markers, in a public institution may violate the law (such as Section 504 of the 1973 Civil Rights Act, the precursor to the Americans with Disabilities Act of 1990), but it also registers such a violation by de-emphasizing the subjective experience of disability.

Keller's intuitive grasp of cripistemology was present from the beginning of her life in public. It was inseparable from her public identity. As a white American woman of considerable resources and celebrity, Keller demonstrated that her role as a public figure was shaped as much by multisensory experiences of the built environment as it was by her status as a deafblind woman. Georgina Kleege has observed that, in *The World I Live In* (1908), Keller's second biographical bestseller, Keller shares with the reader not only "information that is spelled into her hand, but her own interpretation of sensory phenomena which comes to her independent of others' mediation. While Sullivan was the central figure in Keller's first book, she is never mentioned by name in the second."[22] Kleege's observation is an enticement for scholars to challenge the collective tendency to privilege Sullivan's (and, later, Thomson's) mediation of the world, as finger-spelled on the palms of Keller's hands, over those of Keller's own sensorium since it prioritizes language—and, by association, vision and sound—over tactile and olfactory pleasures. Keller's multiple engagements with material and social environments—sipping a cup of coffee at a café or window shopping along a commercial thoroughfare—were indeed mediated alternately through the modality of her companions' hands or the photographer's gaze, but just as forcefully and eloquently through her own subjective physical experiences. No one modality was more important or more powerful or more authoritative than any other.

Keller did not associate her coming to consciousness as a self with the idea of home or, for that matter, even the modality of touch; in her first autobiography, *The Story of My Life* (1904), she wrote, "It was not the sense of touch that brought me knowledge. It was the awakening of my soul that first rendered my senses their value, their cognizance of objects, names, qualities, and properties. Thought made me conscious of love, joy, and all the emotions."[23] Highlighting her sensual relationship to "objects, names, qualities, and properties" fundamentally changes how we think about the many cartographies of disability that coexist alongside the familiar traces of the modern city.

For instance, in 1922, the Nordyke & Marmon Fine Motor Car Company invited Keller to promote its newest luxury vehicle, the Marmon 34. The campaign's advertisement, published throughout the United States in major publications such as *National Geographic* as early as February 1923, featured Keller as its spokesperson, and included an image of Keller sitting in the back of a Marmon motorcar with her hand touching the glass of the right rear window, her head tilted upward, and her eyes closed in a meditative state (see figure 2.3). Eschewing photographic realism, the image of Keller was presented to viewers in the form of a painting by a noted artist, Countess Maria Elizabeth Zichy (née Podvinecz), whose father had built one of the most successful automobile companies in Hungary before the Great War. Keller is depicted wearing a heavy black fur coat and hat over which is draped, cascading down her shoulder, a diaphanous gauzy scarf. Through the windows—obscure to Keller but visible to the magazine reader—is a breathtaking mountain range, giving visual confirmation to Keller's observation, printed in large letters across the page, "I knew we were in the Catskills by the atmosphere."

Nordyke & Marmon's engineers provided Keller with a test drive after securing her endorsement, presuming that the lack of visual and auditory stimulation would leave intact a highly aestheticized experience that would highlight the Marmon's status as a luxury vehicle. Keller did not disappoint. "Recently, we drove over Catskill roads," she writes, "but I hardly felt any difference from pavements. I knew we were in the mountains by the atmosphere and the odors peculiar to high altitudes. Riding in a Marmon is just like sailing: the same smooth, vibration-less motion." The newest designs for Marmon made innovative use of aluminum, which not only made the firm's cars lightweight but gave them a more comfortable advantage over cars made of solid steel. The advertisement's copywriters confirmed this dimension of her test drive, averring that "to [Miss Keller], the chief appeal of the Marmon is its super-comfort and ease of riding."

That a group of automobile executives pinned some part of their financial future to Helen Keller's automotive connoisseurship may well seem like the beginning of a joke in poor taste. So how did Nordyke & Marmon come to select Keller? It was not the first time that Keller was associated publicly with transportation: Keller was known for appearing all over town in the passenger seat co-pedaling a tandem bicycle navigated by Sullivan across Cambridge to attend her classes at Radcliffe. In 1899, she joined famed "trick rider" Alfred St. Onge on a tandem bike, traveling from Newbury Street in downtown Boston to Franklin Park along circuitous routes. St. Onge reported that Keller "seems to understand unusually well the various motions of the wheel, and the minute it begins to descend a hill she realizes that she must 'back pedal' while on ascending a hill or incline she knows

Miss Keller has attained international fame for her mastery of handicaps. Though blind, deaf, and dumb, she now "sees" and "hears" through touch. She converses fluently. She has devoted her life to the helping of others similarly afflicted.

Miss Keller touring in the Catskills
—A painting by the Countess Elizabeth Zichy

"I knew we were in the Catskills by the atmosphere"

By Helen Keller

"I am delighted with my Marmon. To my touch the workmanship seems perfect.

"Borne along on deep, springy cushions, I find a long drive in it lulling and alluring. I do not have to hold on to keep my balance. In other cars I am keenly conscious of curves, but in my Marmon I hardly know when we turn a sharp corner.

"Recently we drove over Catskill roads, but I hardly felt any difference from pavements. I knew we were in the mountains by the atmosphere and the odors peculiar to high altitudes. Riding in a Marmon is just like sailing—the same smooth, vibrationless motion.

"I can hardly say enough in praise of this wonderful automobile. It gives me so much enjoyment."

＊　＊　＊　＊　＊

Miss Keller is one of the many who prefer Marmons. To her its chief appeal is super-comfort and ease of riding. Like other Marmon owners, she also seeks dependability and economy.

The Marmon plan of nation-wide standardized service shows that the average monthly cost for mechanical maintenance of 1922-23 cars serviced at Marmon service stations is $4.71 per car per month.

The Marmon itself is proving its own superiority, based on actual service, not on claims; based on the evidence of owners, not on vague generalities.

M A R M O N
The Foremost Fine Car

1923

FIGURE 2.3. Print advertisement c. 1923, for the Marmon 34, created for the (now defunct) Nordyke & Marmon Fine Motor Car Company, featuring Helen Keller as its spokesperson. In the center of the advertisement is a painting of Keller sitting in the backseat of the car wearing a heavy coat, her head wrapped in a diaphanous scarf, while her right hand touches the window. The text underneath says, "I knew we were in the Catskills by the atmosphere." Author's collection.

just how to assist her fellow rider. She is clever in knowing better than many riders how to reserve her powers and not to overtax her strength."[24] In 1917, after she, Ann Sullivan Macy, and John Macy left the Boston area to set up a group house at 93 Seminole Avenue (now 71-11 112th Street) in Forest Hills, the distance from Queens to Manhattan necessitated a change in medium from tandem bicycle to taxi.[25] In public representations, Keller was often presented as sophisticated and worldly: following her graduation from Radcliffe, for instance, the Havana Cigar Company of London, Ontario, placed an image of Keller sporting her graduation gown and mortarboard, an academic variant on the early twentieth-century cult of product endorsement by athletes and Hollywood starlets on cigarette cards, breakfast cereal packets, and the covers of pulp magazines. Keller's appearance in the Marmon campaign, however, which asks its reader to associate her finely tuned sensory apprehension of the world with a finely tuned connoisseurship of luxury branding, was positively unprecedented. Outside of J. D. Leyendecker's Arrow Shirt man, the advertising icon whose eye-patch marking him implicitly as a veteran of World War I made him a highly eroticized object of (male) consumer identification, advertising that featured people with disabilities was limited to medicalized images involving wheelchairs, elevators, trusses, and prosthetic and orthotic items—ads intended specifically for physicians, hospital administrators, patients, and their caregivers at home or in residential institutional settings.[26] So what, exactly, was Keller ultimately *selling* in such an advertisement—and to whom?

Author Charles Leerhsen argues that Nordyke & Marmon's engineers chose Keller because they were "casting about for someone to bolster [the] company's claim that it manufactured 'The Easiest Riding Car in the World.'"[27] Was the company relying on Keller to help court the metropolitan resident who commuted to the city from the suburbs for work, or else the family that liked to go joyriding as a weekend pleasure? The Marmon advertisements were certainly not for visually impaired readers of national magazines, who would have required some form of translation or interpretation since Braille editions did not feature advertisements, even those with Keller's celebrity endorsement. Something of Keller's cosmopolitanism must have resonated with Marmon's executives in the hope of being competitive with other luxury automobile manufacturers including Mercedes-Benz, Duesenberg, Cadillac, and Rolls-Royce; a basic Marmon 34 cost about $3,500 in 1923, approximately $65,000 a century later. In the Marmon advertisement, the depiction of Keller's hand raised aloft and touching the window is an impressionistic element as well as a deliberately situated activity through which she shows her capacity to use her bodily senses to make meaning of her environment. The language she attributes to this experience—"In other cars, I am keenly conscious of curves, but in my Marmon, I hardly know when we turn a sharp corner"—actively refutes any connotations of pity or deprivation associated with her subjectivity. The advertisement breaks through any negative associations that a deafblind person lives in a "world of darkness" by showing how Keller deliberately *deploys* that darkness—the absence of light or sound—to show how her capacity to feel vibrations could be an experience of refinement, not disorientation. Keller's self-representation of her experience establishes her as a discriminating subject whose sensory modalities are attuned to environments, both natural and built.

The roles played by touch and smell and vibration and other embodied affects in Keller's sensorium were clearly exploited by Marmon's copywriters for commercial purposes. Some of this was layered with the exoticism attributed to accounts of famous nineteenth-century figures like Laura Bridgman and Louis Braille—people who, like Keller, were regarded as living metonyms of sensory connoisseurship. But those embodied affects were routinely, if not obsessively, highlighted in pictorial and textual accounts created or organized by Keller herself. In a famous essay published in 1929, for instance, she recounted waiting on the subway platform beneath Grand Central Terminal in Manhattan:

> Tremulously I stand in the subways, absorbed into the terrible reverberations of exploding energy. Fearful, I touch the forest of steel girders loud with the thunder of oncoming trains that shoot past me like projectiles. Inert I stand, riveted in my place. . . . Before my mind flashes in clairvoyant vision what all this speed portends—the lightning crashing into life, the accidents, railroad wrecks, steam bursting free like geysers from bands of steel, thousands of racing motors and children caught at play, flying heroes diving into the sea, dying for speed—all this because of strange, unsatisfied ambitions.[28]

Media accounts of Keller built upon these insights gleaned from her seemingly preternatural capacity for sensory discrimination, with her hands in particular described as somatic tools of translation that possessed an uncanny otherworldliness in relation to the technological or aesthetic objects they encountered. In an industrial economy, hands were not merely sense organs but material armatures of economic livelihood, as Erica Fretwell and Zeynep Alexander have demonstrated in their respective histories of haptic and kinesthetic sensory research. Thus, observers and onlookers alike imputed mystical characteristics to what Keller could divine through her fingertips.[29] In 1933, for instance, a reporter for the *New York Times* accompanied Keller and Thomson on a visit to the newly opened Radio City Music Hall. "She went to the bronze doors opening from the foyer into the auditorium and felt the figures in relief on them. They amused her . . . She turned to Miss Thomson and said: 'It needs censoring. It's too seductive.'"[30] In a 1937 article written for radio enthusiasts, Keller described how, through touching the cone of a loudspeaker, she could feel the vibrations emanating from a symphonic broadcast and distinguish between woodwind, brass, and string instruments.[31] In 1939, a reporter for the Associated Press relayed the story about a pilot hired to help Keller attend a conference in West Virginia after she had missed her train in Philadelphia. During the flight, Keller asked the pilot if the plane had reached eight thousand feet—at precisely the same moment that the instrument panel indicated they had reached that exact altitude.[32]

Yet, for all these remarkable moments of articulating sensory information, Keller was still regularly pressured, even contractually, to retell dramatic events from her early life, doled out in child-sized portions for eager and often paying audiences.[33] For philosopher of science Justin Lieber, one of the "invidious" aspects of William Gibson's play *The Miracle Worker* (1957) is that it distorts Keller's sensuous intake of the world by reducing everything to the "miracle" of language, emphasizing Keller's ability to speak—her "wawa" moment" at the water pump—rather than presenting her acquisition and use of language as part of a more complex set of cognitive processes involving multiple modalities of sensation of which spoken language was only one component. Lieber argues that this simplification helped to foster the eternally reductive representation of Keller as a female child, locking into place a specifically gendered set of associations with the domestic spaces of the home where, as Lieber witheringly observes, "to learn a language is just to learn a lot of labels for things."[34]

The appearance of such condescending stories in the media was usually not enough to entirely transcend the effects of any juvenile-oriented nostalgia. But for those paying attention, such stories were thwarted by every news editor who sought out ways to foreground, and not marginalize, Keller's urban experiences. In 1932, for instance, the *New York Times* published a photo of Keller on the eighty-sixth floor observation deck of the Empire State Building (see figure 2.4). An editor at the *Times*, John Finley, invited Keller in December 1931 to visit the world's tallest skyscraper and tell him in a letter "what she saw," a distillation of which was published in the *New York Times Magazine* a month later.[35] In the photograph, presented with many of the same mystical qualities the Marmon advertisement had featured nearly a decade earlier but without its deliberate commercial goals, Keller is depicted with her left hand pressed up against the window of the

FIGURE 2.4. Photograph of two well-dressed white women in hats and heavy
coats standing in a small room that has large glass windows. This is Helen Keller
(right) and her secretary, Polly Thomson, standing inside the observation
deck on the eighty-sixth floor of the Empire State Building. Keller touches one
of the large windows and communicates her haptic experience to Thomson,
who receives Keller's message in her right hand while holding Keller's coat
and gloves in her left. The scene was photographed after an editor for the *New
York Times* invited Keller to visit the newly opened skyscraper and share her
experience with the newspaper's readership. Photograph c. December 1931
for Wide World Photos, copyright undetermined. Author's collection.

observation deck, while Thomson holds Keller's other hand and watches
her reaction. What we can perceive in the image is Keller's approach to
public representations of tactility: the sense of pressure from the window,
as well as haptic engagement with the window's surface temperature and
smooth materiality. Indeed, one could argue that the excitement around
the photographic spectacle of Keller's tactile epiphany at the Empire State
Building mirrors the building's own history of the haptic: in May 1931, just

seven months earlier, President Herbert Hoover had made international headlines when he christened the $52 million building by touching a button on his desk in the Oval Office to illuminate its electric lights.[36] The window to which Keller's hand is pressed is infused with sunlight, and yet one cannot discern the city or even the sky or clouds in the distance. In her stylish black hat, double-strand pearl necklace, and elegant black outfit, Keller appears wistful here, another example of a public Helen Keller Moment intended to show off her Sphinx-like apprehension of the world.

By the late 1930s, Keller had retreated to suburban surroundings far from the top of the tallest building in the world. She built a house, named Arcan Ridge, on a bucolic estate near Easton, Connecticut, after having lived in Queens for two decades. "More than ever the outdoor world is a dear necessity to me," she wrote in 1941. "That is not simply for the tranquility it breathes upon me, it releases as yet unspoken thoughts and impulses which were held in check during the years I spent among cities harsh with turmoiled unrest and unmodulated mechanism."[37] She repeated this yearning for the calm of suburban spaces in a guest editorial she wrote in 1951 for a real estate magazine published in Glastonbury, Connecticut: "Every waking moment that I am not occupied with a lecture or an interview, my soul speeds home to the walk by a cedar railing where I have communed with the morning and listened with my hand on the trees as the winds make music in their branches."[38] Literary scholar Diana Fuss has written eloquently about how the architectural features of Arcan Ridge were shaped by Keller's subjective experience of spaces on her own property—the installation of a quarter-mile-long timber railing so that she could take long walks by herself, for instance, or the physical dimensions of or access points in the kitchen, bathroom, bedroom, and office that enabled her to navigate the house alone without having to rely on Thomson.[39] Cameron Clark, a well-known regional architect, specially designed and constructed the house with Keller's spatial needs firmly in mind. "Yours is a different understanding of architecture than that of my other clients," Clark wrote to Keller in November 1939, suggesting that Keller's subjective needs were also a key to her understanding of space in general.[40] This focus on Keller's navigation of domestic space, while an important part of her daily life in later years, has also had the effect of freezing her in the last years of her life as a homebody tethered to ways of navigating space that were entirely predicated on conquering the domestic. But the geographical relocation to Connecticut did not prevent Keller and Thomson from traveling regularly to New York City to attend theater and dance performances, and dine with friends and colleagues.

In 1969, the great American actress Ruth Gordon published a tribute to Keller in the *New York Times*, in anticipation of an autobiography that she never completed, in which she discussed her friendship with Keller from the early 1940s through the end of the 1950s.[41] She first met Keller in 1941, when she was invited to join American author and *New Yorker* critic Alexander Woollcott for afternoon tea along with Keller and Thomson at the Gotham (now the Peninsula) Hotel on Fifty-Fifth Street and Fifth Avenue. Keller's request for a bourbon old-fashioned instead of tea clinched the deal on what would become a two-decade-long friendship. Gordon describes how, two years later, in 1943, she rode in a taxi to Woollcott's funeral at McMillin Auditorium at Columbia University along with Keller, Thomson, the actress Katharine Cornell (Gordon's co-star in *The Three Sisters* on Broadway), and Guthrie McClintic (the play's director and Cornell's husband). Gordon describes the five passengers stuffed into the back of a taxicab that, stopping short, threw Keller to the floor, resulting in peals of laughter from Keller and the rest of the group on their way to the funeral party. The description of the Marx Brothers–like hurly-burly in the back of a New York taxi provides a marked contrast with Keller's ethereal voyage through the Catskills in the back of a Marmon precisely two decades earlier. It also provides evidence for why Keller was so desirable as a companion and friend: for Gordon and so many others, her capacity to heighten urban experiences— having a drink at a hotel bar, driving uptown in a taxi—was made possible because her subjectivity was always on display. This is what gave her public appearances the imprimatur of authenticity even if, in retrospect, they were also the basis for highly choreographed performances for the camera.

Gordon would not see Keller or Thomson for another decade; World War II had encroached on their collective fun. In 1955, Keller came in to Manhattan from Arcan Ridge to attend a performance of *The Matchmaker*, in which Gordon played the lead role of Dolly Levi, at a theater around the corner from the Palace Theater where Keller and Sullivan Macy had performed on the vaudeville stage thirty-five years earlier:

> I remembered [Keller] always came to the plays Kit Cornell was in and I invited her to the Royale Theater on West 45th Street. Polly wrote that Helen would be delighted. A Wednesday matinee would be best. And might they have five tickets and a script of the play for them to read in advance? The script and the five tickets were sent to Helen's house, Arcan Ridge. . . . Back came a check. Well, that wasn't the idea. Back went the check to Arcan Ridge and a few days later there arrived a big luxurious bottle of Gardenia Bath Oil from Henri Bendel's elegant store with

a message from Helen that she was looking forward to Wednesday. One knows great moments. What about bathing in gardenia scented bath oil, the gift of Helen Keller![42]

The power of this anecdote is not simply in recounting Keller's generosity or Gordon's good-natured appreciation of it. Rather, it is the way that it traces the components of Keller's urban knowledge and how for her the geography of the city was a sensual basis for physical action. Her gift of "Gardenia Bath Oil" may have highlighted the branded luxury commodity, but it also made evident a type of urban connoisseurship that was not about seeing or being seen but about embodying the kind of sensorial pleasures associated with the skin, the nose, the mouth—the virtues of which Keller had extolled as spokesperson for the Marmon some three decades earlier. The heady, floral scent of gardenia and the glossy, unctuous feel of bath oil were links in a synesthetic chain comprising olfaction, tactility, urban geography, memory, and the affective glue that holds them all together.

Disabling the *Flâneur*

By 1937, Polly Thomson had become Keller's primary traveling companion. Anne Sullivan Macy had long dealt with illness, and in October 1936 she died; her body was interred in a columbarium in the Washington National Cathedral in Washington, DC. Thomson's first significant journey alone with Keller took place in January 1937 after Keller had been invited to Paris to attend the unveiling of a statue celebrating Thomas Paine installed in the southeast corner of Parc Montsouris in the 13th arrondissement in Paris.[43] The Paine sculpture—which today stands 850 meters from the remarkable house at 50, avenue René Coty built by Jean-Julien Lemordant, whom we first encountered in the introduction—was not formally dedicated until 1948, but it was a labor of love of the US publisher Joseph Lewis, one of the mid-twentieth century's most outspoken atheists and freethinkers. Lewis's decision to invite Keller, well known as a socialist and feminist writer, was an odd fit with his choice of artist: famed sculptor John Gutzon Borglum, who designed the Paine statue at approximately the same time he was completing the monumental heads for Mount Rushmore, arguably inspired by his commitment to white nativist politics and his involvement with the Ku Klux Klan in the 1920s.

An editor for *Le Soir*, one of Paris's many competing daily newspapers, caught wind of Keller's arrival and made arrangements on January 30 to photograph Keller and Thomson window shopping on the fashionable avenue des Champs-Élysées. In the photograph, which we also first encountered in this book's introduction, Keller and Thomson stand side by side in front of a boutique window showcasing a selection of belted and embroidered dresses, patterned chemises with cravats, and form-fitting cloche hats in delicate, light fabrics, suggestive of the coming spring—a sharp contrast to the heavy, textured winter coats worn by the two women (see figure I.6). Their apparent delight in and longing for the consumer goods that have captured their attention is marked not only by the message that Keller is hand-spelling directly into Thomson's hand, the paleness of which is centered against the backdrop of their black winter coats, but also by the reflections of both women mirrored in the window glass that seem to haunt the shop's interior and our reception of the event. Later that day, Keller recorded the event, with self-conscious delight, in the journal that she kept of her daily activities: "Polly and I walked out with [the photographer] and he took pictures of us on the Champs-Élysées beside a shop window resplendent with Paris hats and gowns . . . Seeing everybody here in the pink of fashion doesn't tend to lull my feminine vanity."[44]

Keller, who was fifty-seven when the photograph was taken, clearly had more than a passing interest in clothes, which gave her the space to engage the tactile pleasures of the phenomenological world while simultaneously satisfying her own "feminine vanity." The day after posing for *Le Soir*'s photographer, for instance, Keller described in her diary a visit to the atelier of the *grande couturière* Elsa Schiaparelli, who was only too happy to have her material creations linked to the world's best known deafblind female celebrity. "I was sorry that [one of Schiaparelli's dresses] could not be made for me in a day," Keller wrote disappointedly, "but my hands were crammed with loveliness as one robe after another appeared."[45]

In French visual culture of the 1930s, images of people with disabilities, regarded as exotics who appeared alongside images of racial and ethnic "types," homeless men, itinerant families, and those with bodily differences, were regularly exploited by the camera and spanned a range of both commercial products and avant-garde experiments, used either to demonstrate humanist narratives of endurance in the face of adversity or else, in the case of the surrealists, to explore the uncanny textures of the urban unconscious.[46] But such artistic or documentary images do not exist in isolation from the political and technological spheres where they were shaped. The bodies of male veterans of the Great War with physical or sensory or cognitive disabilities were also highly visible, and highly gendered, subjects of media interest, sustaining the types of associations between male bodily sacrifice and the impassioned defense of civility under duress that has been part of French urban culture for centuries. In one account published in a

French journal for war veterans in 1917, for example, an officer riding on the Paris Métro observes a disabled ex-serviceman board the subway car. Noticing that none of the passengers seems willing to vacate their seat for the veteran, the officer accosts a "young man of robust appearance" and implores him, "Come on, young civilian, give up your seat to this wounded man." The young man tilts his hat deferentially to the officer and awkwardly replies, "Excuse me, Captain, but I have lost a leg."[47]

The photograph of Keller and Thomson window shopping in January 1937 represented a typological shift in the generic conventions used to depict bodily difference. It also marks an epistemological shift in our understanding of the French verb *flâner* and the noun *flânerie*, which have bequeathed the nouns *flâneur* and *flâneuse*, making it possible to historicize nineteenth- and twentieth-century urban culture with greater precision. The phenomenological inspiration derived from *flânerie* has been a central component in genealogies of modern experience that can be traced to the singular figure of the man (and it is nearly *always* a man) in the crowd who observes, but does not participate in, urban culture, his aloofness the basis for his agency. Yet the multiple urban subjectivities of people with disabilities are typically excluded from such discussions because their sensory, physical, and cognitive subjectivities are too regularly subordinated to, and held captive by, the valorized gaze of the *flâneur.* Participating in the ebbs and flows of urban modernity need not rely solely on seeing or hearing or physical movement: as historian Rebecca Scales has written, in 1928, "just a few years after the first radio broadcast from the Eiffel Tower, two new radio charities, Radio for the Blind and Wireless at the Hospital, took up the task of distributing free radios to invalids and the blind, with the goal of putting these 'brave and poor people into contact with *exterior* life' and ending their 'isolation' in the private sphere."[48] By 1939, Theodor Adorno recognized radio technology as making possible a kind of aural *flânerie*, identifying the airwaves as a public space in which virtually all citizens could spatially perambulate and discover new narrative experiences of modern life.[49]

Some have argued that the *flâneur* is not a singular urban type but a multivalent urban icon; as early as 1841, for example, Louis Hart's *Physiologie du flâneur* implied that the *flâneur*'s foppish caprice carried all of the sexual (and, often, queer) connotations of physical and social difference found in nineteenth-century pseudoscientific tracts on physiognomy and phrenology. Such shifting tides of meaning across two centuries track a constant recalibration of the *flâneur:* from the lazy, unproductive figure of the mock-artist, to the perambulating gadfly-about-town, to the solitary, existential figure whose primary association is with enclosed shopping arcades.[50] There are more nuanced exceptions to this paradigmatic approach: in the

1980s and 1990s, feminist scholars carved out space for the *flâneuse* in order to problematize the male privilege implicit in discussions of *flânerie* and reinscribe women's place in the social etiologies of nineteenth- and twentieth-century urban modernity—a challenge not unlike that taken up by Silvia Radelli in her *Métroféminin* project.[51] Yet scholars continue to preserve the notion of the *flâneur* as a paradigmatic example of the modern subject who takes the functions of his or her body for granted. Making any claims for the *flâneur* or the *flâneuse* as an agent of modern experience— female, queer, postcolonial—still presumes that the codes of urban modernity, what counts as urban and/or modern, are organized around narratives of nondisability.

Such limited interpretations of urban subjectivity clearly had little or no effect on Keller, a *flâneuse* who believed not only that one could experience modernity through senses other than sight or hearing, but that one could appear modern, act modern, feel modern, and be modern without relying upon any of the meanings attached to bodily difference as either proscribed by her contemporaries or codified retrospectively by urban historians. Keller, for one, did not think that she herself was excluded from the boulevards of modernity. As she wrote in her diary, on the same day that she posed for *Le Soir*, she and Thomson

> went alone for a stroll . . . The air was soft, the moon was snowing its loveliness upon the city. The traffic was at a low ebb. We went as far as the Rue Royale, passing Maxim's, looking in the shop windows which are the undoing of unwary mortals, Polly noticing especially the jewelry, rare antiques, and Lalique glass. Everywhere I recognized the odor peculiar to Paris—perfumes, powders, wines, and tobacco agreeably blended. . . . This is the real Paris in winter, and the more I see of it the better it pleases me.[52]

Perhaps the willful exclusion of people with disabilities from the literature on *flânerie* has something to do with how the embodied experience of disability challenges and even thwarts cultural expectations of the seemingly firm division between public and private spheres. Victor Burgin has written that "the flâneur who turns the street into a living room commits an act of transgression which reverses an established distinction between public and private spaces . . . [and makes visible] the survival of precapitalist social forms that had not yet succumbed to the modern segregation of life into public and private zones."[53] Burgin's observation echoes that of German cultural critic Walter Benjamin, who wrote in 1929 that the *flâneur* has a tendency to "turn the boulevard into an interieur," and that "the street becomes a dwelling for the flâneur; he is as much at home among the façades of houses as the citizen is in his four walls."[54] One could argue that this is precisely what the body of the disabled *flâneur* does when it circulates or is visibly represented in public spaces. The disabled *flâneur* visibly alters perceptions of public space by exposing that which is usually segregated and hidden—vulnerable bodily differences, the effects of institutionalization, or even networks of caregiving and mutual support that are anathema to narratives of modern autonomy—by the private "interieur."

Keller's particular brand of embodied and multisensory *flânerie* complicates the normative wisdom attributed to some of the foremost theorists of urban modernism of the mid-twentieth century—in particular, the contributions of Benjamin, living in the Montparnasse neighborhood of Paris during the mid-1930s at the height of his scholarly productivity. Benjamin, who fled Berlin for Paris, was attuned to many of the same sensory experiences that Keller described in her writings, though his interest was more in their potential to challenge conventions of cognitive processing so as to realize a revolutionary consciousness. In a famous passage from his most famous work, "The Work of Art in the Age of Mechanical Reproduction" (1936), Benjamin makes a famous distinction between what he calls "contemplation" and "distraction." "Contemplation" is based on a Hegelian separation between subject and object, whereas "distraction" is yielding, a blurring of the lines between subject and object:

> Distraction and concentration form an antithesis, which may be formulated as follows. A person who concentrates before a work of art is absorbed by it . . . By contrast, the distracted masses absorb the work of art into themselves. Their waves lap around it; they encompass it with their tide. This is most obvious with regard to buildings. Architecture has always offered the prototype of an artwork that is received in a state of distraction and through the collective. The laws of architecture's reception are highly instructive.[55]

Benjamin uses the metaphor of architecture as a way of engaging in "contemplation"; one thinks, for instance, of the contemplative program presumed in Le Corbusier's *promenade architecturale* for visitors to the Villa Savoye, which we encountered in the introduction. By contrast, "distraction" takes shape through the largely subconscious elements at the edges of the human sensorium, those "physiognomic aspects of visual worlds, which dwell in the smallest things—meaningful, yet covert enough to find a hiding place in waking dreams."[56] One might wash the dishes in the sink to accomplish a necessary task after dinner, but it is the margins of the senses—the smell of dinner still wafting in the air, the unpainted crack in the plaster, the choreography of a dog scratching and a bug buzzing around—that make for the intimate understandings of what home is. Distraction is at the edges of what we see but in a broader sense at the edges of our understanding of the rational through linear applications of our sensory knowledge. For Benjamin, film and photography are the preferred forms of facilitating this distraction because of how they make visible—through the technological tools of slowing, stopping, freezing, speeding, editing, and rearranging images— the flotsam and jetsam at the margins of culture. Film and photography allow for the edges, the margins, and details, which are not dissimilar from the kinds of dream imagery that Freud seizes upon in his explorations of the unconscious.

Initially, Benjamin's endorsement of "distraction" suggests a primary challenge to the hegemony of vision. As Michael Taussig has argued, in theory Benjamin's approach to distraction can lead to a kind of cultural "rewiring, [with] seeing as tactility, and hence, as habitual knowledge."[57] *But what if the tactile* is *your optical?* What if what Benjamin, a nondisabled person, calls "distraction" is "contemplation" for another person? For people with sensory or physical or cognitive differences, "distraction" is not an experimental medium for revealing "the optical unconscious"; rather, it is a primary medium for accessing consciousness. Touch was for Keller a primary, if not *the* primary, modality of structured, rational thought, not the means either literally or metaphorically for producing "distraction." But Benjamin offers very little attention to the senses as actual modalities of experience; for him, a sensory experience like tactility is only a metaphor, eminently interchangeable with other nonrational sensory experiences; a mere allegory for how the senses operate outside of structured, rational "contemplation."

Literary and cultural historians like Abby Garrington, Sarah Danius, and Michael Davidson have argued that, throughout the late nineteenth and early twentieth centuries, sensory overload in cities (think of noise, fog, pollution, and densely packed streets and sidewalks and apartment buildings) was responsible for producing new forms of psychological and physical anxiety, as well as new forms of aesthetic production—what Erica Fretwell has called "sensory experiments"—in literature, music, cinema, visual art, and architecture.[58] New works employed effects like synesthesia or the blurring of sensory mediums to effectively conjure the dissonance that people experienced in modern urban environments—an endless parade of somatic evidence of the brutality and beauty of Western modernity. For someone like Keller, however, sensory overload did not lead to modern anomie or neurasthenic disintegration of the self. Her engagement with sensory experiences was proactive and generative, synonymous with the ways that cities were integral to the development of a deliberately contemplative urban subjectivity. Benjamin, like so many of his intellectual peers who theorized about aesthetic experience without thinking about the possibility of someone with a disabled subjectivity, equated tactile perception with a form of "liberating" the subject from the constraints of the rational mind. Distraction leads (productively) to more distraction. For Keller, so-called "distraction" was quite literally her method of studied contemplation. And this is why it cannot be successfully applied as a universal critical method, a deep dive into the individual or collective unconscious, because it is fundamentally organized around the singular act of seeing. A revolutionary program built on persuading people to embrace their other senses in order to (re)claim the margin isn't quite so revolutionary when what one person claims as the margin is another person's center.

Fifteen years later, Keller and Thomson would return to Paris for a trip in which their *flânerie* would be documented by a French filmmaker in those sectors of the city well known for touristic performances. Although some of this footage was used in the production of a documentary about Keller, a good deal of it did not make the final cut and exists only in staccato scraps that were left on the cutting-room floor. What survives has been added to the Helen Keller Archives at the American Foundation for the Blind. The footage is a testimony to the continuity of Keller's role as a *flâneuse* that spans more than a half-century, a reputation that would all but evaporate within a few years of the documentary's release when it would be replaced by that of the wild child of Tuscumbia whose sensorial primitivism was tamed by the love-language of rational thought.

À Nous Deux Paris

In early 1952, Keller was named a Chevalier of the Ordre National de la Légion d'Honneur, the highest honor given to civilians by the French government. The receipt of her award would take place in June at the Panthéon in Paris as part of a ceremony to coincide with the centenary of the death of Louis Braille in 1852. In recognition of his contributions to France and around the world, Braille's body would be disinterred from its burial place in the small village of Coupvray outside Paris and ceremonially reburied in the Panthéon, where many postrevolutionary greats have been entombed. During the disinterment process, Braille's hands were separated from his body and left behind at the village's ancient cemetery. The two vectors of subjective experience for which his name earned him global recognition—indeed, the tactile mediums through which he achieved his place in the

Panthéon—were severed from him, isolating his modalities of encounter and communication as if only his body was required for him to ascend to France's equivalent of secular heaven.

During that spring, the American actress and songwriter Nancy Hamilton—famed for such standards as "How High the Moon"—heard about Keller's award and proposed the idea of a documentary film, using the imminent trip to Paris as a way of framing Keller's life for a younger generation potentially unaware that Keller was still productive even if she was less prominently featured in popular media. Hamilton and Keller became friends in the early 1940s through Hamilton's longtime lover, Katharine Cornell; as Ruth Gordon intimates in her autobiographical account, everyone in their social circle (including Keller and Thomson) knew that Cornell and husband Guthrie McClintic were partners in a longtime "lavender marriage" that allowed the two to maintain discreet personal lives while enjoying a public life as two of the theatrical luminaries of the period. The close friendship enjoyed by Hamilton and Cornell and Keller and Thomson was transformed into a productive collaborative relationship. The combination of Hamilton overseeing the production of the film, including much of its direction, and Cornell providing mahogany-voiced narration proved a formidable one; the documentary, *The Unconquered: Helen Keller in Her Story*, was awarded the 1956 Academy Award for Best Documentary Feature. It also, as Hamilton predicted, rekindled public interest in Keller's life and career in a way that may have inspired a "rediscovery" of Keller and initiated the "third act" of her life.

Hamilton understood the sensual intimacies with which Keller carried out her relationships to the world through her interactions with physical spaces and material objects. She knew, for instance, that when Cameron Clark designed Keller's house, Arcan Ridge, in Connecticut, he also made provision for a local carpenter to build a quarter-mile-long fence railing around the perimeter of her property so that Keller could take long constitutionals by herself. As we have already seen, Keller believed that this railing was one of the most important and independence-oriented objects in her entire home design. Hamilton also knew that Keller was a true cosmopolitan and seasoned *flâneuse*, since she and Cornell spent a great deal of social time with Keller and Thomson in the city before heading back to Hamilton's own house at 411 East Fifty-First Street in Manhattan (see figure 2.5). In a letter written in mid-June 1952, shortly before Keller and Thomson embarked for Paris, Hamilton tried to convince Thomson to allow a film crew to shadow her and Keller in order to produce a copious amount of "B-reel" footage from which Hamilton could craft a documentary, since Hamilton and Cornell were unable to accompany them:

FIGURE 2.5. Photograph of four elegantly dressed white women bundled in coats and hats, and smiling while walking arm in arm down a city sidewalk. From left to right: Katharine Cornell, Helen Keller, Polly Thomson, and Nancy Hamilton, Cornell's longtime lover. The four women were friends for at least a decade before Hamilton offered to make *The Unconquered: Helen Keller in Her Story* (1954), for which she won the 1956 Academy Award for Best Documentary Film. Photograph taken c. late 1940s in New York City. Reprinted courtesy of the Helen Keller Archives, American Foundation for the Blind, and the Nancy Hamilton Papers, Sophia Smith Collection, Smith College.

This will probably sound like a terrible idea to you in the midst of all your official duties, but I do think if you have time and strength for it, pictures of you and Helen sightseeing in Paris, going to the Luxembourg Gardens, feeling the statues, standing in the Place de la Concorde, walking in the streets, just anything of that nature, would be a marvelous touch in the documentary. And Jimmy Shute has recommended Jacques Letellier as such a brilliant cameraman, that I'd love to make use of him if possible for a days [*sic*] shooting. If you find you [can] spare the time and toil and blood and sweat and tears, let him come to you . . . to talk with you and get a glimpse of you relaxed, and let him tell you how best you both should dress and make-up so as to photograph at your best.[59]

Hamilton's plea succeeded, and the "cameraman" Jacques Letellier did indeed meet up with Keller and Thomson for at least two days. What Letellier provided for Hamilton is the definition of urban documentary footage, which gives its use in *The Unconquered* an aura of authenticity specific to the documentary form as well to Keller's own subjective experience of the city. Letellier's footage captures Keller and Thomson walking under the Tour Eiffel, strolling along the banks and across the bridges of the Seine, stopping to listen to a street guitarist, drinking coffee in a café, sitting on a bench in the Jardins du Luxembourg watching a little boy push his sailboat into the middle of a pond.

Although Letellier's biography is not as well known as those of other French cinematic figures of the period, he was more than a cameraman; he was in fact the director of photography for the short films of Pierre Kast, the prolific director and writer who was also one of the original *cinéastes* who in 1951 founded *Cahiers du cinéma*, arguably the most influential journal of film criticism of the twentieth century.[60] On Kast's own films, like *Les Femmes du Louvre* (1951) and *À Nous Deux Paris!* (1953), Letellier used the streets of Paris as a mise-en-scène for richly layered narrative fictions as well as studied documentary profiles of contemporary figures, including the documentary *Le Corbusier, l'architecte du bonheur* (1956). Kast and his circle, the *Cahiers* network of French critics-cum-auteurs of the early 1950s, including François Truffaut, André Bazin, Robert Bresson, and Jean Cocteau, were clearly an influence on Letellier. They were as smitten with the moody chiaroscuro of German expressionism and American film noir as with the work of lamented French directors like Jean Vigo. In fact, Letellier's footage for Hamilton's documentary often resembles Vigo's use of Paris in films like *L'Atalante* (1934).

By 1953, when she began to assemble the film that would become *The Unconquered*, Hamilton was able to splice the footage Letellier took with existing newsreel footage from US and European news agencies. In the early 1950s, television news as we know it was nonexistent; people relied on newspapers and newsreels for events of national or global significance. British Pathé, for instance, distributed a complete documentary about Keller's trip to Paris, *Pathway into Light* (1952), a collaboration undertaken with the British National Institute for the Blind. The documentary follows Braille from his humble beginnings in Coupvray and his invention of the embossed printed type that bears his name to the interment ceremony at the Panthéon, along with footage of Keller's acceptance of her title (which she delivered in French) and medieval processions of blind boys and girls, blind priests and nuns, and blind veterans of both world wars through the ancient streets of the Quartier Latin in the 5th arrondissement thronged by nondisabled onlookers.[61] Some of the young, blind male veterans sitting in the narrow seats of the Panthéon—handsome in their Sunday suits and dark sunglasses—would not have looked out of place in a New Wave film set a decade later in the same location.

During their time together, Letellier led Keller and Thomson to some of the most well-trodden tourist paths in central Paris. Letellier also took static photographs to serve as studies for the documentary work. These photographs, preserved in the Helen Keller Archives of the American Foundation for the Blind, were not published during Keller's lifetime, but they capture spontaneous moments of ordinariness that provide a poignant contrast to those scenes staged for the film camera. In one photo, Keller and Thomson stand atop the Esplanade of the Palais de Chaillot, looking out toward the Tour Eiffel and the Hôpital des Invalides (see figure 2.6). Although this had become a famous tourist location owing to its enviable position on the Right Bank facing the Tour Eiffel, it had been made infamous a dozen years earlier as the site of the only known photograph taken of Adolf Hitler in Paris after the Nazi invasion in 1940. A companion snapshot to that of Keller and Thompson on the Esplanade is one in which the two women stand outside the front door of a *boulangerie*; Keller holds two enormous crusty baguettes close to her chest, her face registering a meditative engagement with the texture and aroma of the loaves of bread (see figure 2.7). In a film outtake, which we have already seen in the introduction to this book, Letellier captures a sequence in which Keller and Thomson sit with an unidentified male friend at an outdoor table at L'Auberge du Vert Galant, a once-famous local café formerly located at the corner of Quai des Orfèvres and rue de Harlay on the Île de la Cité (see figure I.7). The short sequence provides a seemingly endless stream of variations on the theme of Keller drinking coffee: she lifts the cup to her face, inhales the aroma, brings it slowly and methodically to her lips, tastes it, holds the liquid in her mouth, smacks her lips, and smiles, registering affective approval. This sequence is repeated two or three times, presumably because Letellier believed it might effectively dramatize the ineffable quality of Keller's subjectivity as she navigated her way through gustatory encounters with French cuisine, whether through drinking coffee or handling (soon to be eaten) baguettes still warm from the oven.

FIGURE 2.6. Photograph, c. late June 1952, of two women wearing dresses and hats standing with their backs to the camera and facing in the direction of the Eiffel Tower to their right. The two women are Helen Keller, left, and Polly Thomson, right. They are standing on the famous Esplanade of the Palais de Chaillot, built as part of the 1937 Exposition Internationale. In the far distance to the left is the rotunda of the Hôpital des Invalides. About a week after this photograph was taken, the Marxist intellectual and future co-founder of the Situationist International, Guy Debord, debuted his infamous experimental film *Hurlements en faveur de Sade* (1952) in the auditorium of the Musée de l'Homme, only a few yards from where Keller and Thomson are standing in this photo. Reprinted courtesy of the Helen Keller Archives, American Foundation for the Blind.

FIGURE 2.7. Photograph, c. late June 1952, of two women wearing dresses and hats and pearls, standing to the right of an entrance to a building marked by the word "Biscottes" spelled out in vertical letters. The woman on the left is holding two giant baguettes in her arms, while the other carries a basket in the crook of her arm. Both women have enormous smiles on their faces. This is Helen Keller, left, and Polly Thomson, right, standing outside of a bakery from which they have just purchased the crusty bread. Reprinted courtesy of the Helen Keller Archives, American Foundation for the Blind.

Letellier's outtakes, like all those that wind up on the cutting-room floor, vary in quality both technical and thematic, and it is clear why Hamilton might have hesitated before choosing not to include some of the footage in her documentary. In one outtake, filmed at one of the outdoor wooden bookstalls that line the banks of the River Seine, Thomson holds out her hand to show Keller the cover of a special theme issue on "L'Art nègre" in *Présence Africaine*, an extremely influential journal of pan-African politics, Francophone fiction, and philosophy (see figure 2.8).[62] Books and magazines, like baguettes and coffee cups, gave Keller and Thomson an opportu-

FIGURE 2.8. Film still of Helen Keller (right) and Polly Thomson (barely seen on
the left edge of the frame) facing each other while in front of an enclosed book
stall. Keller, with her eyes closed, is finger-spelling into Thomson's right hand,
while Thomson holds what looks like a book with the title *L'Art nègre* but which is a
special issue of the arts journal *Présence Africaine* (nos. 10–11, October 1951) on the
theme of contemporary African sculpture. Outtake c. late June 1952 shot by Jacques
Letellier for *The Unconquered: Helen Keller in Her Story* (dir. Nancy Hamilton, 1954).
Reprinted courtesy of the Helen Keller Archives, American Foundation for the
Blind, and the Nancy Hamilton Papers, Sophia Smith Collection, Smith College.

nity to fulfill Hamilton's request for conventional images of the two women
"sightseeing," but they also gave Keller the opportunity to have tactile experiences with objects associated with a particular kind of French cosmopolitanism, albeit one frozen in time. As Roland Barthes observed in a series of
perceptive essays later reprinted in his book *Mythologies* (1957), film footage and still photographs of bookstalls and baguettes and cafés and views
of the Tour Eiffel were like advertisements for Banania, a chocolate drink
featuring laughing African faces wearing fez hats: they appealed to tourists
who wanted a timeless version of French culture unchanged by movements
for postcolonial independence or liberation, let alone one transformed by
a tidal wave of brand-name consumer products from the United States—
Coca-Cola, laundry detergent, margarine—to which members of the aspir-
ing French middle class had already succumbed.[63]

FIGURES 2.9 AND 2.10. Two film stills of a young white girl with long blonde hair whose expressive face is being caressed by white-gloved hands that belong to Helen Keller, whose face can be seen in the upper right quadrant of figure 2.9. The action takes place on the steps of Sacré-Cœur in Montmartre, Paris. In figure 2.10, one can see that the thumb of Keller's glove has been cut out so she can read Braille or, in this case, receive tactile information. The girl's affective responses to the gloved hands in these film stills range from uncertainty to discomfort. Outtakes c. late June 1952 shot by Jacques Letellier for *The Unconquered: Helen Keller in Her Story* (dir. Nancy Hamilton, 1954). Reprinted courtesy of the Helen Keller Archives, American Foundation for the Blind, and the Nancy Hamilton Papers, Sophia Smith Collection, Smith College.

One of the longest outtakes shot by Letellier is particularly challenging to watch. It shows Keller encountering a very young girl on the steps of Sacré-Cœur, the magnificent basilica in Montmartre that overlooks the city from the very top of an inaccessible set of steps (see figures 2.9 and 2.10). In expected fashion, Letellier captured Keller methodically touching the girl's face and her body through her clothes. The discomfort on the face of the girl contrasts dramatically with the ever-present smile and delighted curiosity of Keller, who moves her hands up and down the girl's body in the same way that she would treat any other subjective encounter with another person or object in order to gain knowledge of them. In some of the footage, the girl's mother or caregiver tries to instruct the child, presumably to be more flexible and less rigid, but it is to no avail. The little girl is too young to understand what is being asked of her in that moment, and she never gives Letellier what he clearly wants to document, which is confirmation that a complete stranger—in this case, a young girl no more than five or six years old—will replicate the same feeling experienced by any other person whose face and body are touched by the world's most famous deafblind woman.

Keller understood that her role was not to expect to be touched except through an affectionate nudge or as a linguistic translation spelled into her hand. She was the holy vessel into which the experiences of the world were poured. This is why, throughout her travels, popular media regularly photographed Keller with famous people who agreed to be touched; in such images the smiles on their faces serve to index their ability to let Keller break a social convention and enable a form of intimacy typically frowned upon, if not outright forbidden. The political and cultural figures who allowed Keller to touch them took seriously the implications of her outreach and her political advocacy, but they maintained their power by allowing themselves to be temporarily vulnerable and to relinquish control. To *be* touched by Helen Keller, in this context, was to hold power. But unlike adults, who can not only give consent but also perform consent for the camera, the young girl on the steps of Sacré-Cœur cannot give her consent; instead, she is spoken for, since she has neither the life experience nor the politeness training to perform consent for the camera. In the sequence, Keller cannot register the little girl's affect; sighted viewers, however, can see it all, since Letellier's camera frames the girl's reactions to Keller's gloved hands. We may not impute any ill-will to Keller, but what Letellier's camera preserves is a record of an intersubjective encounter gone terribly awry.

Sociologist Kevin Hetherington argues that touch is more than just a blind person's "confirmation of the real."[64] The act of touching is constituted by both touching *and* being touched. Touch, ontologically speaking, is always a two-way street. This is why, as psychiatrist Adam Philips observes, we are unable to tickle ourselves; the power to tickle is reserved in the materiality of another person's touch.[65] Letellier's unused footage taken on the steps of Sacré-Cœur exposes the illusion that Keller's encounters with other people were always received as a positive interaction. Reaching out her gloved hand, the fabric of which has been deliberately cut at the thumb so that Keller can receive more tactile information, Keller touches the young girl's skirt, then her blouse, then her hair, all the way to the top of her head; then her cheek, then her chin, then the back of her head before tenderly kissing her hair as if blessing it. This is, one imagines, the same gestural grammar of interaction that Letellier tried to capture in his footage of Keller drinking coffee. What makes the sequence at the café charming is that the coffee is an inanimate object on which Keller's subjectivities are all temporarily focused and entangled, an experience of intimacy not unlike that of Joseph Merrick and the Mainz Cathedral model we first encountered in chapter 1. It is one thing to grapple with intimate interactions that involve human beings and objects—Merrick putting the model together, Keller feeling the fabric at a dress shop—but it is quite another to grapple with those that involve two human beings whose miscommunication cannot be explained or resolved. It can only be forgotten.

After Keller's return from Paris, Hamilton added to the storehouse of still photographs by following Keller and Thomson around midtown

Manhattan with a portable movie camera and a still camera. The figuration of Keller and Thomson in these settings had no other purpose than to conceive of interesting potential locations for the documentary. The photo on the cover of this book, for instance, was taken on an afternoon in spring 1953 during which Keller and Thomson were photographed crossing the intersection at Fifth Avenue and Fifty-Seventh Street, with the iconic Tiffany's jewelry store in the background; standing in front of the elegant Henri Bendel department store; moving along the sidewalks and through the crowds. As Ruth Gordon recalled in her autobiographical sketch, Keller was particularly enamored with Bendel's. In another film outtake, the camera documents Keller patronizing the perfume counter, choosing a hat, and attending a live fashion event in the days when select customers were invited to a private salon for a viewing with live models. In one sequence, Keller runs her hands up and down the body of a model wearing a Christian Dior–inspired "new look" dress with a tight A-line skirt and cinched waist, to understand the outfit's contours and the feel of the fabric.

As with the footage of the young girl on the steps of Sacré-Cœur, it is hard to imagine anyone else breaching, or overreaching, the conventional divide in quite the way that Keller does. As Elspeth Brown argues in her history of the twentieth-century modeling industry, the ever-present eroticism of the model, whether on the runway or on the front cover of a magazine, was always bounded by their physical inaccessibility, their position as an object to be consumed visually by audience members.[66] In this unused footage, the erotic potential of such encounters is made real, upending the ways that Keller's public touching, however sexually charged, was always transmuted into an information-gathering exercise. Whatever Keller's own private understanding of her sexuality, her perceived asexuality enabled her to practice forms of intimate touch in public. And perhaps such unrestrained, and uncontested, forms of tactile intimacy were bittersweet for Hamilton and Cornell, a couple who could not reveal the intimate nature of their relationship in public, to witness.

At the end of June 1952, a week after Letellier took the photograph of Keller and Thomson on the Esplanade of the Palais de Chaillot, the young Marxist intellectual Guy Debord debuted *Hurlements en faveur de Sade* (1952) in the screening room (now the Jean Rouch Auditorium) of the Musée de l'Homme, only a few yards from where Keller and Thomson had stood. The auditorium, well known as an informal home for members of Paris's Ciné-Club, provided Debord with the ideal environment in which to introduce his experimental "film." After the house lights were turned off, members of the audience sat for long, uncomfortable stretches of time in complete darkness, with only intermittent bursts of recorded sound consisting of quotations from political texts. When the "film" finally began, the house lights came on, and audience members were confronted with wall text in place of a screen offering inflammatory comments about the death of cinema. Unhappy *cinéastes* balked and left in anger, failing to recognize that Debord had produced sensorial disorientation in the service of a radical critique of film as a bourgeois medium and film audiences as creatures of convention. In many ways, the film owes less to the cinematic avant-garde of the period than to high-concept performance pieces like John Cage's *4'33"*, which debuted in Woodstock, New York, in August 1952, just two months after *Hurlements en faveur de Sade.* Both Debord and Cage plunged their respective audiences into unfamiliar and even uncomfortable environments that violated expectations of seeing and hearing in an auditorium or venue and asked audience members to accept disorientation, even temporarily, for the purposes of new types of meaning-making.

Debord's provocation was an opening salvo to the kinds of political critiques through mediated performances that he and his colleagues would engage in over the next decade. Debord belonged to a group that was developing its own methods for producing and interpreting urban experiences and reimagining how those methods could support a Marxist analysis of postwar urban planning and renewal schemes that often resulted in the destruction of those ineffable urban qualities that make a city like Paris unique. Within a year, Debord's group became known as the Situationist International, their name drawn from their desire to provoke urban "situations" and encounters (some accidental, some deliberate) during which participants and observers might radically alter familiar tropes of urbanism and liberate themselves from the stultifying effects of contemporary life. Their methods, the most famous of which are the *dérive* (drift), *détournement* (rerouting), and the insights derived from *psychogeography*, have been absorbed into the critical traditions of urban sociology and urban ethnography, and have inspired the practices of artists and art collectives for the better part of six decades.[67] These are highly theatrical techniques intended to produce alternative geographies of the city based on the political value of urban memory, the insights gleaned from marginalized spaces (and the people who occupy them), games of chance, and sensory impressions based on a color or smell or texture. As urban historian Simon Sadler observes, "the situationist 'drifter' was the new *flâneur* (the Parisian 'stroller,' dandy spectator of the urban scene)...[who] skirted the old quarters of the city in order to experience the flip side of modernization."[68]

Of course, the Situationists were not alone in drawing attention to the "flip side of modernization" in cities like Paris; it is precisely what director Jacques Tati tried to highlight in his wistful comedy *Mon Oncle* (1958), in which an ultra-hygienic automated home—a machine for living in fear in—takes over the lives of a Parisian family in the suburbs and makes them bend to its will. While in many ways *Mon Oncle* seems to point its finger at soulless American-style consumerism through the figure of the modernist house—imagine the Villa Savoye but as designed by a drunk Rube Goldberg—the tension is not between the United States and France but between the terrifying suburban modernist house and Tati's urban corner, which glows with golden nostalgia even if it shares in the same urban deprivations of postwar Paris as depicted in films like Albert Lamorisse's *The Red Balloon* (1956). The modernist critique front and center in *Mon Oncle* would take on a more sinister aura in Tati's magnum opus *Playtime* (1967)—released the same year as Debord's *The Society of the Spectacle*—which gave a critical language to everything that students, workers, and revolutionaries of all stripes saw failing in French society during the spring of 1968.[69]

For Sadler, a canonical genealogy of creative protest and political resistance to urban modernity would start with Charles Baudelaire's formulation of the *flâneur* in the 1870s and lead inexorably to the semiotic reveries of Walter Benjamin in the 1930s and to the revolutionary counter-urbanisms of the Situationists in the 1950s. Yet neither Baudelaire nor Benjamin nor Debord unsettles or challenges those conventional modalities of encounter, such as looking, hearing, and mobility, through which they aspire to revolutionary states of counter-hegemonic consciousness. As David Gissen has observed, there has been a fundamental absence of—perhaps even a resistance to—any kind of critique of the perspectives of the Situationists: nondisabled European male intellectuals whose engagements with urban space, however radical, were always a choice and never an organic part of their subjectivity.[70] For Baudelaire, Benjamin, and Debord, using methods that "disabled" their subjectivities was always an alternative (and always a temporary) rejoinder to the arc of urban modernity. Meanwhile, as we have seen throughout this chapter, Keller's proactive, rather than reactive, engagement with urban spaces anticipated by decades how intellectuals, artists, and activists have come to talk about embodied encounters with the built environment. For Keller, an urban sensibility did not emerge from the contrast between conventional or unconventional states of being, or between conventional or unconventional modalities of encounter, because her subjective experience as a deafblind woman did not distinguish convention from lack of convention, orientation from disorientation, presence from absence. Keller's urban sensibility was wholly constituted *through* her subjectivity, not in compensation for or as an adjustment to her subjectivity. The energies expended by Baudelaire, Benjamin, and

Debord to build a new psychic, emotional, and political counter-urbanity was for Keller just another walk in the park.

∵

In 1980, folklore scholar Mac E. Barrick described the rise of a particular genre of humor encompassed by the phrase "the Helen Keller joke"—a type of riddle used reductively as cultural shorthand to intimate, and ridicule, the complexities of Keller's life for popular consumption.[71] Based on the time period in which Barrick was writing about these jokes, some of the most common (in all senses of the word) include the following examples:

Q: How did Helen Keller burn the left side of her face?
A: She answered the iron.

Q: Why did Helen Keller go crazy?
A: She was trying to read a stucco wall.

Q: How did Helen Keller's parents punish her?
A: They rearranged the furniture.

On one level, such jokes are unworthy of reflection or acknowledgment; they exhibit prurient forms of abuse and cruelty, fantasies of psychosexual drama focused on Keller's vulnerable body, a descent into humor's subterranean subgenre of humiliation as an authorized form of consensual bonding between teller and listener. But for jokes like this to have any kind of ontological coherence, one would have to assume, among other things, that Keller was incapable of distinguishing a telephone from an iron, or that she routinely confused a book for a stucco surface. Technologies such as telephones and irons were regularly refined through design innovations that differentiated handheld consumer objects, thus making their aesthetic and material conflation much less likely. Keller, like her sighted and hearing counterparts, would have been able to distinguish the temperature, weight, and triangular shape of an iron through tactile means and feel the electrical vibrations, Bakelite smoothness, and distinctive mouthpiece of a period telephone. Yet in the context of the low-tech appliance that is the joke, the physical artifacts and domestic spaces of ordinary life do not permit for a comfortable landscape of variation or discovery. Physical objects, in other words, can be only meaningful or offer utility if they can be visually differentiated.

There is a poignant irony to the proliferation of Helen Keller jokes, which persist into the present. For architectural historian Anthony Vidler, many of the traits that we associate with urban modernity were often the targets of control by experts in medicine, psychology, and environmental engineering.[72] Doctors and social scientists coined words like *anomie* and *neurasthenia* to characterize the physiological impact of noises, smells, dangers, and tricks of the unconscious that, for many, made subjective distortions experienced by urban dwellers into often nightmarish material realities. But if the normative modalities of sight, sound, and mobility are typically the conduits to experiences of modern anomie, anxiety, and disillusionment, then at least having access to those modalities must be better than not having access, since those who do can participate in a shared understanding of the so-called "modern condition." Thus, the source of the Helen Keller joke is the tacit conviction that, without access to those particular modalities of experience normalized as modern, *the world as we know it* would be unintelligible or else simply collapse in on itself. But this is only one definition of the world as "we" know it, just as this is only one definition of modernity that "we" recognize. Perhaps this is why the worst of Keller's detractors—those who today post cruel or derogatory comments about her on social media—cannot reconcile the "wawa" image with that of a deaf-blind woman who was educated at Radcliffe, became a prolific author and outspoken activist, and knew the best places in New York and Paris to be a *flâneuse*. In any case, Helen Keller jokes say more about profound lack of imagination on the part of the teller of those jokes than about Keller's capacities or lack thereof. Keller's subjectivity did not develop in the absence of sight and sound, but rather was made possible *because of* the absence of sight and sound.[73] The spatial clumsiness and sensorial disorientation attributed to Keller's imagined mishaps are not, and have never been, by her own hand.

CHAPTER THREE

Disabling the WPA

In his masterful study of President Franklin Delano Roosevelt's first two terms, known collectively as the New Deal, historian William Leuchtenberg relates that the Works Progress Administration, one of the numerous agencies created by FDR to combat the economic effects of the Great Depression, "built or improved more than 2,500 hospitals, 5,900 school buildings, 1,000 airport landing fields, and nearly 13,000 playgrounds. It restored the Dock Street Theater in Charleston; erected a magnificent ski lodge atop Oregon's Mount Hood; conducted art classes for the insane at the Cincinnati Hospital; drew a Braille map for the blind at Watertown, Massachusetts; and ran a pack-horse library in the Kentucky hills."[1] For Leuchtenberg, as well as for other historians of his generation, enumerating the wide range of projects undertaken and completed by the Works Progress Administration (hereafter WPA) was an efficient way to capture the variety of its projects and, one extrapolates, the cumulative benefits of the New Deal to the US economy and society before its programs ended in 1943. One could argue that for Leuchtenberg the WPA's "art classes for the insane" and "a Braille map for the blind" were not in themselves of particular interest. Yet today there are compelling reasons to make them so: the "Cincinnati Hospital" was most likely Longview Asylum, a state-funded behemoth built by the state legislature of Ohio in the 1850s. Longview benefited from landscaping and small construction jobs (administered by the Public Works Administration, another New Deal agency that awarded contracts to existing firms) as well as from the services of WPA-sponsored gardeners, woodworkers, and teachers of art, music, and cosmetology.[2] Leuchtenberg's phrase, "a Braille map for the blind," was likely a reference to the Perkins School for the Blind, the oldest school for the visually impaired in the United States and home briefly to blind "royalty" like Laura Bridgman and Helen Keller during the nineteenth century. During the 1930s, the WPA contributed funds to the school to expand its resources for its students, which included the making of local, national, and global world maps. In fact, tactile learning was pioneered domestically by the Perkins School when it was still in its original location in South Boston before moving to Watertown in 1906.

While Leuchtenberg's phrase of "a Braille map for the blind" was meant to invoke a humanitarian response similar to that of "art classes for the insane," it was clearly directed at readers who had no understanding of how tactile objects work for people, especially children, who live with visual impairments. This is because Braille is a linguistic medium, not a medium through which maps are constructed. When Braille is incorporated onto such maps, it is usually used to indicate place names of natural or built landmarks, or else to provide a key for conveying information about distance. The "Braille map for the blind at Watertown, Massachusetts" may suggest a neutral, even a banal object that is a straightforward, one-to-one physical translation of the geography of a place into a miniaturized form, crafted to be accessible to anyone who has the requisite mobility to touch it. But a hand has to be carefully taught *how* to read a tactile object in the same way that a hand must be taught how to write. The primary medium of maps for users who are visually impaired is not the raised dot but the raised line, produced through a printing press using brass embossing plates, which can be made as thin or as thick as necessary (to mark a street, for example, or a national border) or to correlate with the properties of the environment (a mountain range, a coastline). For the mapmaker as well as the user, the success of the map is based not on translating language into a tactile form but, rather, on translating size, scale, distance, or terrain into a form that can be apprehended and learned through touch over time (see figure 3.1).

In the first two chapters of this book, I discussed particular individuals—Joseph Merrick, Helen Keller—and how the spaces and objects they encountered effectively (and affectively) shaped, and were shaped by, their disabled subjectivities. This chapter is focused less on specific individuals and more on the spaces and objects that people with disabilities experienced within a particular cultural moment: the crucible of FDR's New Deal administration and its efforts to transform the spheres of education as well as employment. As economic and pedagogical objects produced in relation to the needs of students, artifacts such as the maps for students at the Perkins School for the Blind, Watertown, Massachusetts, give us a unique opportunity to think more critically about a historical era in which, we are told, people with disabilities may have been supported by government agencies but were not recognized for their own bodily capacities or, for that matter, their own particular subjective experiences.[3] As I will show, some New Deal agencies shaped not only the experiences of people with disabilities but also employed people with disabilities as producers of crip

FIGURE 3.1. Photograph c. 1938 of a group of five young white girls with fashionable hairstyles who are seated around or standing next to tables on which have been placed tactile maps of Central America. In the background we see a globe, desk chairs, and tables, indicating that this is a classroom. The girls are students at the Perkins School for the Blind; the maps were produced for the school as part of a project to build a comprehensive archive of tactile "Maps of the World." The Massachusetts Works Progress Administration provided funding to employ workers at its Boston-based Museum Extension Project workshop to design and fabricate the maps. Reprinted with permission of the Perkins School for the Blind Archives, Watertown, MA.

objects, a phrase that we first explored in chapter 1. The recognition that some workers would be valued in an industrial workforce for their bodily capacities makes it more difficult to assert that the WPA was across the board a discriminatory agency.[4] Indeed, in many cases the WPA recognized disabled subjectivity as a job qualification.

These projects of the WPA offer an alternative, and even competing, history of the entanglements of disability and the culture of the New Deal era through what we might call the agitations of modernism. Architecturally, this was manifested in the form of new designs for public schools that recognized the subjective capacities of children with disabilities and new pedagogical innovations that contributed to a broader conception of education that included and in many cases centered disability among its curricular innovations. As I argue, some disability objects such as Braille maps and tactile models were shaped not only by new forms of pedagogy but, in a broader educational context, the influential work of US social scientists, such as Harold Lasswell and Walter Lippman, who argued for fostering democratic values through media forms (newspapers, radio, advertising) in order to protect vulnerable populations from the rhetorical sway of authoritarian regimes that dominated global politics in the 1930s.[5] As media historian Fred Turner has argued, many European and American educators working in response to "the visual and social chaos of industrial Europe" in the 1920s and 1930s sought to centralize art and design in the curricula of young people. Their purpose was twofold. First, they wanted to create new "built environments—in books, in museum exhibitions, in classrooms, and in their own photographs, paintings, and designs—that modeled the principles of democratic persuasion that were being articulated by American social scientists at the same moment."[6] They also wanted to help these students embody the sensorial possibilities of living in a democratic society; as Turner writes, educators believed an art-oriented practice for all students could help students "find their way to authentic free expression of their innermost selves . . . Students could [integrate] their exposure to various skills into their professional practices, and their exposure to different sensations into their personalities. They could, in short, become whole."[7]

Of course, among psychologists, medical professionals, and educators during the 1930s, the notion of becoming "whole" was never a neutral endeavor free of ontological baggage.[8] Most social scientists of the era relied on presumptive definitions of what "wholeness" was or could be, one tacitly dependent on an unproblematized white, male, cisgender "self" for whom integrating "different sensations into their personalities" was as straightforward as adding decorative mirrors to the walls of an existing gallery already filled with reflective surfaces. Indeed, the social science ideal of an actualized "whole" self was dialectically productive with the mythological power and cultural authenticity accorded to the kind of bodies depicted in WPA-sponsored photography, paintings, sculptures, posters, and—perhaps most notoriously—in the murals that still decorate many schools, post offices, community centers, and libraries across the country nearly a century later.[9] Given this context, the selective prioritizing of certain workers with disabilities and certain projects organized around disabled subjectivities seems even more extraordinary, challenging ideas about what kinds of architectural spaces, what kinds of employment opportunities, and what kinds of disability objects are remembered as constitutive of the economy and culture of the 1930s. As we will see, in so many cases the WPA's elevation of difference reflected both its economic ambition to keep ordinary citizens employed and its cultural ambition to nurture new types of educational environments and encourage thousands of crip objects to bloom.

New Deals for New Schools

Before the 1940s, the vast majority of US students with physical or sensory impairments or cognitive differences did not attend public schools with their neighborhood fellows or playmates.[10] Although most were taken care of (or, perhaps, neglected) within the domestic spaces of home, those fortunate enough to have access or resources were able to attend day schools or residential schools funded and built by individual states, often sited in bucolic rural locations where architects could either transform former estates or build new institutions that mimicked the grand estates built by nineteenth-century industrialists and other members of the genteel class. Beginning in the early nineteenth century, institutional architecture that was developed to house and educate people with disabilities deployed recognizable architectural styles that not only conveyed visual authority but also communicated civic care in built form. In many private and state-sponsored residential institutions, it was not uncommon to find spatial layouts or ornamental features resembling college and university designs for libraries, classrooms, and dormitories as well as those of the period's luxury hotels, apartments, and private estates. The regular appearance of details such as double-height ceilings, gender-segregated parlors, grand staircases, oversize corner turrets, dormer windows, gingerbread moldings, terracotta brickwork and roof tiles, and exaggerated bay windows was never meant to belie the intended efforts to contain and segregate residents from the mainstream but, rather, to make those efforts more palatable to the philanthropists, charitable organizations, and the genteel public for whom these were forms of civic investment.

Architects hired to build for asylums, state residential schools, and private houses located in rural or suburban locations chose such building styles as much for their fashionable appearance as for their normative sensibilities of care. In 1934, a forerunner agency of the WPA initiated the Historic American Building Survey, which gathered details about the construction of such buildings as well as taking copious photographs to build an archive of vernacular American architecture. The survey included photographic and measurement studies of residential institutions for children who were, in the parlance of the day, "crippled" or else blind, deaf, "mute," or some combination thereof in states like Kentucky, Indiana, Michigan, Pennsylvania, and Iowa. Many of these schools resemble the campuses of private colleges and were clearly designed to encourage taxpayers and charitable organizations alike to marvel at the architectural munificence of grand manor houses, gardens, and athletic facilities that were designed more for show than to accommodate the needs of the children who lived there. By the early decades of the twentieth century, many such institutions had gone through a period of neglect or abandonment due to dwindling financial resources (especially after the Great Depression hit in 1929), leading some trustees and legislators to regard such schools as overdone and resource-depleting behemoths of Victorian fussiness.

During the 1920s and 1930s, a handful of day schools and residential schools in Europe and the United States began to experiment formally with architectural and pedagogical designs characterized as the "International Style," the phrase and design typology popularized by architectural critics Henry Russell Hitchcock and Philip Johnson in their program/manifesto for the style in a seminal exhibition at the Museum of Modern Art in 1932. As architecture and design historians such as Beatriz Colomina and Juliet Kinchin have argued, modern design as applied to hospitals, clinics, and asylums for short-term and long-term care stripped down everything—external decoration, interchangeable parts, historical references to past styles—to an austere design of simplified forms specific to the function of the building.[11] Projects by Josef Hoffmann (Purkersdorf Sanatorium for people diagnosed with tuberculosis, Vienna, 1904), Otto Wagner (Lupus-pavillon, for people diagnosed with lupus, Vienna, 1908), and Alvar Aalto (Paimio Sanatorium, for people diagnosed with tuberculosis, Finland, 1927) introduced an architectural vocabulary of hygienic surfaces (e.g., white tiles that could be cleaned easily) and ventilated spaces (e.g., patients' and common rooms with plentiful light and access to large windows, open terraces, and balconies). All of these had a profound effect on school design across Europe. Schools in this category became associated with the white hygienic spaces of hospitals and sanatoriums, where students learned new pedagogies of interactive discovery by educators and psychologists such as John Dewey, Friedrich Froebel, Maria Montessori, Jean Piaget, and Rudolf Steiner in open-air classrooms framed in cement and glass.

Among the most influential of these was the Cliostraat Openlucht-school voor het Gezonde Kind (Open Air School for the Healthy Child), designed by Jan Duiker, which opened in Amsterdam in 1930. The Cliostraat Openluchtschool was built in a direct dialectical relationship with disability, since Duiker adapted architectural features used for a tubercular population—access to fresh air, sunlight, open spaces—in order to instill values of personal and civic cleanliness through what Duiker called a "strong hygienic power."[12] Daybeds and ample room for rest typically featured in these designs, while customized furniture made of lightweight materials, such as plywood or hollow tubular steel, made everything mobile and child-friendly. Eight years later, the Skolen ved Sundet (School by the

Sound), a river-proximate school in Copenhagen designed by Kaj Gottlob in 1938, was specifically made *for* children who had contracted respiratory-related illnesses like tuberculosis. This is why the "sickly child" implied in the designs of Duiker for the Cliostraat Openluchtschool was not the client but their clearly articulated inverse, a child *without* illness or disability, thereby confirming and strengthening the relationship between a child's (already) healthy status and its parallel in modern design.[13] As modern architecture avatar Philip Johnson, himself sympathetic to Nazism, opined in 1932, "the International Style is especially adapted to school buildings because functional planning, the fundamental principle of the new architecture, is exactly what schools need to develop in sympathy with modern trends in scientific education."[14]

The eugenic implications of these investments in education perfectly capture the competing modernisms that took shape during the early decades of the twentieth century. Yet the sensorial freedoms and possibilities promoted as part of the vocabulary of architectural modernism were apparent to some educators and psychologists thinking about the environmental influences on pedagogy as well as health and socialization, a nexus of concerns amid the often soul-crushing demands of industrial modernity. Some opportunities were shaped less by design and more by charitable activities; in 1920, for instance, the Shriners charity initiated a program to raise enough funds to provide free hospital care for children with physical disabilities. By 1941, it had funded 60,000 children—"only charity patients, whose parents or guardians cannot afford expensive services" and without discrimination "on account of color, race or creed"—at fifteen purpose-built hospitals across the United States. As journalist Farnsworth Crowder explained in 1941, the Shriners hospitals functioned for these residential patients as "a home, a school, and a club. It is a convalescent's paradise," where children encounter "schoolrooms designed with special seats . . . [that] give the feeling of really going to school as against endless hospital confinement." Murals, both painted and wallpapered, abound in dormitories, playrooms, lunchrooms, and in classrooms, where one could find "floor and wall decorations from Mother Goose and Fairyland." Above a young girl's crib, a daintily articulated Cinderella floats in a diaphanous gown; on a ward for older boys, "a mural illustrating the development of transportation from the covered wagon and sailboat [*sic*] to the modern China Clipper, winging for Manila over Golden Gate Bridge . . . The radio loudspeaker in the room is concealed behind a scout blowing his bugle."[15]

In other schools, architectural modernism was a free-floating signifier of "progress," which, depending on one's political or ideological commitments, could be either utopian or dystopian—a light-filled zone to offer civilization to people of discrepant subjectivities, or a cement bunker to protect civilization from people of discrepant subjectivities. Building design became a civic investment in nondisabled children, the designated members of a future workforce and healthy nation-state. Schools in the 1930s, as design historian Juliet Kinchin has written, "were viewed as crucial to the absorption and spread of modernist values. Harnessing the language of abstraction as well as new materials and industrial production, the new modern schools were simple, light, and flexible; a tabula rasa upon which the modern child could inscribe his or her identity."[16] The highly influential Wiedikon Kindergarten, designed by Hans Hofmann and Adolf Kellermüller in Zurich in 1932, did more than promote health through its modern architectural features of light and air. The structure itself—a kind of Bauhaus version of the Hanging Gardens of Babylon, with vertical gardens dangling from open glass walls—was also a combination kindergarten, community center, and after-school care facility, a sociospatial crossroads of civic care that extended from children to the elderly. Similarly, the Suresnes School, designed by Eugène Beaudouin and Marcel Lods in Suresnes, near Paris, in 1936, was built in consultation with health experts as well as nonexperts such as Louis Boulonnois, a French public school teacher, who had grown up with the lived experience of having tuberculosis. The Suresnes School featured classrooms with glass doors on three sides and convenient adjacent patios where children could rest nestled among trees.

Many schools, less stylistically ambitious than their functionalist counterparts, followed designs that built upon recognizable historical styles—Federal, Georgian, Queen Anne, and Romanesque, among others—that were part of the civic vocabulary of nineteenth- and early twentieth-century aesthetics for institutions across the social, political, and educational spectrum. Some modern approaches to school design, however, such as William Lescaze's Oak Lane Country Day School (Blue Bell, Pennsylvania, 1929), Richard Neutra's Corona Avenue School (Los Angeles, 1934), and Eero Saarinen's Crow Island School (Winnetka, Illinois, 1940), are routinely cited as the best domestic variants of the International Style (see figure 3.2). Even today, their functionalist features—open transitions between minimalist interiors and patios and balconies, curvilinear walls of glass bricks—could easily serve as appropriate mise-en-scène for a production of a Cole Porter musical set in a Manhattan penthouse. Yet many less well-known schools were part of this group as well, their design the primary aesthetic medium through which new curricula as well as new types of classroom environments could be realized. For instance, the Washington Boulevard Orthopaedic School, a day school in Los Angeles, opened in 1936. Designed by

FIGURE 3.2. Photograph c. 1955 of two white buildings set against a backdrop of sky and trees; the building on the left is a geometric cube with inset glass windows, while the building on the right has a curved roof supported by thin pillars. In the foreground, a young white boy is showing his tongue to a woman wearing a long white coat who is sitting on a sculpted wooden bench with a jar full of tongue depressors. This is the outside play area and back exposure of the Oak Lane Country Day School in Blue Bell, PA, just outside Philadelphia, designed in 1929 by Swiss architect William Lescaze. It is often regarded as the first instance of the International Style in the United States. Photo originally published in the *Philadelphia Evening Bulletin*, 1955. Reprinted with permission of the J. W. Boone Jr. collection, Special Collections Research Center, Temple University Libraries.

local architect William. F. Ruck as a series of white cubes overflowing with sunlight from ample wall-sized windows, not unlike the mansions Ruck designed in Bel Air and Beverly Hills, the school was heated and cooled with modern ventilation systems that brought comfort to classrooms as well as "rest areas," rooms filled with cots where physically exhausted students could plunge into soothing darkness. The Washington Boulevard School was featured in the November 1937 issue of *Architectural Record*, where photographs and blueprints depicted a minimalist entrance directly adjacent to individual lanes separated by railings that enabled students with varying physical needs to queue up for the bus ride home to different parts of the greater metropolitan Los Angeles area (see figure 3.3). These railings

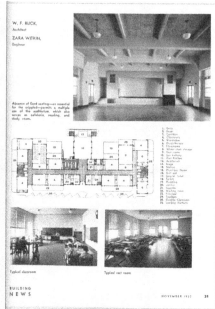

FIGURE 3.3. Reproduction of two pages from the November 1937 issue of *Architectural Record* featuring the Washington Boulevard Orthopaedic School (now the Sophia T. Salvin Special Education Center) in Los Angeles, designed in 1936 by William F. Ruck. Under the headline "Los Angeles Builds a School for the Crippled" are diagrams, descriptive text, and photographs of building interiors and exteriors with children inside and outside the buildings. Images courtesy of George Smith and USModernist.

also provided a way of organizing students into different groups depending on their relationship to their assistive technology, so that kids on crutches would line up behind other kids on crutches, while kids in wheelchairs would line up behind their fellows using similar mobility devices. Photographs of the students depict children across a range of ages and racial and ethnic identities, and prominently show a day bed for children who may have needed a comfortable space amid the activities of the day. Because the classrooms needed to be open and flexible, the wheelchairs parked next to the windows around the perimeter of the room take the place of traditional chairs and desks, making the space functional for multiple users rather than only for those who can easily navigate grids of tightly-packed desks. Only a small table and chairs centered in the room, piled high with books and pieces of construction paper, indicate that the classroom is as much a workspace as a place for affording social time for children who in a previous generation would have been isolated at home or sent to a residential school in some far-flung location.

Architectural historians like Beatriz Colomina have argued that the hygienic principles associated with hospital and clinic architecture transformed modernist design across a range of functions and needs: from the mid-century ranch house to urban renewal projects of cities after World War II, Colomina sees in postwar architecture a direct distillation of hospital modernism into more palatable, and less ideological, consumer forms. But it is difficult to read about the application of "hygienic" designs to public schools built in the name of either "the healthy child" or their "sickly" opposite without placing such language in the context of the contemporary interest in eugenical science, the rise of which long precedes its most infamous implementation in the policies of the German Third Reich. Public schools that inherited the principles of hospital design went beyond what Juliet Kinchin calls "the interdisciplinary convergence between progressive pedagogy, medical expertise, and a high modernist architectural and design ideal."[17] Indeed, on both sides of the Atlantic, it was the moment when many schools became functionalist mediums of social engineering. The desire to improve the population and control the reproductive capacities of future generations may have tapped into the modern association between bright, sunlit, clean white surfaces and bright, sunlit, and clean white children. As disability studies scholars David Mitchell and Sharon Snyder have described, from the 1890s through the 1940s a "transatlantic eugenics" was practiced and shared between scientists, intellectuals, social reformers, and lawmakers in Britain, France, Germany, Italy, the Soviet Union, and the United States.[18] One could observe in Duiker's school design a transfer of architectural knowledge from strengthening models of care to meet the needs of the "least fit" to strengthening models of care to encourage the hygienic power of the "most fit." While most day schools may have moved the site of education closer to home, many continued to practice the same eugenic logic of segregating own their students and discouraging their students from dating or intermarrying.[19] They followed a pattern characterized by historian of medicine Rachel Elder in her study of Detroit's White Special School for Epileptic Children, which operated between 1935 and 1959. Students received a rudimentary education, but it was always secondary to the institution's goals of providing "a gentle and holistic regimen of 'hygienic living.'" Some schools took this further than others and encouraged aggressive medical interventions on their students: eye surgeries for students with visual impairments; leg, knee, and hip surgeries for students with physical impairments; and, in the case of the White Special School in Detroit, experimental injections of sheep brain lipoids to suppress seizures, the result of a partnership brokered between the Parke Davis pharmaceutical firm and the city's Board of Education and Department of Public Health.[20]

With so many examples of institutions exercising control over the bodies of children and adults with disabilities, it is easy to associate aspects of these new school designs, or any school designs for that matter during the first half of the twentieth century, with the didactic side of modernist architecture as a form of social engineering. Scholars like philosopher Sven-Olav Wallenstein, for one example, have underscored the degree to which the "emergence of modern architecture" highlights modernity's proclivity toward controlling all people scrutinized under the unyielding gaze of the state or institutional power.[21] Such a narrative has been a fundamental part of disability study scholarship for at least four decades, which is why histories of architectural modernism have not fared particularly well within disability history.

Common attitudes and prejudices toward disability or difference were not miraculously suspended by new architectural designs for public institutions. The Sunshine School for Crippled Children in Oakland, California, for example, completed in September 1937, reflected a collaboration between WPA architects, physicians, and members of the San Francisco Board of Education that was typical of New Deal public works projects. According to Charles Short's and Rudolph Stanley-Brown's 1939 public buildings survey, the design for the Sunshine School was chosen to "create the most cheerful possible atmosphere in order to encourage the children to *forget as far as possible* their disabilities."[22] The school used familiar elements, such as exposed arches, wraparound terraces, decorative column finials, and an enormous interior courtyard reminiscent of early twentieth-century architectures of transit and entertainment, such as World's Fairs and Coney Island, as well as the kinds of exotic colonial and Orientalist architecture styles used throughout California and in US territories in the Pacific, including Hawaii and the Philippines.[23] In 1934, the Kate Critcher Orthopaedic Buildings at the Children's Hospital in Los Angeles inaugurated a new pool large enough for a dozen children and their nurses. Promotional materials touted the pool's size as well as "its adjacent heat treatment booth by the 'electric stretcher,' the most modern device available for moving *helpless patients*."[24] In May 1938, the West Virginia School for the Deaf and Blind in Romney announced its reopening after it had been redesigned and rebuilt with funds from the WPA. The school boasted "classrooms and auditorium [that have been] specially wired for amplification of sound to prosecute *auricular training, the latest step* in educational methods for the deaf."[25] By privileging hearing and oralism over sign language, the school was presented to the public as a cutting-edge institution, reflecting the emphasis on oralism that dominated education for students with hearing impairments during the twentieth century.

Yet to cast *all* architectural modernism in a villainous role is to discredit the important and neglected work of some architects and educators who wanted to foster more direct associations between design innovation and people with disabilities who might thrive in ways that had never been seen before in public architecture. During the New Deal era, the push–pull of state support and philanthropic support for children institutionalized through state- and charity-run schools helped give shape to a transitional period during which children who depended on the care of the state were caught in between different economic and educational philosophies regarding their care. Interestingly, none of them is featured in *Built in USA, 1932–1944* (1944), an important survey of architectural projects made prior to and at the tail end of the WPA period that served to celebrate the adaptation and influence of the International Style on US architecture.[26] Yet these same buildings neglected by the editors of *Built in USA* are vital to any holistic understanding of the role of architecture in civic life during this transitional period, caught between a purely didactic architectural modernism, on the one hand, and an increasingly empathic architectural modernism, on the other.

Throughout the 1920s and 1930s, city and state officials began to see the economic, if not direct educational benefit of keeping children with disabilities in their local areas and exploring their inclusion in mainstream classrooms or the creation of what came to be known as special education classes.[27] Private residential schools did not disappear, of course, but the transition from thinking about public education for children with disabilities as only segregated in the countryside to thinking about children with disabilities attending their local school or perhaps a regional day school that met their needs became a standardized practice. The PWA and WPA assisted enormously in this transformation. The Willis and Elizabeth Martin Orthopedic School, for instance, completed by the WPA in 1938 in the Fairmount neighborhood of Philadelphia, was among those specifically built to address the needs of vulnerable populations that could benefit from new facilities. Designed by Irwin T. Catherine, famous as the long-standing architect for the Philadelphia public school system, in a style that one might call Depression Georgian, the Martin Orthopedic School featured specially equipped classrooms with tables and chairs that folded down to accommodate wheelchairs and other mobility devices, as well as an accessible gymnasium, a vocational arts workshop, and an auditorium. Within the walls of the school was an open courtyard containing gardens for helping students learn about cultivating vegetables. In one photograph (see figure 3.4), a young girl takes a sip from a water fountain using a safety bar for gripping and balancing her body with the assistance of a teacher. This appliance,

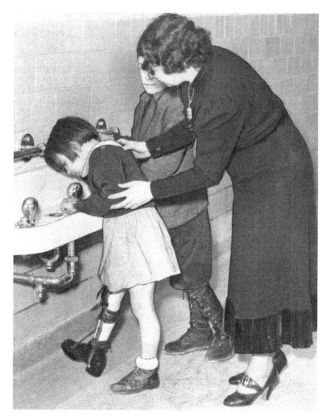

FIGURE 3.4. Photograph of Adaline Latina, a student at the Willis and Emily Martin Orthopedic School in Philadelphia, who is wearing a short dress and leg braces on her legs. Adaline is being supported by Rose Zacca, a woman wearing a long dress, to enable Adaline to drink from a water fountain. The photograph shows a stainless-steel grab bar, an uncommon feature in public schools of the era. Photo dated February 6, 1936, and published in the *Philadelphia Evening Bulletin*. Reprinted with permission of the George D. McDowell collection, Special Collections Research Center, Temple University Libraries.

uncommon enough in any public setting, was virtually unknown in public school settings. Other architectural innovations for students with disabilities were made possible by the vertical expansion of educational space by elevators, rather than relying only on stairs. In 1939, the WPA built a three-story addition onto the A. Harry Moore School in Jersey City, New Jersey, which included a solarium on the roof of the building offering views across the river to midtown Manhattan and provided seating and beds for several dozen children. In publicity photographs for the solarium taken in November 1939, one can see the racial makeup of the students on the rooftop, indicating that these special schools were not racially segregated and were also open to children along a broad continuum of disabilities, from those who used crutches and wheelchairs to those who needed an attendant or nurse to move around the school. Furthermore, many schools that received funding from the PWA and WPA made innovations to and expansions of disabled subjectivities possible. Audiovisual technologies, such as lantern slides, record players, and overhead projectors, that served multiple learning styles and modalities were echoed in the availability of furniture like molded plywood desks and daybeds that were crafted with the bodies of children of varying capacities firmly in mind. Not all schools could afford tubular steel–framed furniture by high end designers like Marcel Breuer or Charles and Ray Eames, of course, but these forms (or their inexpensive knockoffs), which we often associate with high-end living in middle-class homes, were great innovations for schools that designed classrooms as well as furniture for students with special needs.

Perhaps no other school embodies the convergence of technology and innovation in the service of a new kind of education imagined for children with disabilities as much as the Charles A. Boettcher School for Crippled Children, opened in 1940 directly across the street from the Children's Hospital (now St. Joseph's Hospital) in Denver, Colorado, and designed by Burnham Hoyt, a regional architect in the Midwest (see figure 3.5).[28] Hoyt's name is absent from most architectural histories except for recognition of his design for the Red Rocks Concert Venue, about fifteen miles outside Denver, an organic auditorium carved into the living rock by the Public Works Administration in 1939 that is often used as a model of what the public works of the New Deal were able to accomplish. The Boettcher School, however, deserves recognition as the most ambitious design of its kind in the United States, featured in popular magazines like *Time* and professional journals like *Architectural Forum* (in a special issue devoted to "architecture and health"). Boettcher, a mercantile millionaire, donated half of the $348,000 cost, with the other half paid by federal funds, for the construction of a school to be affiliated with the Children's Hospital but open to children with physical impairments throughout Denver. This public-private partnership was rare in the 1930s, but it led to enormous aesthetic freedom for Hoyt, which translated into enormous spatial freedom for the children for whom the school was designed. As *Time* reported in 1940, students "found handrails along every wall, adjustable chairs and tables, two lavatories, a drinking fountain and a grassy outdoor playground next to each classroom."[29]

Some features of the school would be recognizable to anyone who spent time in Dessau or Amsterdam during the 1920s: large white cement spaces

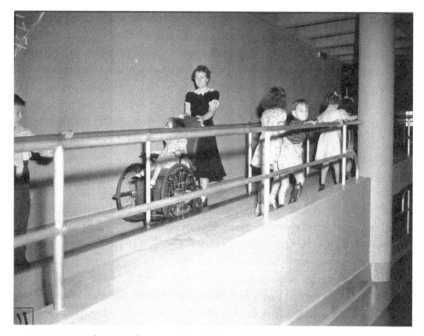

FIGURE 3.5. Photograph c. 1941 of a middle-aged white woman and several white children on a ramp, all of whom are going in different directions. The woman is pushing a child in a wheelchair down the ramp, while on the right side several white children are going up the ramp. This is the central thoroughfare between floors used by students and teachers at the Charles A. Boettcher School for Crippled Children in Denver, Colorado, designed in 1937 by Burnham Hoyt. Reprinted with permission of the Denver Public Library, Western History Collection, X-28337.

supported by spindly industrial columns interspersed with walls of plate glass; modern riffs on familiar architectural details like a *porte-cochère* held aloft by cement pylons; a wide building footprint resembling that of a factory or department store; double-height windows overlooking interior courtyards and green spaces for eating lunch or enjoying the sunshine; stainless steel used for banisters as a hygienic surface that played against white-painted cement walls and tiles. In 1943, the Boettcher School was even referenced as a successful example of private investment in public good, sparking one journalist to observe that there was "a striking difference between this time-lasting structure of steel, concrete, and glass and the basementless, wooden structures built for the Japanese relocation center at Granada, Colo.," as part of FDR's notorious Executive Order 9066. The Granada relocation shells—three of them—are to cost the American taxpayer $300,498 . . . [while] private enterprise in Denver built a structure

FIGURE. 3.6. Photograph of a large, white open interior space with a ramp
on the left side and a glass wall on the right side. This was the main public
area and heart of the Charles A. Boettcher School for Crippled Children in
Denver, Colorado, designed in 1937 by Burnham Hoyt. Photograph c. 1992 by
Roger Whitacre for the Historic American Building Survey one year before
the school was demolished to make room for a parking garage. Reprinted
courtesy of the Prints and Photographs Division, US Library of Congress.

that will last an eternity."[30] The editorial praised the involvement of "private
enterprise" in funding enduring architecture while criticizing expenditures
of federal monies on poorly built temporary structures, though neither position addresses the racist decision to build internment camps for Japanese
Americans in the first place.

Hoyt's pièce de résistance, however, was the double-lane ramp that he
designed to take the place of the central staircase at the entrance to the
building, which connected the first floor, mezzanine, and second floor (see
figure 3.6). This double-lane ramp, which replaced a staircase and allowed
for traffic in both directions simultaneously, meant that anyone traveling
between floors of the school would need to use the same ramp, thereby
neutralizing the typical division between those who might climb a staircase
and those who would need an elevator or some other device for traveling
from one floor to the other. The stainless-steel tubing that connects all three

levels is reminiscent of the kind of nautical-inspired tubing one finds in the architecture of Walter Gropius's Fagus Factory (1911) or Le Corbusier's Villa Savoye. But whereas for Gropius, Le Corbusier, and their adherents these details were intended as a tongue-in-cheek blurring of designs for ships and factories with the interior spaces of private homes to produce the machine-like environment so valued by high modernist architects, at the Boettcher School the metal tubing makes transparent the ways that staircases privilege those who can climb them, whereas ramps make all users equal by virtue of the incline and decline that do the work of moving a body through space. Similarly, a promotional photograph shows four children and the school's principal, Catherine Hays, standing near one of the building's three half-circle glass enclosures that lead to an interior courtyard (see figure 3.7). The all-glass frontages include doors embedded into them, thereby minimizing any structural elements that might obscure sunlight and fresh air from entering into the interior of the building. One young boy, sitting in a wheelchair, rests his arm on a circular stainless-steel bar that wraps around one of the massive cement pylons that support the ceiling, while another boy with a cane sits on a half-circle padded leather bench that surrounds the cement pylon in much the same way that a bench in an upscale hotel lobby might be positioned for maximum visibility by hotel patrons. The repetition of circular or half-circular elements, from the seating to the window bay, provides a dramatic contrast to the kinds of institutional architectures common to residential schools and hospitals during the 1930s because it takes as its premise the idea that a sophisticated modern vocabulary of shapes without corners and volumes of physical space both horizontal and vertical could enable a way of embodying space that was not about obscurity but about illumination.

Despite the Boettcher School's capitulation to the contemporary use of the word "cripple," the building defied every existing stereotype and expectation for what a school for children with physical disabilities might encounter. For Hoyt, the capacity for a building to neutralize the perceived differences between a child with a physical disability and a nondisabled teacher or administrator was precisely the point: no user's experience, no apparatus, would be elevated above another. In retrospect, the Boettcher School was more like schools in Amsterdam and Copenhagen in terms of its deployment of open space for its students as well as for its teachers and administrators—space that did not constrain bodies into forms of navigation that made them conform to existing conventions of spatial movement but instead provided a wide berth for moving through space on one's own terms. For many students, this freedom was enacted by the mere act of traveling to school. One of the design elements stipulated by Children's Hospital

FIGURE 3.7. Photograph of a white woman in a jacket and skirt standing in front of a glass wall with four white children, all of whom hold a mobility device or wear leg braces. This is a publicity photo for the Charles A. Boettcher School for Crippled Children, Denver, Colorado. Identified in the photograph are (from left to right) Darline Whalen, age seven; John White, age ten; Ronald Eady, age ten; and Betty Tap, age eight; and principal Mrs. Catherine D. Hays. Photograph dated August 26, 1940. Author's collection.

was that Hoyt connect the school to the hospital via subterranean tunnel in recognition of the fact that some students lived in the hospital year-round. Hoyt designed a long, weatherproof corridor running from the basement level of the hospital to the school; students who traversed it would move from a tunnel lit by dim electric lights and into a vestibule before entering a two-story lobby flooded with sunshine from banks of windows at the building's entry.

In 1993, Children's Hospital declared its intention to expand space for its facilities and razed the school, though not before making sure that it was comprehensively documented by photographers for the Historical American Building Survey. The former Boettcher School site is currently occupied by a three-story parking structure for St. Joseph's Hospital, its low, wide horizontality matched to the school's original footprint. At street level one can find several upscale commercial tenants, including a restaurant and a private gym called the Body Shaping Company. One wonders if customers or gym members know that mere feet below the rubberized and carpeted flooring is a tunnel through which children once traveled—some pushing themselves in wheelchairs, some balanced on crutches or canes, some in leg braces helping their peers—to facilities built not to change them or rehabilitate them but to accept them on their own terms.

Working with Your Hands

Public schools were not the only sites where, during the New Deal era, people with disabilities experienced a dramatic shift in sensibility toward physical or sensory difference. WPA-sponsored workshops across the United States employed workers who were both skilled and unskilled, nondisabled and disabled. This is a surprising dimension of New Deal economic and cultural production that has been neglected by historians of labor as well as by historians of disability.[31] As historians such as Kim Nielsen and Sarah Rose have demonstrated, during the nineteenth and early twentieth centuries, labor itself was not a universal wedge with which all people with disabilities were historically excluded from employment across the board: young (white) men who were deaf or hearing-impaired, for instance, apprenticed at printing press facilities because they could endure loud industrial environments better than their hearing counterparts; the fates of (white) men and women who had been institutionalized in asylums were adjudicated in the courts where they were discerned to be intellectually "competent" enough to participate in the labor force.[32] Meanwhile, scholarship on disability and labor activity during the 1930s remains relatively thin. For the late historian Paul Longmore, the WPA has negative associations given its checkered history of discriminating against workers with physical disabilities and fostering a paternalistic attitude toward people with disabilities in general.[33] Longmore uncovered the existence of the League of the Physically Handicapped (1935–37), a protest group organized to demand participation in the economy rather than "handouts," which they believed to be undignified. Yet the existence of workers with disabilities has not been rescued from obscurity in the way that, for instance, the existence of African American workers during the period has undergone a significant recovery by scholars such as Cheryl Lynn Greenberg.[34] As researcher Algernon Austin has written, "The WPA provided jobs for hundreds of thousands of Black people but within a system of racial hierarchy. Despite some new federal requirements requiring equal treatment, Black workers were often placed at the back of the line for jobs, and they were often relegated to the lowest paid positions regardless of their skills."[35] This does not mean that nonwhite people with disabilities were any more successful at challenging racial hierarchies. The Atlanta branch of the Georgia WPA, for instance, hired African American workers who were visually impaired in the production of Braille books for members of their extended community. A 1937 documentary photograph by the Federal Arts Project, for instance, does not indicate whether this was a segregated workshop or merely one located in a Black community, though the fact that, as Greenberg demonstrates, African American workers were brought on to build or improve segregated schools, colleges, hospitals, and public housing across the South suggests that Black workers with disabilities were not miraculously exempt from racial hierarchy.[36]

Because the New Deal's emphasis on the physicality of work was shaped by the imperatives of an industrialized nation, it seems excluding people with physical disabilities from WPA projects or judging them as incompetent or incapable would be a fait accompli. Indeed, for art historians such as Barbara Melosh and A. Joan Saab, the proliferation of conventionally gendered, heterosexual, and nondisabled representations of industrial and agricultural workers was an ideological bulwark of democratic culture, projected as works of and by "the people" and thus normalizing nondisability as a standard of US labor identity. But as Melosh and Saab argue, such mythological representations were anything but consensual; images of productive bodies and reproductive family units, portrayed as the intended recipients of economic commitments to "ordinary" people and families, maintained a nondisabled physical standard that squashed the hopes and desires of those who wanted to join them. Such mythological representations extend as well to the figure of FDR himself and his dissembling over his own disability status; as historians such as Nielsen and Daniel Wilson have discussed, FDR's "splendid deception"—a phrase popularized by disability scholar and activist Hugh Gallagher, who also drafted the legislation that would become the Architectural Barriers Act of 1968—required an entire production team as well as the complicity of the public.[37]

Even before Roosevelt's first administration began in January 1933, a series of laws passed by Congress during Herbert Hoover's administration ensured that the WPA's employment of people who were legally blind would be a priority, given the number of veterans blinded during the Great War as well as people born with congenital visual disabilities. A tax surplus made possible by the Smoot-Hawley Tariff Act of 1930, for instance, provided $100,000 for the federal purchase of "Talking Book" machines, otherwise known as record players, and for the translation of books into vinyl format, the earliest form of what we would think of today as audiobooks.

As Matthew Rubery and Elizabeth Ellcessor have described, vinyl and Braille copies of popular books, from the Bible to the latest mystery novel, were made available to blind and visually impaired subscribers; publishing houses and authors took the unprecedented step of waiving copyright costs and royalty payments.[38] Six years later, the Randolph-Sheppard Act of 1936 stipulated that owners of vending machines, newsstands, and other kiosks give priority to blind proprietors, forging an association between self-reliance and entrepreneurial independence that had a profound effect on public perceptions of people with disabilities.

Although the talking book programs were initiated in 1931 under the Hoover administration, they reached their maturity as a technological and social intervention with the WPA's expansion of training of visually impaired apprentices for workshop labor in private industry after the war. Corinne Frazier Gillett, a correspondent for the national publication *Outlook for the Blind*, observed in 1941 that, in Georgia, "boys' clubs have been asked to make a special effort to interest blind boys in their activities, and blind adults with meager education are being brought into touch with the adult education department of the WPA for possible enrollment in blind classes in counties where teachers for the blind are available."[39] In New Jersey, Gillett described a WPA-funded project that paired

> two men, taken from the ranks of the state's needy unemployed . . . One is sighted, the other blind—the latter, a man who has had considerable experience with machinery. . . . The sighted member of the team describes to the sightless one the operation to be undertaken, and the blind man sits down and attempts it. When machinery is involved, the sighted man describes its structure and function to his partner, helps him to find and test the operation of the controls, and then looks on as the blind investigator operates the apparatus.

As both workers recognize how mutual dependence can produce excellent work, the typical hierarchy that puts the nondisabled worker ahead of the disabled worker is deliberately inverted. One commentator opined that blind workers could not only "keep up with their sighted fellow-workers . . . in some of the processes requiring sensitive finger tips, their skills exceeded that of any sighted person." In one case where the momentum of the assembly line required the placement of a tiny screw, three sighted workers proved to have butterfingers while a blind man with "sensitive fingers, accustomed to 'reading' the tiny dots of the braille alphabet, handled the screw easily, fitting it into place without hesitation the first time he tried." At the Milwaukee branch of the Wisconsin WPA, carpenters created miniature and life-size models of various objects of educational interest to be used as educational aids for blind students who must 'see with their fingertips.'" And at the Columbus branch of the Ohio WPA, "miniatures of ocean liners, locomotives and air transports, built by WPA artisans, and raised geographical maps, have helped give the sightless a physical picture of the world around them." Gillett estimated that blind workers employed by literacy projects of the WPA accounted for the transcription of four million book pages, a large amount of them produced as Braille textbooks for visually impaired readers attending state schools for the blind or for patrons using the blind services of public libraries.[40]

WPA-supported workers with sensory impairments helped to produce not only books, records, and magazines, but also the very Talking Book machines on which their words would be reproduced as well as the outlets where they could be found. In 1936 the New York City branch of the WPA hired a dozen blind workers as technicians; working on the tenth floor of one of the WPA's main production sites at the corner of Thirty-Sixth Street and Tenth Avenue in Manhattan, workers were taught how to build record players using their sense of touch to install screws and adjust wiring so that the machines would reproduce sound. A construction team for the WPA even designed a special roof garden for the workers where they were encouraged to take lunch, smoke cigarettes, and play cards with a Braille deck. This was not unprecedented in New York City; some banks and insurance companies created rooftop gardens for their blind customers, such as the roof garden constructed by the Bank of New York on Allen Street for wealthy depositors who were visually impaired. But these technicians were workers, not rich customers, and recognition of their own leisure time and the construction apparatus available to activate it underscored the ways that new configurations of work under the WPA also created new forms of inclusion for workers with disabilities that had previously been available only to members of the bourgeoisie.

Numerous WPA projects followed a similar formula, hiring locals to do work that not only kept them employed but also tapped into their specific skill set. The argument for employing blind technicians was that their tactile dexterity—a skill set made available *because* of, rather than despite, their disability—would enable them to make and repair record players with greater precision than their sighted counterparts. Their specialization, which may have seemed rarefied, also made these blind technicians similar to all workers who labored for the WPA. The tactile expertise of the blind worker, or the tactile knowledge of the average blind person that could be adapted for work experience, made such employees valuable to the WPA's broader understanding of employment as a necessary precondition for democratic participation. And as part of the same subset of users who would go on to use the very record players that they were making, they represented a kind of vertical integration that made their employment status and their consumer status coequal.

At the beginning of the New Deal, Roosevelt's mandate to create agencies like the WPA and the PWA was to achieve full-scale employment for American workers shut out of the labor market, which was famously extended to those who were deemed "unskilled." But it also extended to some workers with disabilities: a 1938 study conducted by the WPA's Division of Research, for instance, featured an interview with a deaf worker, Bernard DiMarco, who had been hired to help build an airport near Dubuque, Iowa, by the Civil Works Administration, a short-lived emergency relief program established by the Roosevelt administration in 1933. As it was designated as "relief work," DiMarco was paid in groceries, not cash. Even so, as a deaf worker DiMarco was routinely harassed by a city manager on the site who "wanted him sent home but the men on the job stood up for Bernard & and he remained." Two years later, DiMarco found paid employment in a more welcoming atmosphere after the WPA granted $200,000 to help expand and improve the majestic Eagle Point Park in Dubuque; DiMarco stayed on the project for more than two and a half years.[41]

Other WPA projects underscored the degree to which the experiences of workers with disabilities were often a catalyst for generating access to knowledge that might otherwise be beyond the purview of sighted workers or those without the embodied forms of expertise to carry it through. Some of this work was not primarily or exclusively technological. In Fargo, North Dakota, for instance, the WPA supervised numerous community-based recreational activities including "reading to shut-ins" and "producing Braille books."[42] Meanwhile, the Wisconsin WPA was successful in recruiting and employing workers in its statewide Braille Program, including several dozen blind transcribers and proofreaders, and eleven blind students enrolled at the University of Wisconsin's central campus in Madison. A 1939 report prepared by the Wisconsin WPA's Professional Services Division announced that "Braille projects in Wisconsin have been in operation since July 1936," and in just three years had produced or translated for the Wisconsin School for the Blind "1,707 books . . . [and] 3,871 pages of Braille music," increasing the school's library resources "by approximately 200%." The number of academic titles produced by WPA-employed workers for the Madison Braille Project enabled some members of the WPA to imagine Wisconsin as "the first university anywhere in the world where a sightless student may come with the knowledge that he can do most of his reading for himself."[43] In addition to incorporating blind workers, the Wisconsin WPA also provided employment opportunities for 2,600 women from Milwaukee County, 90 percent of whom could not find jobs elsewhere. In her memoir of working with the Milwaukee Handicraft Project, Mary Kellogg Rice describes the normative assumptions about these female employees that persisted despite the inclusive character of the project. Many of the women were characterized as "uneducated, untrained, some illiterate, some speaking only a foreign language, and a few who were mentally deficient." The Handicraft Project's visionary leader, trained artist Elsa Ulbricht, stipulated to supervisors and foremen, in a tone of ambivalent compassion, that in leading the women they should "watch each worker" and "be able to distinguish between laziness, lack of ability, maladjustment, or willful lack of application."[44]

Many projects under the aegis of the WPA, such as the Federal Art Project, underscored the degree to which the promise of design for multiple senses could inspire cultural engagement even if the primary purpose was not pedagogical. In 1937, for instance, sculptor Irene Emery was hired by the Federal Art Project to produce a bas-relief sculpture of multiple birds, their overlapping bodies in mid-flight, for use on the wall of the sunroom built for the Carrie Tingley Hospital for Crippled Children at Hot Springs, New Mexico. Deliberately textured and set at a height only a few feet above the ground, the heads and bodies of Emery's bird sculptures could easily be seen by the sighted as well as traced by the hands and fingers of children with visual impairments attending the school, a form of cross-accessible design available to those standing as well as to those who used a wheelchair.[45] Community art programs sponsored by the Federal Art Project, often at buildings that were also designed and built by the WPA, included courses specifically designed for children with disabilities. In June 1938, for instance, a civic group in Salem, Oregon, established the Salem Federal Art Center to offer free art classes, including sculpture courses, for blind and visually impaired children, many of whom received instruction from nondisabled teachers for the Federal Arts Project who were sponsored as employees of the WPA (see figure 3.8). A contemporary portrait taken at the Salem Federal Arts Center by a WPA photographer captures a group of five blind young women working with their hands on what appear to be both conventional and abstract clay models, while a sighted instructor in a knee-length white smock observes them, all under a tricolor patriotic sign emblazoned with the words "USA—WORK—WPA."[46]

Similarly, *Work Pays America* (1937), a documentary film produced by the Federal Art Project and nationally distributed to cinemas as daily newsreels, highlights various WPA projects that depict workers across a spectrum of abilities producing "a new generation of good citizens."[47] Under

FIGURE 3.8. Photograph c. 1938 of five young women standing at tables on which they are making sculptures out of clay with their hands. Behind them is a man with glasses and a mustache who is wearing a white smock coat. Above their heads is a small sign with stars and stripes that says "USA-WORK-WPA." This is a workshop for blind and visually impaired students at the Salem Art Center in Salem, Oregon, taught by art instructors employed by the Works Progress Administration (WPA). The teacher, the architect and builders of the Art Center, and the photographer of this image were all employed by the Oregon WPA. Reprinted with permission of Alpha Stock / Alamy Stock Photo.

the swelling dramatic orchestration common to documentaries of the era, a sober male voice narrates to us that "new interests have vanquished *the darkness and despair in the lives of thousands of sightless men and women* as the result of several projects in which books and maps have been translated into Braille, the written language of the blind." The documentary shows us Braille-embossing typewriters and "talking machines" (record players) for producing audiobook disks for circulation to libraries and for home use by users who were visually impaired. The documentary also observes that "the proofreading of these works is done by sightless experts; in some cities, instruction is given in the reading of blind maps." Such observations about "sightless experts" continued well into the late 1930s as various programs for the WPA either evolved or solidified. In 1938, for instance, the *Baltimore Sun* reported that the city's Enoch Pratt Library employed a blind man,

Solomon Sibel, to oversee nineteen blind female technicians—referenced by the *Sun* through the nondisabled synecdoche "38 eyes"—to do Braille transcription work for the WPA.[48] The images that punctuate this narration include nondisabled workers fabricating embossed maps intended for use by the blind and a pan across a room of "sightless experts" running their hands slowly across the pages of Braille books, thereby both revealing and mystifying blind reading practices for sighted viewers.

WPA-sponsored projects famously promoted a complex, progressive vision of cultural pluralism that often bordered on the radical, a charge not infrequently made by conservatives who sought to defund areas of the WPA that they believed were promoting a left-wing agenda.[49] In the first wave of New Deal initiatives created to address infrastructure, the Public Works Administration, a forerunner agency that paralleled the WPA, commissioned the esteemed African American artist Sargent Claude Johnson to carve two decorative wooden screens for use in the auditorium at the California School for the Blind in Berkeley: one, in redwood and steel, to cover the cylinders of the school's massive pipe organ, completed in 1934; and the other, in walnut and steel, to serve as a proscenium that would hang permanently over the curtains at the front of the stage, completed in 1937. The proscenium offered sighted visitors a tableau of details celebrating "drama" and "music" all surrounded by lush trees and flowers, rabbits, deer, and birds, as well as a variety of stylized, carved masks (see figure 3.9). The face of what appears to be a European conquistador with a groomed and pointed Vandyke beard is sandwiched between two profiles: on the left, an African warrior bearing ritual markings; on the right, an elongated skull stripped of its flesh. Johnson's rendering of a trio of faces sparely suggests an intertwined history of colonialism and death, which gives a darkly ironic twist to the surrounding flora and fauna, though it may have required a teacher's reinforcement to communicate the artist's vision.

Today, the proscenium hangs in relative obscurity. When the state of California moved the location of the School for the Blind to Fremont in 1980, Johnson's sculptures were removed and put in storage while UC Berkeley converted the school's former buildings for its new Clark Kerr Campus. When it opened in 1986, the school placed the proscenium in a conference room. The redwood and steel organ screen, however, remained in storage for another three decades until 2009, when UC Berkeley began a process of deaccessioning its holdings. The organ screen was purchased by a furniture dealer for $164.63 with tax, unrecognized as either a masterwork by an important African American artist or as an important object of disability history.[50] Eventually, after a series of public humiliations, Berkeley's error was corrected; the organ screen was rescued from an ignoble fate and

FIGURE 3.9. Photograph of what looks like an elaborately decorated arch-shaped painting. This is a decorative wall sculpture, c. 1937, crafted of walnut and steel by African American artist Sargent Claude Johnson as a proscenium that hung over the curtains at the front of the stage in the auditorium at the California School for the Blind in Berkeley. Photograph taken 2012 by Harvey Smith for the Living New Deal (www.livingnewdeal.com) and reprinted with permission of Harvey Smith.

is now on display at the Huntington Library in Pasadena. The proscenium still hangs in a conference room next to an air conditioner, unavailable to and presumably unknown by the general public.

Learning at Your Fingertips

The "Braille map for the blind at Watertown" made for the Perkins School for the Blind was a product of the Massachusetts WPA in coordination with a Boston-based branch of what was known as the Museum Extension Project, a semi-autonomous program administered at the state and local levels with an enormous amount of flexibility in its hiring practices as well as in the creative projects it undertook. According to James Findlay and Lillian Perricone, twenty-four of the forty-eight US states funded and maintained their own versions of the Museum Extension Project (MEP), one of the longest running and yet one of the most historically neglected projects organized under the auspices of the WPA.[51] Inexplicably, however, the Museum Extension Project is not even mentioned by name in the WPA's final report, which was published in 1947; a minuscule paragraph under the heading "Museum Projects" describes how "WPA workers assisted museums in the making of dioramas, models, maps, lantern slides, and other visual-aid devices for extension work in public schools." But the phrase "visual-aid devices" does not even begin to convey the variety and complexity of MEP projects: not only the numerous people who used such "devices," many of whom were children with disabilities, but also the economic and social stability of the people who facilitated their construction and distribution, many of whom were workers with disabilities.[52]

The statewide work of the MEP, which began in 1935, was distributed among major cities or regional centers until 1943, when unemployment had been effectively eliminated and the US government was mobilizing for World War II.[53] This means that half of the US states supported workshops involved in a multitude of ambitious projects specifically identified with the goals of the MEP. In a 1937 progress report, for instance, the Connecticut WPA highlighted the work of its MEP among a list of projects that spanned everything from school lunches to veterinary science, a whirlwind of buzzwords without explanation or follow-up that were seemingly engineered by an anonymous writer to protect the WPA's funding from the red pen of even the most circumspect bureaucrat. The variety and scale of these objectives and products is tantalizing:

> Community Service Projects, including Music, Art, Index of American Design, Writers' Racial Studies, Educational and Recreation, Adult Guidance, Nursery Schools, Library Service, Visual Aids, Museum Work, Crafts, Silk Screen Posters.

> Welfare Projects, including Health, School Lunches, Nursing Assistance, Housekeeping Aides, Household Employees Training, Toy Lending, Sewing Pattern Exchange, Legal Aid, Food Stamp Plan;

> Research and Records, including Historical Records Survey, American Imprints, Federal Archives, Historic American Building Survey Indexing and Restoring Public Records, Establishing Files for Public Agencies, Surveys and Analysis, Blister Rust Control, and Mastitis Survey.[54]

In MEP branches across the country, the design, construction, and distribution of objects intended for public schools, libraries, and community centers—including maps, models, toys, lantern slides, clothing, and literally hundreds of thousands of other pedagogical objects—were central to the purpose and significance of their public orientation. There was already a strong precedent for this kind of public activity; beginning in the 1890s, large urban institutions such as the Field Museum in Chicago and the Metropolitan Museum of Art in New York City initiated outreach programs for rural and poor urban schools without access to the rich artifacts in museums' historical collections. According to historian of education Nicole Belolan, schools for children with disabilities were among those identified as the most likely beneficiaries for the educational (as well as social) opportunities provided by the now-conventional museum field trip (see figure 3.10). In her history of educational programs developed for children with disabilities at the Metropolitan Museum of Art, Belolan argues that Progressive Era administrators, influenced by educational theorists like John Dewey, were committed to the idea that "exposure to art prepared all children, regardless of disability (or ability), to live their adult lives as productive, enlightened citizens engaged in many aspects of public life, including appreciating and, perhaps even, creating art."[55] Students who traveled to the museum met with curators and docents who introduced them to physical examples from the museum's collections—taxidermy animals, plant specimens, suits of armor, antique coins—which often included special dispensation to touch objects that were otherwise off limits to visitors.

Belolan argues that these kinds of educational outreach programs for children with disabilities disappeared by the end of the 1920s and did not resume until the 1970s with the return of "workshops and lectures for visitors with disabilities, the likes of which became more common following the passing of several national laws that secured disability rights."[56] This is because the vast majority of educators of the visually impaired shifted pedagogy away from tactile learning and toward visual- and text-based learning in order to emphasize normative conventions of social communication, paralleling in significant ways how sign language was replaced by oralism and technology-based solutions at many schools for the deaf and hearing-impaired.[57] New pedagogical mandates, as historian Brad Byrom has argued, shifted power away from distinctive cultures of organic communication and instead trained students to be "productive" within more recognizable mainstream forms of communication.[58] Not everyone agreed with this pedagogical shift; Thomas Cutsforth, a blind psychology instructor at the University of Kansas and the author of *The Blind in School and Society* (1933), caused controversy after lamenting that blind educators were thoughtlessly ignoring opportunities for encounters with objects that are shaped outside of conventions of language-based pedagogy.[59] "Socially and educationally," Cutsforth argued, "the blind are expected to appreciate things not as they themselves experience them, but as they are taught how others experience them. For example, a lamb, which is a kinky, woolly, bony, wiggling object, possessing none too delightful an odor, whose feet are generally dirty and sharp and whose mouth and nose are damp and slobbery, is not described as such, but as the snow-white, innocent, gamboling lamb."[60]

The object-oriented pedagogies stimulated and made possible by the MEP suggest that the shift to language-based pedagogies may not have

FIGURE 3.10. Photograph c. 1912 of one young girl and two young boys, all dressed in formal clothing, who have their eyes closed and their arms outstretched to embrace a large globe resting on a large metal pedestal. These are children with visual impairments invited to the American Museum of Natural History in New York City to learn from tactile objects like the globe. Beginning in the late nineteenth century, many prominent museums in the United States and Europe developed educational outreach programs for poor children, children in rural areas, and children with disabilities. Many of these programs inspired the Works Progress Administration to sponsor its Museum Extension Project. Image no. 335068, reprinted with permission of the American Museum of Natural History Library.

happened at the same time for all students or at all institutions, providing a necessary corrective to the assumption that pedagogy for the blind has a singular narrative arc. This is perhaps because workers and administrators in the WPA were deeply inspired by the values held by educators a generation earlier; Progressive Era educators elevated museums during the early twentieth century as sites that enabled children's creative and experiential engagement with the world and also pushed them outside of the classroom to get involved in civic institutions if they lived in or near cities with such resources. For many social critics, this move was not entirely unproblematic; most objects highlighted at local museums or historical societies were drawn from the gilded detritus of the wealthiest and/or most storied residents. As Mabel Wilson and Carol Duncan have argued, these institutions were intended to serve as guardians of culture, preservers of social hierarchies, and disseminators to the unwashed masses of nativist values organized deliberately around a white historical past.[61] The MEP's innovation, however, was to democratize access to the museum as a public institution by taking it out of its gilded setting and utilizing and directing the vast surplus of skilled labor in large parts of the country, especially those in urban locations, to make museum-quality objects that could be purchased at low cost by libraries and school systems on a permanent basis. The MEP synthesized progressive educational theory and urban pedagogy through the medium of the museum object, which brought modern understandings of object-oriented educational theory to teachers, parents, and students who might not otherwise be recipients of forward-thinking pedagogical projects. With objects purchased from the MEP, they could create objects with which teachers and students could curate exhibitions, make dioramas, and engage in creative play, or which they could send home as the basis of homework assignments.

Surviving documentation of the work of the MEP as well as that which was materially produced—much of which still appears at garage sales and on internet auction sites—demonstrates the wide variety of historical and contemporary objects with which the MEP sought to engage students and teachers. Many of these were crip objects. The Columbus branch of the Ohio MEP, for instance produced an entire catalog, *Models for the Blind* (1941), which not only provided descriptions and ordering information but also included numerous photographs of the kinds of objects that one could purchase and the various pedagogical uses to which such objects could be put.[62] From the catalog, one could order models of a Chicago skyscraper, the Eiffel Tower, a zeppelin, a lighthouse, or a Le Corbusier–inspired white modernist house. In photographs taken by a WPA-sponsored photographer to accompany the catalog, a boy and girl with outstretched hands feel the spires and flying buttresses of a model of Salisbury Cathedral in England, the expression of discovery on their faces reflected in the austere white surfaces of the cathedral model, while a worker prepares a model of the Washington Monument to be used in the classroom. On nearly every page, the catalog emphasizes that these objects could be used to teach children or adults with visual impairments about their city, their state, and even the long stretch of history from eighteenth-century origins of agriculture in Ohio to the present day in the state's capital of Columbus.

In some ways, tactile renderings of famous buildings produced for children at schools for the blind were extensions of mystique imputed to buildings, particularly in the era of the skyscraper—one thinks of the gestalt of the image of Helen Keller standing on the eighty-sixth-floor observation deck of the Empire State Building (see figure 2.4) we examined in chapter 2. But tactile models had been around for at least a century in the United States before the MEP and for much longer within the tradition of vernacular folk arts. In the 1830s, as new types of books became formalized at the Perkins School "in Watertown," tactile models were instrumental to comprehensive education for the blind. In other parts of the world, especially in Europe and Scandinavia, tactile models were deployed by educators and rehabilitation specialists to ensure that those with visual impairments were included in knowledge-building exercises that pertained to all citizens. As media historian Yvonne Eriksson has shown, specialty book publishers in England, France, Germany, Italy, and the Scandinavian countries produced books that introduced blind readers to modern houses and apartment buildings—a form familiar to those living in nations whose public housing, schools, factories, and civic buildings had been influenced by the architects and designers of the Bauhaus—as the basis for teaching students about spatial arrangements of modern living. As Eriksson demonstrates, these included efficient spaces for living and sleeping, galley kitchens, rooms for toileting and bathing, and addressed how to move down a corridor, enter rooms, and even to ascend a staircase in an apartment building, with the suggestion that one could live by oneself if one understood how to navigate the small space of a modern apartment.[63]

The modern elements at play captured in the Ohio MEP's *Models for the Blind* convey the notion that students would not only have an opportunity to become sensorially acquainted with famous buildings or maps of cities rendered through tactile means; such objects would also insert them into the present moment, enabling them to become active participants in an urban environment in which knowing urban cartography would be useful to their status as engaged citizens. In one compelling image from the catalog, a young girl stands above a large tactile map of downtown Columbus, where miniature versions of important civic buildings and skyscrapers are prominently featured in proximity to the river, each tiny block of wood or rivulet of paint bearing a tiny strip of Braille text to indicate names and locations. (see figure 3.11). Wearing a fashionable blouse with a late 1930s Art Deco–inspired print, she runs her hands across what would be identifiable to a sighted onlooker as the downtown business district. In another photograph a young girl stands in front of a tactile relief (cutaway of a model) that depicts an underground drainage system that uses sedimented layers

FIGURE 3.11. Photograph of a young girl wearing a modern dress who is standing over a large tabletop model of a city and, with her arms outstretched, is touching buildings on the model. The girl, a student at the Ohio School for the Blind in Columbus, is showing how to interact with the model of Columbus, which was made by skilled carpenters and model makers working for the Museum Extension Project of the Ohio branch of the Works Progress Administration. Photograph c. 1940 published in *Models for the Blind* (Columbus: Ohio State School for the Blind, 1941). Reprinted with permission of the Ohio History Project, SA1039AV_B11F04_31_001.

of rock to show how water is absorbed into the soil (see figure 3.12). The girl wears a soft calico dress and has her hair in pigtails, suggesting not only her youth but also the importance of showcasing traditionally gendered female students in the pursuit of knowledge that for many would be associated with male farming labor or male scientific expertise. A ruler in front of the relief indicates that the scale of tactile models was deliberately thoughtful about the size of the hands of the children who would be the end users of these tactile projects. While the fingertips of the girl's left hand touch a row of horizontal rocks at the bottom of the relief, those of her right hand

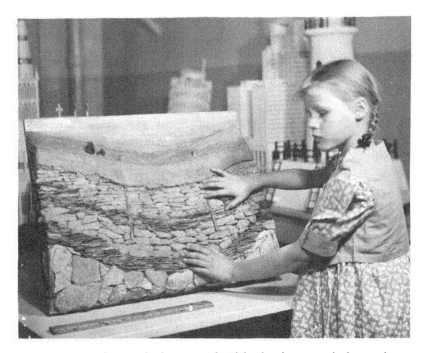

FIGURE 3.12. Photograph of a young girl with her hands outstretched to touch a large, square wooden tactile model into which horizontal lines have been cut. The girl is a student at the Ohio School for the Blind in Columbus, who is showing how to interact with a model showing how moisture saturates sedimented layers of soil, made by skilled carpenters and model makers working for the Museum Extension Project of the Ohio branch of the Works Progress Administration. Photograph c. 1940 published in *Models for the Blind* (Columbus: Ohio State School for the Blind, 1941). Reprinted with permission of the Ohio History Project, SA1039AV_B11F04_29_001.

touch a vertical model of a pipe that connects to the surface of a represented flow of water.

As with the photograph of the girl touching downtown Columbus on the map, the suggestion here is of a form of knowledge that has practical value—the girl may have firsthand knowledge of living in a rural environment still organized around agriculture—but also that she is directly involved in understanding a meta-process that she could never personally experience with her own hands. Drainage systems in rural locations and skyscrapers in urban cities are enormous physical and environmental undertakings that typically would involve some kind of visual assessment in order to make them comprehensible. In both instances, however, the tactile is the means through which large abstract concepts unavailable to the visually impaired become meaningful.

Touch operates on a triangle-shaped system of meaning-making similar to that defined in the analysis of the photograph of Helen Keller and Polly Thomson window shopping on the Champs-Élysées in the introduction to this book (see figure I.6). There must be a person or system that embeds presumptive knowledge into the object; a person or system that encounters the object through the modality of touch; and a person or system that interprets meaning from their encounter with the object. In a pedagogical setting, however, such as a classroom or a museum, the triangle is shaped by the habituation that an educator wishes to impart to the user. In the archival collections of Berlin's Blinden-Museum, for instance, there is a photograph of young schoolgirls at the Johann-August-Zeune-Schule taken in the late 1930s. The photograph depicts the girls, all blind, touching the sculptures of heads representing different racial groups, with one white "European" head and one Black "African" head at their fingertips.[64] These were not designed as tactile sculptures for the blind; they were made and distributed around Germany as conventional representational models that use both visual and tactile cues—such as the shape of the nose or size of the skull—for classrooms or museum exhibitions. That such sculptures rely upon the phenotypic exaggerations typical of racist science is not surprising given the setting (a classroom in Berlin at the height of the Third Reich). What may be surprising to sighted viewers is that those representational exaggerations were exploited in those circumstances where the modality of touch could be used to substitute for the modality of vision. If touch, and not vision, is one's primary mode of experiencing the world, then what does representation even mean, and how does one prepare for it? Such preparation may borrow directly from histories of classical art in ancient Greece or Rome and the long tradition of creating busts to honor political leaders. It may also borrow from phrenology, the nineteenth-century pseudoscience of extracting meaning from the shape of the head as a precursor to creating social hierarchies based on bodily features.

The "meaning" of touch, in any case, is never natural even if the modality used to experience it—the hands or fingers—is. Some form of instruction, whether through the words of a teacher or text (in Braille) or both, must be in place during an encounter with these sculptural objects that will help a person translate what a particular aspect of the sculpture "means," and into what areas of knowledge they needed to enter (or, in some cases, descend) in order to make sense of it. Woodworkers and model makers employed by the MEP in Lansing, Michigan, for instance, engineered a model of the Empire State Building for the Michigan School for the Blind. The model was made with sandpaper edges and thick, glossy paint to give users an opportunity to experience its dimensionality and also to understand the stages through which such a building was made. Unlike a photograph that can only be seen, however, a person using the tactile model of the Empire State Building could gain some broader conceptual knowledge of the whole building and its construction, even if they were unable to visit. That a tactile model of the Empire State Building, or a model of any building, imparts any information at all is not just a matter of design—as if design were a pure form that could be disaggregated from its use—but a matter of habituation by the user. *How* one accesses it and *what* one then makes of it mark two entirely different questions. There is no inherent meaning to a tactile model or map, though the presumption may be that it is as easy to "read" as a visual map. This is because the modality of touch (how one feels something) is separate from the object of touch (what is being felt). Interpretation, as a cognitive act, is separate from the physical act of touch that makes meaning between the two actions. For children at state schools for the blind in Michigan or Ohio, these uses of tactile objects in the classroom were not simply aesthetic counterparts to book learning; they were a method for helping students conceptualize physical space and their relationship to it through the subjective medium of their bodily experiences.

For some scholars, like Susan Stewart and Margaret Gibson, physical objects like dollhouses, model trains, and tiny books produce an aura of astonishment and melancholy, tapping into the original Greek meaning of the word *nostalgia:* "homesickness," a longing for a time and a place (and perhaps a history) that has never happened or else can never happen.[65] An odd mixture of nostalgia and melancholy hovers over a small diorama called *Chronic Illness* (1937) produced by the New York Scenic Designers and Model Makers Project of the Federal Art Project.[66] Made for sighted viewers as a teaching tool to dramatize public health, the diorama used doll furniture and figurines to depict a crowded tenement space—a dilapidated and unhygienic single room occupied by multiple generations, heated by a rickety coal-burning furnace and ventilated by a single window—visited by a smartly dressed female social worker.[67] Although *Chronic Illness* follows the same narrative contours of poverty and deprivation that contemporary photographers like Walker Evans and Dorothea Lange were capturing in their depictions of the Dust Bowl, harking back to images produced by reformers like Jacob Riis or Lewis Hine a generation earlier, it is difficult to discern visually what it is trying to convey, as dioramas like this one are passive representations or objects made exclusively for looking. In stark contrast, tactile objects are interactive, functional devices that activate knowledge *through* a specifically crafted form that does not merely invite touch but relies on touch as its principal form of engagement even if other elements, such as color or aroma, provide supplemental information.

In the early decades of the twentieth century, tactile objects were deployed in a multiplicity of contexts, with meanings imbued in them that did not inhere to the objects as forms of conventional representation. In his book *Downcast Eyes*, Martin Jay argues that many European artists and intellectuals during the 1920s and 1930s deliberately sought out nonvisual and nonauditory modalities such as tactility and olfaction to challenge bourgeois norms and to open up possibilities for aesthetic and political protest.[68] Such artists were motivated and inspired to disentangle sensation from meaning, using the shock of the uncanny to undo rationality and in the process rewire the secure self. For instance, in his "Manifesto of Tactilism," first delivered as a lecture at the Théâtre de l'Œuvre in Paris in January 1921, the Italian Futurist provocateur Filippo Tommaso Marinetti declared that the tactile could become a tool of both experiential and psychological liberation—formidable ideas that had a eugenical cast to them, undergirded by Marinetti's own infamous relationship to fascism after the election of Mussolini the following year.[69] Marinetti treated the immersion of the self in the modality of the tactile as a starting point:

> I started by submitting my sense of touch to an intensive treatment, pinpointing the confused phenomena of will and thought on various points on my body, and especially on the palms of my hands. This training is slow but easy, and *all healthy bodies can, through this training, give surprising and exact results....* On the other hand, *unhealthy sensibilities, which draw their excitability and their apparent perfection from the very weakness of the body, will achieve great tactile power less easily, without duration or confidence.* I have created a first educational scale of touch, which is, at the same time, a scale of tactile values for Tactilism, or the Art of Touch.[70]

The single surviving art object constructed by Marinetti, which he called a *tavola tattile* (tactile table), has at its core a presumption about the experiential differences between European subjects and colonial others subordinated to their rule: "One of these abstract tactile boards made by me, and that has as its title *Sudan-Parigi* (Sudan-Paris) contains, in the part representing Sudan, rough, greasy coarse, prickly, burning tactile values (spongy material, sponge, sandpaper, wool, brush, wire brush); in the part representing The Sea, there are slippery, metallic, fresh tactile values (silver-coated paper); in the part representing Paris, there are soft, delicate, caressing tactile values, hot and cold at the same time (silk, velvet, feathers, down)."[71]

However one might interpret Marinetti's aesthetic experimentalism, the premise of the *tavola tattile di Sudan-Parigi* is that it exploits a perceived nonvisual "poetics of space" as experienced by the privileged metropolitan urban dweller, mixing tactile and olfactory exoticism in an arrogant attempt to confirm the difference between the African Other and the normative European. Such a mixing of sensory modalities, however, is rooted not in the practices of nonrepresentational art but rather in the practices of scientific claims of genetic truth, a central intellectual and political tenet of the international eugenics movement of the early twentieth century. During the Third International Congress of Eugenics, for instance, held in 1932 at the American Museum of Natural History in New York City, the US Eugenics Record Office featured an interactive display of ten different fur samples that patrons were invited to touch. The exhibit, part of a group of displays that historian Devon Stillwell has identified as "eugenics, visualized," was created to demonstrate that the ability to distinguish "quality" fur through tactile means was scientifically verifiable as an inherited trait, not merely a sensibility learned through breeding or education.[72] A sign hanging above the samples reads "Specialized Test for Sense of Elegance: Quality in Fur" and offers special instructions for closing one's eyes, feeling individual pelts, and gauging one's experiential capacity to "know" which samples are authentic mink or silver fox and which are squirrel or rabbit.

The exhibit's interior logic, in which one can embody proximity to "quality and elegance" via the modality of touch, implicitly argues for the putative transparency of genetic superiority, guided by the putatively neutral claims of rational science and conspicuous consumerism. Before the advent of washable wool and the commercial availability of synthetic blends like polyester and rayon, animal furs lower down on the luxury food chain than mink and silver fox were readily available to many middle-class consumers and thus were somewhat unremarkable—so unremarkable, in fact, that a few years after attending the Third International Congress of Eugenics a person might have encountered the work of German Surrealist sculptor Merit Oppenheim, who in 1936 produced her best known art piece, *Object*, which consists of a bright yellow department-store-bought tea cup and saucer and stainless-steel teaspoon purchased at a Paris flea market covered extravagantly in the downy fur of a baby gazelle. The intention, as with much work of the Surrealist movement, was to force the viewer to encounter an ordinary domestic object that had been transformed or recontextualized in some way in order to lay bare the uncanny and erotic qualities hidden in its recesses or else in the recesses of the viewer's brain. Much less well known, but equally uncanny and suggestive, is Oppenheim's piece called *Fur Gloves*, also from 1936, which consists of a sculpture of two hands covered in fur pelts with cut out and exposed fingertips on which the fingernails have been painted with garish red varnish—an object that seems to deny the possibility of touch even as it invites speculation about its pleasures and discomforts.

The MEP's investment in the possibilities of tactile pleasure for its students reflected the larger goals of the WPA in its commitment to creating and preserving architectural and environmental projects that were associated with American history and technology symbolic of national values in the mid-twentieth century. While model makers in Ohio and Pennsylvania created tactile scale models of important national buildings like the US Capitol and the Washington Monument, they also produced models of log cabins, Cape Cod bungalows, steel and cement office buildings, and even underground drainage systems used on farms and suburban estates. These various projects, both contemporary and historical, were commensurate with the kinds of recovery and preservation projects that were associated with the WPA in so many of its local and federal instantiations. In all of these examples, we see how tactility as a modality of communication travels quite literally in multiple directions at the same time between the subject (that which is doing the touching) and the object (that which is being touched). Touch, like smell, is always relational in a way that vision is not: its meaning is contingent on the conventions or expectations encoded in or expressed through a particular scent or a tactile surface. The meaning is entirely dependent on the person who is doing the interpreting, the object being touched, and the experience (or lack thereof) that each party brings to the situation. The object-oriented epistemologies of the WPA were clearly interested in promoting educational content through other means.

∴

There is something peculiar about the way that touch in much contemporary scholarship—in art history, in cinema studies, in science and technology studies—is discussed for its metaphorical potential rather than its literal properties. In her influential book *Meeting the Universe Halfway* (2007), for instance, feminist science studies scholar Karen Barad describes the use of an electron microscope to "touch" atomic particles.[73] Extending some of the ideas of feminist film theorists like Lara Marks, the epistemological distinction between "seeing" and "touching" in Barad's example becomes negligible due to the literal inaccessibility of such minute particles.[74] Yet the optical is still the singular modality of observation and interaction, with vision as the ultimate mediating factor in encounters with the world. During the first year of the COVID-19 pandemic, some even argued that virtual touch via Zoom and other technological interfaces was akin to or at least a parallel with physical touch given the constraints that people endured without access to physical touch (except perhaps with people within their epidemiologically protected "bubble").[75] The metaphorical uses of touch in these ways is not unlike what Walter Benjamin was describing in the 1930s in his (arguably specious) distinction between contemplation and distraction, a point of contrast that we explored in chapter 2 in relation to Helen Keller and her challenge to vision as the primary and exclusive modality of the modern. Benjamin conceived of cinema and photography as prosthetic extensions of the body in terms of their capacity to "know" something through the visual, and Barad recognizes Benjamin's connection to her own theories of touch and vision in some of her later work.[76]

The expectation in all of these metaphorical comparisons is that someone who is sighted will be able to experience a version of tactility through some form of technological mediation. Yet knowing through touch is *not* the same as knowing through vision. Touch cannot be easily reduced or, at its most reductive, simplified to a parallel with vision. Indeed, most of the aesthetic philosophers of the early modern scientific era were more apt to talk about the synesthetic experience of vision and touch happening simultaneously than they were to separate them out as later scientists tended to do. Those who want to use visuality as a metaphor for tactility—or for any other sensory modality—must recognize that a person with visual or other sensory impairments cannot participate in this metaphor. It is so anchored in a nondisabled epistemology that its sense of proportion is incommensurate with the radical disorientation of the senses that it seems to suggest. The expectation that one stands for the other as a matter of breaking down boundaries or else productively disorienting the normative practices of a given modality of experience comes from a place where vision, rather than touch, is the organizing principle of knowledge production. In the end, this is not so much an *expansion* of the experience of vision as it is an *attenuation* of the experience of touch. None of this is to suggest that touch is superior to vision; rather, it is to recognize that to endeavor to make touch and vision comparable in some way already starts from a faulty premise that does not pay due diligence to the literal (and not metaphorical) dimensions of touch.

Touching something or someone, unlike looking at or listening to something or someone, is a modality that cannot be fixed at a distance; it is constitutionally and experientially unfolding in proximity, in the here and now, in a state of unsuspension. Yet as the aforementioned examples from the WPA demonstrate, the challenge is to acknowledge that all uses and meanings of touch are relevant when it comes to historicizing the presence or absence of disability in a given moment in time, and within a particular cultural context. The workers who produced touch-oriented objects and technologies for the WPA and its associated programs like the MEP imagined individuals with disabilities with their own understanding of the world. Their sensibilities were understood to be already in process so that the objects built or manufactured for them met them at their level. The sensory worlds brought into being by those experiences became the basis for building educational and economic resources that were deeply intertwined with a vision of what government institutions were capable of producing if their focus was trained on connecting the most vulnerable to a public sphere in which their needs were foregrounded rather than pushed to the margins. Clearly, the historiographical argument that by the 1930s schools for blind and visually impaired students had abandoned object-based learning is not only inaccurate but fails to take into account the radical potential that was clearly recognized by programs like the MEP, which regarded pedagogy as something multisensorial and beyond the linear structures of oralism and visuality. It fails to take into account the fact that teachers and students in schools for the blind were working with Talking Books that were regularly produced by adult members of the same community in federally sponsored projects established to employ them. Indeed, their employability was constructed around the presence of disability, rather than in compensation for something else. The variety and complexity of architectural and material objects designed by and for people with disabilities offers ample evidence that, when it comes to disabled experience and disabled subjectivities, thinking by way of comparison not only keeps the experience of touch at a distance but keeps the experience of disability at a distance as well.

CHAPTER FOUR

Overdue at the Library

In December 1954, the US architect Philip Johnson gave a speech at the Harvard Graduate School of Design, his alma mater, entitled "The Seven Crutches of Modern Architecture."[1] Paying frisky homage to British art critic John Ruskin's famous 1849 book and lecture series, *The Seven Lamps of Architecture*—one of the most influential Western aesthetic manifestos of the nineteenth century—Johnson provided a manifesto of his own. Johnson's perspective on what he saw as professional "crutches" was deliberately confrontational in an era when most architects and students had adopted the principles of modernism, as practiced by giants in the field such as Frank Lloyd Wright and Le Corbusier, as unofficial orthodoxy. These principles included the Crutch of Pretty Drawing ("the illusion that you are creating architecture," he quipped), the Crutch of Comfort, the Crutch of Serving the Client, and the Crutch of Structure, which, he admitted, "gets awfully near home because, of course, I use it all the time myself." Johnson, who identified himself as a neoclassicist in the same way that T. S. Eliot defined himself as such, argued that adhering to the canons of early twentieth-century modernism (which one might gloss as prewar modernism) had become so doctrinal, so unadventurous, that it stifled creativity. The problem, as he saw it, was that too many young architects put all their eggs into the basket of modernist design principles—many of which, ironically, Johnson himself had helped to institutionalize in the 1930s during his time working with the Museum of Modern Art.

What made Johnson so hostile to the type of architectural modernism he had advocated for two decades earlier? In the mid-1950s, the kinds of designs that Johnson associated with "the Seven Crutches of Modern Architecture" could be seen in nearly every sphere of domestic, civic, and corporate architecture in the United States as well as around the world: in suburban homes, in government buildings, in schools and universities, but perhaps more routinely in hospitals, clinics, and institutional facilities. Many of these designs, which took shape in some of the educational spaces we examined in chapter 3, had gained popularity in the mid-twentieth century when euphemisms for architectural modernism, such as "midcentury modern" and "Danish modern," recast building forms for the postwar generation by disentangling them from earlier associations with prewar European antecedents. In mid-1955, for example, the Crippled Children's Hospital in New Orleans received national attention by decorating its walls in "a dozen colors ranging from persimmon through grays, greens, beiges and ultramarines . . . there is no white in the hospital, not even in the sterilization room."[2] With features like washable plastic walls, kitchens with automatic appliances, glass windows and walls throughout the public and private spaces, and individual beds that could be adjusted according to the needs of each child, the hospital took seriously the idea of customizing the convalescent experience according to the unique characteristics of the child, rather than expecting the patient to adjust or conform to expectations of how a body should yield to the physician's and physical therapist's demands. Here was spatial attunement to children with disabilities, as we saw in chapter 3, not as experimental or avant-garde but as normative, even expected, applications of modernism. The hospital's classroom design, which provided a setting for children to continue their education while convalescing, looked more like a lounge than a traditional classroom, with round tables and chairs made of molded plywood interspersed with small adjustable metal desks under which a wheelchair user could roll up without needing to conform to a regular desk design. The metal desks had a center panel that tilted upward to create a comfortable surface for reading or writing at a 45-degree angle and could be adjusted to the height of the reader with the touch of a button.

It is hard not to acknowledge the deliberate opprobrium that Johnson attached to "crutches" as a metaphor used to invoke intellectual or creative "weakness," inasmuch as they were material objects synonymous with physical weakness. Crutches for Johnson were clunky technologies that not only stigmatized their users but also immobilized their creative autonomy. Any mention of crutches, especially as linked to weakness, was also part of a very particular historical moment when such disability objects had a wide range of interpretive meanings. Crutches may have been perceived before the war as evidence of dysfunction to be hidden from public view, as with President Franklin D. Roosevelt, or else as objects to be tossed aside ceremoniously, as with those "healed" by religious conversions or medical miracles. After the war, however, men, women, and children on crutches were part of a constellation of visible disabilities in the public sphere that were shaped (some might say exploited) by patriotic themes: from veterans of World War II recuperating and reintegrating into the wider postwar world, to those living with polio, to the seemingly incongruous visibility of crutches in the spheres of culture and celebrity. Tennessee Williams's *Cat on a Hot Tin Roof*, for instance, which debuted in March 1955, famously used crutches as its symbolic device—surely an example of what David Mitchell and Sharon Snyder have called "narrative prosthesis"—to symbolize not only Brick's fragile ego but also his complex relationship to his closeted sexuality and his secret relationship with another man.[3] Indeed, crutches seemed to be everywhere in the popular media of the early 1950s—from political hopeful John F. Kennedy, who appeared in public during his bid for Congress in 1952 while perched on crutches, to celebrities like Marilyn Monroe who, in 1954, famously broke her ankle while filming *Red River* and maneuvered herself on crutches while wearing 6-inch-high heels.

Perhaps it might be more useful to think about Johnson's description of "crutches" as an anxious declaration stemming from a nondisabled set of professional and personal presumptions during a moment of transition for architects and architectural critics after World War II.[4] Despite the ubiquitous presence of modernism in hospitals and schools, rejecting modernism would sever or at least diminish its associations with political ideologies such as socialism and communism, knocking the "Crutch of History"— ostensibly the most dangerous crutch of all—out from underneath the arms of its youthful practitioners (see figure 4.1). As Monica Penick has shown, even Elizabeth Gordon, the editor in chief of *House Beautiful*, claimed that the austere, white glass-and-steel cubes of European modernism were nothing short of a communist takeover.[5] For geographer Rob Imrie, this is why many people in the United States and Europe rejected anything that resonated with prewar modernism or at least its most recognizable features:

> While [prewar] modernism was premised, in part, on the idea of liberation, of universal freedom, its claim to transcend politics and power, to overturn the bourgeoisie, was never evident in the developments of postwar urbanism . . . [Instead it pursued] an abstract, intellectual purity of rational, geometric forms, and a mass produced industrial technology. Any sense in which it could relate to differences in body, human behaviour, or access requirements were all but lost in a style that many have referred to as "non contextual" architecture.[6]

Johnson was apparently smitten with the work of British architectural critic Geoffrey Scott, whose 1914 book *The Architecture of Humanism* gave the closeted classicist in Johnson the permission to reach back before modernism's social and political influence in the 1930s while also castigating his peers and warning future students.[7] Several years earlier, in 1949, Johnson's

FIGURE 4.1. Photograph of an enormous room with tall ceilings presenting two different activities. On the left is a woman wearing a hat and glasses and a long shimmering coat, with her back to the camera, who uses crutches while reading an information poster. On the right is a group of four white men in suits who are deep in conversation. In the center is a 22-foot vertical poster of what looks like a giant pencil. This is a press conference for Frank Lloyd Wright's proposed skyscraper, "The Illinois," which if constructed would be a mile in height, or approximately four times the height of the Empire State Building. The spatial separation between the solitary female visitor on crutches and a collective of nondisabled male architects captures something about the incompatibility of conceiving of disability within the ambitions of the immediate postwar era. Photograph taken October 16, 1956. Reprinted with permission of Douglas M. Steiner, Edmonds, WA.

Glass House at his compound in New Canaan, Connecticut, became headline news in design circles; within a decade, his 1958 Seagram's Building became the ultimate touchstone for those who wished to carry forward some of the architectural principles of modernism while leaving others behind in the dust. Co-designed with his Dutch mentor Mies van der Rohe, the Seagram's Building appropriated elements from the Bauhaus of the 1920s and the International Style of the 1930s to make a sybaritic triumph of modern design that was deliberately disconnected from the social or political concerns that had originally brought many of those ideas into being three decades earlier. In the end, many architectural theorists and practitioners challenged the "crutch" of modernist orthodoxy and proposed manifestos and projects of their own that would come to be called a *post*-modern approach to architecture and design: from the playful urban aesthetic of Aldo Rossi's *The Architecture of the City* (1966), to the antimodernist "complexity and contradiction" (to invoke the title of Robert Venturi's 1966 book), to the kitsch and pastiche associated with clever historicism, as embodied in the flamboyantly antimodernist *Learning from Las Vegas* (1972) by Robert Venturi, Denise Scott Brown, and Steve Izenour. People who abandoned modernism's associations with socialism or colonialism or simply unchecked Western arrogance became smitten with the possibilities of the postmodern.

In the previous chapter, we saw how architectural modernism was used a resource for designing for and with disability in the 1930s. This chapter examines the postwar critique and demonization of architectural modernism that emerged concomitantly with the rise of postmodernism. It does so through a close analysis of one work of architecture that, I will argue, sits on the cusp between these architectural typologies: the Illinois Regional Library for the Blind and Physically Handicapped, which opened in Chicago in 1978. It was designed by Stanley Tigerman (1930–2019), a US architect known for his wry wit and playful sense of humor. Any preliminary assessment of work by Tigerman might have expected him to embrace postmodernism's allure of eclecticism and irony wholeheartedly as inspired by distrust of or skepticism about modernism. I will argue, however, that Tigerman was someone who believed in many of the essential aesthetic and social tenets of early twentieth-century modernism that could be applied to public architecture. While Johnson regarded forms associated with modernism as "crutches of history" that were anathema to the future of architecture, Tigerman embraced so-called "crutches of history" as a form of adapting or massaging modernism, even in a period when critiques of prewar modernism were at an all-time high, for the purposes of highlighting disability. The version of modernism Tigerman found most compelling—that which was bequeathed to hospitals and clinics and schools—could be put into the service of public architecture beyond that of hospitals and schools. His design for the Illinois Regional Library for the Blind and Physically Handicapped (hereafter IRLBPH) puts disabled experience at the center, and not the periphery, of architectural experience—a deliberate subversion of the mythos of the heroic architect whose genius towers over the user (see figure 4.2).

FIGURE 4.2. Photograph c. 1976 of an intersection of two streets with an unusually shaped building in the distance. The left side of the building has a thick, rounded pillar supporting the second story, while the right side of the building features a window with undulating waves installed across the horizontal length of the building. This is the exterior of the Illinois Regional Library for the Blind and Physically Handicapped, at the corner of Roosevelt Road and Blue Island Avenue in Chicago, designed by Stanley Tigerman, taken during its construction. From the G. E. Kidder Smith Image Collection © Massachusetts Institute of Technology. Reprinted with permission of MIT Libraries through CC BY-NC 3.0. https://creativecommons.org/licenses/by-nc/3.0/legalcode.en.

Whether one wants to categorize Tigerman as a modernist struggling to define work on his own terms or as a postmodernist eager to join his colleagues' denunciation of modernism may be a matter of interpretation. But in assessing the relationship of Tigerman's IRLBPH to the typologies of 1970s postmodern architecture, I argue that Tigerman's engagement with modernism might be better understood not as something to undo or overthrow but, rather, as something he sought to transform. No matter how much Johnson or his acolytes advocated for either demolishing or revisiting modernism, their embrace of an eclectic dissonance in the name of postmodernism still relied on a fantasy of a nondisabled user, a phenomenon not unlike the politically radical but sensorially reactionary activities of the Situationist International that we examined in chapter 2. As Wanda Katja Liebermann has written, this backstory to architectural movements like postmodernism—its default to a the normative body of a nondisabled user despite its seeming investment in avant-garde designs—is part of a much longer history of the tyranny of the normal that has become so interwoven into the life of architectural education and professional practice that even today it is still the tacit brief for students learning how to design public projects.[8]

Both during his lifetime and following his death in 2019, Tigerman's work was and continues to be acknowledged for its dry humor and semiotic play, a way of both mocking and distilling formalistic elements and mythic ideas not unlike better known architects of the era associated with postmodernism, such as Robert Venturi or Paul Rudolph, the latter one of Tigerman's professors when he was an architecture student at Yale in the late 1950s. But whereas figures like Venturi were galvanized by their repudiation of early twentieth-century modernism—captured famously in his antimodernist declaration "less is a *bore*," his arch appropriation of Mies van der Rohe's well-known dictum, "less is more"—Tigerman saw his architectural projects in the 1970s as an opportunity to revisit modernism's influence while also embracing, and even stirring up, an inevitable backlash against it. He became increasingly interested in exploring architectural features that encouraged or at least facilitated sensual and even erotic spatial encounters.[9] Tigerman, in this sense, prefigured Frederic Jameson's observation that what we call "the postmodern" marks not so much an end to the movement known as "the modern" as a recurring and continuing flow of the concept of periodization itself.[10] It is a form of historicity that strikes over and over again, ad nauseam, exposing periodization as a useful fiction that never truly ends (or perhaps never even begins). As Nathan Brown has observed, "the term 'postmodernism' no longer seems to tell us much about the present."[11] As I will show, through his work on the IRLBPH, Tigerman demonstrated how and in what ways a fair reassessment of the productive possibilities of disability design that treated prewar modernism with openness and curiosity was not only due; it was overdue.

Between Signifier and Signified

Tigerman's innovative work for the IRLBPH has often appeared in surveys of contemporary architecture, both as a unique artifact of late 1970s US architecture and as a unique artifact of Tigerman's oeuvre. Throughout the late 1970s, the library garnered Tigerman numerous industry awards and professional citations. Even before it formally opened in spring 1978, the IRLBPH was lauded in the national and international press as well as in influential period publications like *Progressive Architecture* and *Design*

Quarterly (see figure 4.3).[12] *A+U*, the monthly Japanese architectural journal, devoted an entire section of its July 1976 issue to a retrospective of Tigerman's best known works up to that time, concluding with an overview of proposed plans for the IRLBPH.[13] Tigerman always made a point of describing the IRLBPH as a spatially and sensorially empathic approach to the experience of disability, which enabled him to rescript the terms of architectural modernism.

The original designs for the IRLBPH were carefully considered in order to meet the needs of the library as a building typology: after all, libraries are both more generic and more specific than other types of public spaces. But they are also designed to be more than mere repositories of books—as much of a motivating factor for nineteenth-century philanthropists like Andrew Carnegie, who hired architects to design local branch libraries as temples of civic virtue, as it was for contemporary architects like Rem Koolhaas, who redesigned Seattle's award-winning Central Library (originally a Carnegie structure) as a civic public space. When it was originally conceived in the late 1960s, the IRLBPH was intended to function for three distinct though overlapping populations: (1) a local and regional branch lending library and distribution center for Braille and large-print books and magazines, along with books recorded to cassettes and LPs, on the first floor; (2) a community-oriented social space for those in the vicinity, complete with meeting rooms, conference rooms, and areas for local volunteers to record books to tape; and (3) a small local branch lending library with open stacks and reading areas for adults, teens, and children.

Tigerman's original plan for the IRLBPH deployed an impressive array of spatial and sensorial devices that drew upon the then-fashionable idea of built forms as semiotic systems: from the mimetic function of the original two-car garage, with its Pop Art exterior and gull-wing doors, designed for library staff (demolition date unknown), to the metonymic effect of the 165-foot waveform window that is emulated in the smooth, continuous surface of the massive circulation and reference counter.[14] The deliberately odd mismatch of contextual elements resulted in a kind of delightful disorientation, not at the expense of the user but with the aesthetic possibilities generated from being partially sighted. For Tigerman, the interactions of signifier and signified were not just one-note jokes caught up in the self-satisfied smirk of postmodern cleverness. Rather, they were empathic, albeit performative, methods for rethinking the experience of disability as a neglected resource for expanding humanistic design.

Tigerman came of age professionally in the early 1960s among an ascendant generation of architects who, as Barbara Penner has written, saw a need for "more complex and sensorially rich spaces." Penner argues that

FIGURE 4.3. Photograph of a magazine with the title *Progressive Architecture* at the top. The cover features, on the left, interior structural elements and the long white circulation desk of the Illinois Regional Library for the Blind and Physically Handicapped as lit by sunlight coming from the enormous undulating waveform window, on the right. In the center, a white man with glasses who is using a wheelchair is holding a book in his right hand and interacting with a white woman with long hair and glasses whose head and shoulders can be seen on the far left just above the circulation desk. Photograph by Philip Turner c. 1977; first appeared as the cover image of the April 1978 issue of *Progressive Architecture*. Reprinted with permission of the Tigerman McCurry Archive, Ryerson and Burnham Art and Architecture Archives, Art Institute of Chicago.

these architects' commitments to using design to cultivate new forms of empathy and generate new forms of sensorial complexity provide evidence that challenges the reductive idea that "postmodern architecture's defining characteristics were always ambivalence, surface irony, and formal game-playing."[15] As Paul Goldberger observed in 1978, "Tigerman was searching constantly for materials and form that would satisfy his own visual sense of duty, yet somehow convey the idea of beauty equally well to users who could understand it only through shape and texture."[16]

Tigerman's design may have been sui generis for library architecture in Chicago, but it emerged at a very particular moment in the city's history and, more broadly, the ways that histories of architecture and race in US cities were inextricable in the late 1960s and early 1970s. The IRLBPH was sited on a parcel of public land that abutted many so-called "empty spaces" of Chicago's West Loop, and its relationship to and within the community was decidedly different from those of the fortress-like institutional spaces created by Walter Netsch for the campus of the University of Illinois at Chicago, the Brutalist features of which emerged during the same period when the IRLBPH was being designed and built.[17] Architectural historian Reinhold Martin has characterized built forms like housing projects and public facilities for Black inner-city populations, typical of cities like Chicago, Detroit, Philadelphia, and Los Angeles, as redemptive gestures of municipal white guilt.[18] But Tigerman's library design was not tied to any long-term schemes for urban uplift or, for that matter, urban renewal. Long before the 1960s, the state of Illinois, and the city of Chicago in particular, already had a history of circulating Braille books and newspapers as well as a first generation of "talking books" (vinyl records to be played on special phonographs) after those technologies were first funded and distributed by the US Congress in the early 1930s.[19] During the second half of the 1940s, as Aimi Hamraie has shown, the University of Illinois became the first public university system in the nation (initially at Galesburg, before shifting to its main Urbana-Champaign campus) to fund building projects specifically aimed at disabled veterans, including classrooms, dormitories, and gymnasiums.[20] Disability was thus an acknowledged part of public discourse at the state and city levels, and was addressed through environmental access and community building at least two decades before more well-known projects galvanized urban redesign in US neighborhoods in Berkeley, Denver, and Seattle.

Tigerman's philosophical approach to the IRLBPH is worth quoting at length, not only in terms of the architect's stated goals but also for the ways in which Tigerman deliberately adopted certain tenets of disability as a differential of design. As he wrote in 1978:

Metaphorical allusions are implicit in a program that is loaded with poignancy (blindness) rather than the current modish thinking that superimposes metaphors on unsuspecting programs. Anthropomorphism abounds (circulatory system "printed" on the building's face and the win-

FIGURE 4.4. Photograph of a long, dark rectangular shape with a single undulating wave shape cut into it, with large trees and two people walking in the foreground. This is the western wall of the former Illinois Regional Library for the Blind and Physically Handicapped facing Blue Island Avenue, converted to a bank building in 2012. Tigerman designed the 165-foot-long waveform window at a height that would allow a person using a wheelchair to see from the inside as well as from the outside. Photograph taken July 2019 by Brian Selznick and reprinted with his permission.

dow shape) and inversions and reversals are everywhere and nowhere (the apparent lightweight steel panels are made opaque while the apparently heavy concrete wall is made transparent through the device of the horizontal, undulating cut). Therefore, the building represents not just the specific program, nor just the general state of the art, but significantly, the author's own schizophrenic, inconclusive struggle with both.[21]

One takes Tigerman's use of "schizophrenic" here not as a prescient gesture of designing for neurodiversity but as a self-effacing comment about the desire to meet the needs of people with disabilities while also meeting the spatial, economic, and social demands of the site. Yet the architectural features designed by Tigerman for the IRLBPH were not intended solely to produce (or highlight) forms of spatial disorientation. Rather, they were devices intended to *produce* forms of spatial orientation for their disabled patrons. For instance, the 165-foot wall facing Blue Island Avenue, embedded with a seemingly gravity-defying, undulating waveform window, was built more or less as a nonrepresentational sculpture or painting projected outward to the entire community (see figures 4.3 and 4.4). Once this is spatially understood, users can find and/or memorize the distance to the public entrance to the site. The essential semiotic character of the waveform window is replicated in several of the building's exterior and interior designs—from the pill-shaped lightwells to the undulating reference desk to the public staircase with its curvilinear railing and balustrades to the porthole windows to the exaggerated bracing walls, originally painted canary yellow, that were organized both to support and offset circulation areas and built-in seating arrangements.

Flexibility Is Not for Every Body

In a 2013 interview, Tigerman observed that some of his test subjects for the original library design found movable furniture "very difficult, so we fixed everything instead. And used a linear plan so they could flow down the line of the building, engaging their other senses, their tactile senses, while feeling safe."[22] For patrons who are partially sighted or who are wheelchair users, fixed features can be memorized and navigated far more easily than flexible or mobile ones. But Tigerman's interest in the built-in was not merely one that used the architectonic language of fixed structures to address the experiences of disability; rather, he gravitated to built-ins for their dual promise of ergonomic and experiential predictability. Among contemporary scholars and practitioners of designing for disability, such as Sara Hendren and Graham Pullin, such features have been assigned a new status in facilitating more user-centered experiences and, ultimately, a more meaningful disabled *habitus*.[23] Habitus is the concept popularized by sociologist Pierre Bourdieu to describe those "systems of durable, transposable dispositions" of bodily habits, actions, behaviors, and gestures through which bodies occupy social spaces and through which bodies are identified.[24]

Consider the person for whom fixed kitchen features and toilet and bathing functions necessitate predictable surfaces and interfaces that can be cognitively mapped even if they cannot be seen. Built-ins placed at fixed intervals and appropriate height, such as storage spaces or kitchen counters, are not just matters of convenience but also transformational tools of domestic autonomy, not unlike ramps connected to a front porch or breezeway that make possible circulation between exterior and interior spaces. Built-ins, as Bess Williamson has traced in her design history of access before the Americans with Disabilities Act (ADA), were key to helping polio survivors living in group settings during the late 1950 improve their domestic arrangements and make them more easily navigable.[25] Similar design imperatives advocated by architectural educators such as Elaine Ostroff and

Raymond Lifchez drew inspiration from students and disability rights activists in Berkeley and Oakland during the early 1970s.[26]

For people who are blind or partially sighted, or for people who use wheelchairs, sustaining a particular disabled habitus is not a constraint on liberty and imagination; rather, it is what makes liberty and imagination possible within a finite range of options. In the spaces of the IRLBPH, Tigerman's imaginative use of habitus echoed his delight in aesthetic confrontation; like a waxed eyebrow arched before a laconically phrased observation, it also was earnest acknowledgment that disability could serve as inspiration for deliberately controlled spatial experiments. At the curved apex of the second-floor public reading area, for example, and sited beneath four jaunty porthole windows, Tigerman designed a reading section incorporating carpeted play tunnels that invited children to crawl in and find their own private spot away from the (sighted) eyes of librarians, teachers, and parents (see figure 4.5). A child's experience of having low vision, which for many adults would be presumed to be isolating and terrifying, became in Tigerman's hands a design inspiration that gave them the confidence to read Braille books in privacy while enjoying not a small amount of mischief in the process.

By the mid-1970s, conceptual and practical challenges to modernisms became the order of the day. In 1978, for instance, Michael A. Jones and John H. Catlin, two architects and rehabilitation specialists working for the state of Illinois, used modernism's putative inaccessibility as a way to challenge the nondisabled tenets of high modernist design: "Buildings with symmetrical plans are also confusing, especially when no attempt is made to distinguish different areas within the building . . . Cantilevered structures may also create a sense of fear in people and prevent them from using the building."[27] As a result, many designs that we retrospectively might identify as postmodern emphasized flexibility or portability over what were perceived to be modernism's fixed and static forms. The bodily habitus imagined—or, perhaps more accurately, feared—by many postmodernist architects deliberately demonized modernism, perceiving its structuralist goals of bodily and social regimentation as anathema to the poststructuralist goals of freedom, play, and mobility. This is why so much postmodern design in the 1970s emphasized (however exaggeratedly) materials that advocated portability and modularity, an aesthetic embedded in the period's existential restlessness as well as its jet-set ambitions.

Many architects and designers of the era regarded the potential for material, and thus social, flexibility through the rearrangement of (literal and figurative) plastic elements as the postmodern solution to the "problem" of designing for the future. For example, at the 1972 exhibition at the Mu-

FIGURE 4.5. Photograph of the interior structure of a room dominated by four large white circles across the center. In the foreground is an unusually shaped set of stair-shaped platforms or levels. A white man with a mustache using a wheelchair is on the far right side of the photograph, while a white woman with shoulder-length hair is reading a magazine on the far left side underneath one of the white circles. This is the children's play area on the second floor of the Illinois Regional Library for the Blind and Physically Handicapped. The white circles are four porthole windows that bring light into the space. Tigerman designed the stair-shaped platforms as part of a carpeted, multilevel play structure complete with tunnels in which children with visual impairments could read tactile or Braille books on their own. Photograph by Philip Turner c. 1977; first appeared in the April 1978 issue of *Progressive Architecture*. Reprinted with permission of the Tigerman McCurry Archive, Ryerson and Burnham Art and Architecture Archives, Art Institute of Chicago, digital file no. 201703_240417-001.

seum of Modern Art entitled "Italy, the Domestic Landscape," Gaetano Pesce, one of the curators, described designers presented within his contribution to the show as offering "a commitment to design as a problem-solving activity." As Felicity Scott has described, designs included examples of "molded red plastic architectonic elements that could be multiply rearranged"; "independent, reorganizable, and predominantly plastic components"; and "gray plastic container units on wheels, understood as neutral, pre-prototypes that could be filled in with different aspects of a domestic program and rearranged."[28] Such designs were presented as organisms with the DNA of modernism (inexpensive materials and industrial

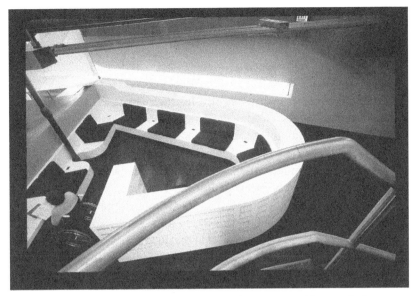

FIGURE 4.6. Photograph of a white triangular structure with curved edges into which dark squares set at intervals have been installed. A person in a wheelchair at the far left side is reading a book. In the foreground are two curving shapes. This is an overhead view, taken from the top of a staircase with stainless-steel hand railings, of the Braille card catalog on the first floor of the Illinois Regional Library for the Blind and Physically Handicapped, c. 1978. The drawers of the card catalog are on the curving exterior walls of the triangular structure, allowing for an intimate interior reading area with built-in seating. Black rubber floor tiles, used throughout the library, facilitate safe movement without navigating steps. Photograph by Philip Turner c. 1977; first appeared in the April 1978 issue of *Progressive Architecture*. Reprinted with permission of the Tigerman McCurry Archive, Ryerson and Burnham Art and Architecture Archives, Art Institute of Chicago, digital file no. 201703_240417-002.

production in the vein of Italian design classics like the Bialetti espresso maker and the Olivetti typewriter) but shown as mutants programmed to be endlessly recombined into subjectively pleasing microworlds of individualized distinction.

These proposed individuations of spaces and objects, for all of their seeming liberatory potential, are just pretty words for a person whose habitus *depends* on an environment in which flexibility is vanquished, at least until the next move, and predictability is grounded and unchanging (see figure 4.6). As David Gissen has argued in his account of his experience navigating the uneven multilevel spaces of Rudolph's original plan for the Yale School of Architecture (1963), the emancipatory discourse of postmodern design is almost always organized around a tacit privileging of being nondisabled.[29]

This is why some of the most iconic buildings of the postmodern era—the disco Brutalism of John Portman's Westin Bonaventure Hotel in downtown Los Angeles (1976), for instance, or Philip Johnson's AT&T Building in Manhattan (1984), a neoclassical fever dream of blue-blood capitalism, as if Jay Gatsby had designed for it for Restoration Hardware—have been acknowledged, albeit controversially, for their smart-ass antihumanism, which has often had the effect of insulating them from conventional expectations of spatial legibility while simultaneously absolving them of the sins of urban disorientation and unequal access.

While such postmodernists were exploring nondisabled presumptions about the potentially liberating qualities of dissonant embodiment, Tigerman deliberately used the practical affordances of architecture to improve spatial orientation for people with disabilities while also critiquing normative approaches to architecture that produce spatial disorientation for people with disabilities. The tropes Tigerman deployed spatially throughout the library hark back to modern forms that involve both a physical *and* metaphysical experience with space that cannot be reduced to mere architectural functionalism. This is an important dimension of the design since the planning and execution of the IRLBPH was directly linked to the passage of the Architectural Barriers Act (1968), which mandated that all post-1968 architectures supported by federal or state funding must be accessible. Another architect working in the same era might have turned to architectural forms with the paternalistically remedial, rehabilitative, or "special" properties often associated with designing for disability or for its intended beneficiaries. In this sense, Tigerman's work stands in stark contrast to that of architects of the 1960s and 1970s like Charles W. Moore and James Wines, for whom the disorientation of habitus was imagined as an exotic rejoinder to modernism. Even Venturi's famed Guild House in Philadelphia (1963), built as a somewhat self-conscious attempt to design for an elderly population, offers a presumptively nondisabled version of habitus masquerading as a site of community care. But whereas the aesthetic codes Tigerman deployed throughout the IRLBPH site are used to anchor the experiences of the user and give agency to their senses, however they are accessed, Venturi's Guild House invokes the aesthetic codes of a dignified classicism, although these ultimately feel like superficial decorations intended to mock, not uplift. The building's features rest on the façade like a pair of Groucho Marx glasses shoved onto the face of a patient in intensive care.

In Venturi and Tigerman, we can see two opposing legacies of modernism, as bequeathed by two of the late twentieth century's most celebrated practitioners of postmodernism. For Venturi, architecture was a medium of semiotic play, but one through which the architect used form to assert smug insider knowledge. For Tigerman, by contrast, architecture was also a medium of semiotic play, but one through which the architect used form to promote social access—and, importantly, access that did not come at the expense of aesthetic pleasure.

For architects like Tigerman, modernism was not just a ghost in the machine, a false consciousness to overcome.[30] As we saw in chapter 3, architectural modernism throughout much of the twentieth century has always meant multiple and contradictory things, and always simultaneously. This suggests something about the coexistence of architectural modernisms in terms of programs or visions intended to rehabilitate the past through the spatial politics of the present. It is no accident that the design phrase "mid-century modern," a consumer-driven category of contemporary design, is meant to telegraph a specific set of images—the modular functionalism of Scandinavian designers like Georg Jensen, or the sleek corporate minimalism of American office designers like Herman Miller or Charles and Ray Eames, or the groovy decadence of European designers like Verner Panton—that are intended to contrast with and erase the grimness associated with the 1930s and early 1940s. The inability to acknowledge these multiple modernisms ultimately prevents us from understanding the ways that form and content, or, perhaps more accurately, aesthetics and politics, continue to be separated out from one another.

In *Behind the Postmodern Façade* (1993), her study of leading US architects during the late 1980s, sociologist Magali Sarfatti Larson observed that for many architects of Tigerman's generation "the political activism of the 1960s merged with the architectural criticism of corporate modernism, going against both its style and its favored building types. The early phase of postmodernism harbored hopes of developing a different type of urbanism and significant public commissions. The hopes floundered in the recession of the 1970s and disappeared in the political reaction of the 1980s."[31] For Tigerman, however, "hopes" of a different world was not a false consciousness to overcome. Rather, postmodernism provided a political and aesthetic platform through which to explore how designing *for* difference rather than *against* it might be one way of keeping modernism's legacies perpetually refreshed.

Banking on Postmodernism

Philip Johnson's metaphor of "crutches" may have suggested the limits of the architectural imagination. But for architects like Tigerman, crutches suggested the metaphor's capacity to capture new ways of thinking about the relationship between disability and architecture. Perhaps one of the most important ways to think about architecture and disability in the mid-twentieth century is to recognize that many of the principles of modernist architecture that neoclassicists like Johnson were railing against were deliberately put into practice by architects like Tigerman who refuted Johnson's claim that mobility impairments represented a weak or dependent form of professional practice. In the late 1940s, for example, Kenneth and Clare Laurent of Rockford, Illinois, contacted Frank Lloyd Wright and asked him to build a house that would be fully accessible for Kenneth, who used a wheelchair. Few people knew about the existence of the Laurent House during its heyday (1951–2012), but as a museum it preserves for visitors an expanded Wrightian vocabulary of built-ins and ready-mades, including lowered cabinets and surfaces, and accessible bathing and toileting features, all of which enabled Kenneth Laurent to move easily from one space to another. In the master bedroom, Wright installed a floating wood desk that one could wheel up to, which was also true of the vanity in another bedroom. Although it is adapted from one of Wright's Usonian houses, it is a magnificent example of modernism that was designed deliberately decades before such features became more widely available, and surely before they would become mandated or expected. Like the IRLBPH, the Laurent House's dual relationship to architecture and disability tells a much more nuanced history of architectural modernism than we might have otherwise.

Tigerman's approach to the experience of disability paid tribute to the formal elements of prewar architectural modernism while also leaving the doors wide open to something beyond that particular iteration of modernism. However "contemporary" the building seemed by the recognizable conventions of 1970s postmodernism, the modernist tropes within which Tigerman was working were part of a longer history of modernism's relationship to disability that we have explored throughout this book. It was a bold move to appear at the height of 1970s postmodernism with a public building, let alone a public building designed for users with physical and sensory impairments that typically would have been treated as remedial.

Sadly, Tigerman's reassessment did not produce the kind of rapprochement with modernism he may have imagined. In 2009, Lakeside Bank, a

Midwestern financial institution, purchased the IRLBPH building from the state after it had lain fallow for nearly a decade and transformed it into the bank's flagship headquarters. At the turn of the twenty-first century, the IRLBPH had been abandoned by local and state authorities, and the building had fallen into noticeable disrepair. The arrival of voice-operated reading software and widespread access to deep databases at the touch of a button, along with the affordability of portable devices like laptops and MP3 players, had supplanted the necessity of a physical site outfitted with thousands of books in Braille, large-print, cassette, and LP formats. Meanwhile, the expansion of residential and commercial interests into Chicago's West Loop, especially the neighborhoods of Little Italy, Pilsen, and the blocks surrounding the University of Illinois at Chicago, had increasingly galvanized speculation in both built and unbuilt sites in and around the library as potential engines of capital redevelopment. The library's original mandate—to serve as a centralized reading and distribution hub, branch library, and community space for library patrons who were blind or partially sighted, or who used a wheelchair—had become all but irrelevant.

The firm of Pappageorge Haymes Partners, a Chicago-based architectural firm, was hired to complete renovation, a provocative choice since one of the firm's two principals, George Pappageorge, was not only a member of the Lakeside Bank's board of trustees but also had been a former student of Tigerman's when the architect taught at the Illinois Institute of Technology, the modernist campus master-planned by Mies van der Rohe less than four miles from the IRLBPH. Lakeside's contemporary conversion of the IRLBPH made the building fully accessible to bank patrons, complying with guidelines for commercial properties under the Americans with Disabilities Act of 1990, a dozen years after the library first opened. Some functional alterations—such as replacing the library's original sheet-metal eastern exposure with a glass curtain wall incorporating a drive-through lane and teller bank window—update Tigerman's design without compromising structural or conceptual integrity. In the end, however, the conversion eliminated or else damaged beyond recognition many of the features that Tigerman created specifically for library users with sensory and mobility impairments. The play structure and tunnels for children, along with the built-in seating arrangements installed throughout the library, disappeared with the swift dissolution of the wrecking ball, extinguishing not only any traces of the building's former clientele but also anything that presumably reminded its new owners of the disabled experiences marked by such design features.[32] Lakeside also removed Tigerman's original choice of black Pirelli rubber floor tiles, embossed with raised bumps, a prescient use of tactile surfaces decades ahead of its time. A minuscule remnant of the original circulation desk that graced the cover of *Progressive Architecture* in 1978 was made into a privacy wall to separate employees from potential clients.

In statements about the renovation process, Pappageorge Haymes Partners vigorously defended its choice to preserve certain stylistic elements of Tigerman's building, asserting that any changes "were carefully measured to sympathize with the building's primary forms and essential character, while meeting the needs of its new commercial occupant."[33] The "essential character" was one that reflected, or confirmed, what the bank believed were the visual aesthetics of "postmodernism" and the building's status as an iconic (and, not insignificantly, a *local*) example of 1970s postmodernism. The bank retained some of Tigerman's original rhetorical gestures, such as the porthole windows punched into the elongated sheet-metal outer structure of the second-floor areas, which continue to create the effect of the bow of an ocean liner, while their elevated position, just above the heads of bank employees, provides bursts of quasi-clerestory lighting within an industrial container. The wall's semiotic relationship to the patrons for whom it was originally designed, however, has vanished. The renovation team removed the mysterious convex "gateway" marker originally installed to mark the eastern edge of the site as a way to give patrons a brightly colored entry point. The team even repainted the former library's interior and exterior spaces with the bank's signature colors of "neutral white with blue accents," thereby stripping Tigerman's choice of "Mondrian like" primary colors—red for perimeter walls, yellow for structural system, blue for ventilation and mechanical—to help visually impaired patrons navigate the site.[34]

By attaching itself to the most recognizable elements of Tigerman's design for the IRLBPH, Pappageorge Haymes Partners' renovation shut down Tigerman's interest in the humanist legacies of modernism and his incorporation of them with an emergent postmodern aesthetic. By failing to restore the IRLBPH's original Crayola-bright exterior and interior primary colors and, instead, choosing to paint in shades of Crate and Barrel white and West Elm blue, Lakeside Bank's flagship branch became just another bland caricature of contemporary design—one that moves backward in time beyond postmodernism to the womblike safety of "midcentury modern" or "Danish modern"—that can be found at any upscale housewares store. The conversion preserved what was most superficially associated with postmodernism, while erasing the building's multiple material and conceptual commitments to disability.

In 2023, Lakeside Bank announced the sale of its flagship property to St. Ignatius College Preparatory School, a private Catholic school that stands across the street from the bank building on Roosevelt Road. During the summer, St. Ignatius revealed its intention to use the building not for expanding its education programs, but for its sports programs, since its current floorplan offered space for athletes' conditioning and weight training. The building will serve this purpose until such time as the school decides either to alter the interior or demolish the building.[35] The idea that Stanley Tigerman's original library design, which drew its aesthetic and political inspiration from the disabled subjectivities of users to serve the needs of education and community building, would be converted to serve the needs of nondisabled athletes is an ignominious fate too sad to contemplate.

1968

Toleration has come in a form that is slightly insulting. One imagined the message, when it came, would read: *Forgive us for having for so long allowed our prejudices to blind us to your true worth. Cross our unworthy threshold with your broadminded feet.* Instead, the message now reads: *Oh, come in. The place is a mess. You'll love it.*

—Quentin Crisp, 1968[1]

It was the late Queen Elizabeth II, and not an ancient Roman poet, who popularized the phrase *annus horribilis*, "a horrible year." Elizabeth, then beginning her fourth decade as reigning sovereign, used the phrase to describe 1992, a year in which members of Britain's royal family were caught in scandals both personal and political. But one would be hard pressed to find a year during the twentieth century in which the phrase *annus horribilis* was more apt than 1968. Only six months after the famed 1967 Summer of Love, there began a year of events that were horrible, and in such concentrated form: from the surprise Tet Offensive attacks against US soldiers in Vietnam (January) to the assassinations of Martin Luther King Jr. (April) and Robert F. Kennedy (June), to the eruption of organized campus protests against university complicity with weapons development (April), to organized protests against government in Prague and Paris and London and Tokyo (May), to disruptions and violence at the Democratic National Convention in Chicago (August), to the murders of student activists in Mexico City just days before the start of the Summer Olympics (October), to the election of Richard Nixon (November). Many ordinary people across the globe reacted to the *annus horribilis* by transforming urban spaces created by the hierarchies of modernity and capital—on city streets and university campuses, in favelas and ghettos both historic and of recent vintage—into zones of resistance and confrontation.

By the late 1960s, the media landscape included satellite transmissions of news programs and color television broadcasts, along with an emergent independent cinema and liberalized television, radio, and recording industries, jostling against the power of networks and conglomerates trying their best either to quell the counterculture or else to appropriate it in order to sell it to a younger and hipper demographic.[2] In May 1968, among the images coming out of the revolutionary protests in Paris and Prague, one could see news footage from Rome of a man with one leg amputated hoisting himself atop the roof of a police car before climbing the walls (while holding on to a single crutch) of the Palazzo Chigi, the historic residence of Italy's prime minister, to call attention to the Italian government's poor record of support for people with disabilities, including veterans (see figure E.1). Also in 1968, the Japanese filmmaker and disability rights activist Kazuo Hara began work on his groundbreaking film *Goodbye CP*, released in 1972, by documenting himself thrusting his body into different public settings around Tokyo and recording the reactions of otherwise polite Japanese people who would shun and ignore him. In Stockholm, the Danish designer Susanne Koefoed attended a conference on radical design and proposed a stylized symbol of a wheelchair, of a size that could be observed from a distance, which could be applied to signs, buildings, airports, parking lots, and other public spaces. The following year, in 1969, Koefoed's original design was altered by adding the humanizing element of a circular head before becoming adopted as the now recognizable International Symbol of Access.[3]

In spring 1968, I was barely six months old, the youngest of five children, living in the suburbs of Los Angeles, and unaware of the extent of the *annus horriblis* that engulfed everyone and everything around me. I was one of many inflection points for the world to which I belonged: a second-generation offspring of Polish and Russian Jewish immigrants who had arrived in Brooklyn five decades earlier after the outbreak of World War I in Europe. Many of them must have witnessed the events of 1968 as they did the walls of the shtetl being attacked by Cossacks: the world that they thought they knew, falling down all around them, exploding into shards of broken glass, unrecognizable and incomprehensible.

[That same spring, in May 1968, painter, decorated war hero, and amateur architect Jean-Julien Lemordant, with whom this book began, died from complications related to a canister of gas thrown by a protester outside Lemordant's remarkable house at 50, Avenue René Coty, in the 14th arrondissement, an unfortunate echo of the mustard gas that had blinded him during the Great War.]

Many people of my mother's generation, middle-class and nondisabled boys and girls raised in the crucible of the New Deal era and the victory culture of World War II, saw divisions and violence all around them as daily visitations even if they did not personally experience them. It was the water in which many members of the Greatest Generation swam but never drowned. Many regarded structural inequalities as something that a normative major-

FIGURE E.1. Photograph of a well-dressed, bearded white man who is kneeling on the roof of a taxi and swinging two crutches above the heads of people in a crowd, many of whom are gesturing for him to get down. This is an image of a disability protest action, c. May 1968, on the Via del Corso, Rome's symbolic thoroughfare, by people demanding improved disability benefits from the Italian government. In another image from the same action that circulated in the news, the same man, an amputee, uses his crutches as climbing instruments to scale the outside wall of the Palazzo Chigi, then residence of Italy's prime minister. Reprinted with permission of Bettmann / Getty Images.

ity tolerated, however reluctantly, and addressed, if they addressed it at all, through paternalistic sympathy. But during the 1950s and 1960s, the federal government under both Republican and Democrat presidencies began to reassess the privileges and claims of a normative majority and to confront the status of civil rights as a matter of both constitutional interpretation and a sense of moral obligation. Recall that the Supreme Court's 1954 decision to strike down the century-old tradition of "separate but equal"—a tradition deemed not only constitutionally illegal but morally untenable—had come only fourteen years earlier. And while it would be naive to think that one Supreme Court decision transformed a national consciousness overnight—it most certainly did not—it effectively captured for many, especially many young people, a sense of optimism that relied on the moral injunction of fair play and equal opportunity for all.

In the early 1950s, my mother worked at a law office on the forty-ninth floor of the Empire State Building during the day and studied Chaucer and

Keats at Brooklyn College at night. On weekends, she ran around Greenwich Village in a beret, black turtleneck, and Evan-Picone skirt, sipping cappuccinos with her girlfriends and watching films like *Les Vacances de Monsieur Hulot* (1953) directed by and starring Jacques Tati. She eventually settled down and married my father in 1956; before that, she briefly dated a young man who attended Columbia University, a commuter from his home in the Bronx to the school's neoclassical, McKim Mead & White–designed campus on the Upper West Side of Manhattan, who studied poetry to please himself but studied engineering to appease his family. Such a young man would have hardly recognized the campus a decade later when, in April 1968, about two weeks after the assassination of Rev. Martin Luther King Jr., Columbia students took control of several campus buildings, including Hamilton Hall, Avery Hall (which houses the School of Architecture), and the offices of university president Grayson Kirk in Low Memorial Library.

The heart of the Columbia protest concerned the design of a new gymnasium, which university administrators and trustees believed would make Columbia more competitive with its Ivy League peers.[4] In the mid-1950s, the university sought out land on which to build a new athletics facility, and the space it identified, and subsequently desired, was a parcel of public land on the edge of campus that abutted Morningside Park, one of the few green spaces in Harlem and one enjoyed by local residents who were primarily Black and Hispanic (see figure E.2). Following a series of unpublicized backroom deals brokered between Kirk and then parks commissioner Robert Moses, Columbia seized approximately three acres of Morningside Park for its private use, an action that was immediately condemned by neighborhood groups across Harlem that challenged appropriations of urban public space. Columbia offered local residents access to the gym when it was not in use by Columbia's athletic teams. But to facilitate this use, Columbia proposed carving out a separate backdoor entrance on the gym's lower level rather than allowing people from the neighborhood to use the structure's elegant front entrance on the higher elevation of Morningside Drive. When, in April 1968, the university announced that it would move forward with its plans and break ground on land in Morningside Park, Columbia students and local community activists joined forces to occupy university buildings in defiance of what they immediately identified as "Gym Crow."

That the controversy was ignited by a gym—and not, say, a library or an auditorium or an art gallery, institutions for which disenfranchised groups might demand equal access—has much to do with the investment in spaces like gyms to protect and enhance normative bodies, especially those that will go on to compete against other normative bodies in athletic events as well as in life after graduation. Gymnasiums, especially those of elite

FIGURE E.2. Photograph of an illustrated map c. 1966 showing (left to right) the Columbia University campus (left), Morningside Park (middle), and the majority Black and Hispanic neighborhood surrounding and east of the park (right). The large white square indicates the proposed entrance on the upper level of the new gym, intended only for Columbia students, at the corner of 111th Street and Morningside Drive. The large white circle and three white arrows indicate the proposed entrance, intended for community members, accessible only from the gym's park entrance on the lower level. Those opposed to Columbia's plans characterized its blatant spatial segregation through the poignant phrase "Gym Crow." From the 1966 brochure "The Columbia Gymnasium Fund." Reprinted with permission of the University Archives, Rare Book & Manuscript Library, Columbia University Libraries.

institutions, are layered with other, less savory histories oriented around norms of "fitness" that betray that word's relationship to the eugenics movement. Even today, no gym is merely a space of exercise or athletic training; it is always a space that produces and protects hierarchies of value, the co-valent bonding of nondisabled fitness to that of social and sexual fitness.

[On July 20, 1968, Soldier's Field in Chicago played host to the 1968

Special Olympics World Summer Games, the first athletic competition of its kind for young people with intellectual disabilities from the United States and Canada. Sponsored and organized by the Joseph P. Kennedy, Jr. Foundation and championed by Eunice Kennedy Shriver, the arrival of the Special Olympics signaled a sea change in terms of its recognition of the athletic capacities of a population of young people not associated in the public imagination with competitive sports.]

The 1968 protests by Columbia students against the building of the new gymnasium has been characterized by some scholars as a convergence point of almost every strand of youth activism of the period.[5] People who identified with a counterculture (in terms of alternatives to crass 1950s commercialism) or with a counter-consensus (in terms of opposition to the Vietnam War) were eager to challenge normative conventions, guided by a moral imperative to address and overturn the systemic inequalities that purportedly were at the core of public school and civic education. Theirs was an imperative to action based in affirming legal and moral equality. Apparently, two decades of Henry Luce–inspired propaganda about American exceptionalism and the democratic way of life had actually seeped into the consciousness of the postwar generation, much to the chagrin of their parents and teachers. Indeed, the Columbia story unfolds like the plot of a proletarian drama performed by the WPA's Federal Theater Project: an elite white institution encloses public land used by poor brown and Black people to provide more room and better resources for superior bodies to compete with other superior bodies at other elite white institutions—and, when asked to be accountable, creates a separate entrance so that the two populations might not ever have to occupy space at the same time, let alone shower together. That is why the phrase "Gym Crow" became so resonant, and so accurate: it sutures together both the problematic occupation of public space as well as the problematic solution to the occupation of that space. In doing so, it makes transparent all of Columbia's misguided motivations, like a poorly wrapped bandage exposing scars that had never really been given enough time to heal.

[In spring 2024, as the world observed students at US universities like Columbia struggle over the unfolding fate of the Palestinian people in Gaza, it was often remarked that the events of April 2024 resembled those of April 1968. The inspiration for students' activism in both eras has been treated as interchangeable, with certain obvious parallels, such as ending war and defunding institutional support for military research, as part of a common narrative of history repeating itself. In retrospect, the inspiration common to both eras for Columbia students was not just about war but about land use: who controls it, who has access to it, and what the impact of spatial segregation will be on the future generations of people living next door to one another. It is this unending struggle over space that most deeply connects the events of spring 1968 at Columbia to events there fifty-six years later.]

∴

One of the few teaching faculty who openly joined with the students and community members in protest of Columbia's proposed gym was a young graduate student instructor named Raymond Lifchez, a middle-class Jewish boy from Charleston, South Carolina. At the height of the campus riots in April 1968, campus security guards and local riot police dragged Lifchez from the doorway of Hamilton Hall, beating him bloody until he surrendered.[6] The experience of surviving the violence and the tensions that ensued was such that, when Lifchez was offered a postdoctoral fellowship at the University of California, Berkeley, he seized the opportunity and left New York City for the Bay Area. There Lifchez witnessed a thriving community of students with disabilities, like the Rolling Quads (in playful homage to their favorite British rock band), who had channeled their frustration with medicalization into a vibrant disability culture. Luckily, Lifchez was hired as an assistant professor at UC Berkeley and was able to focus his teaching and research energies on creating a lab that studied how local people with disabilities (in collaboration with roommates and friends and lovers) had become designers and architects in their own apartments and group houses, inventing new devices and jerry-rigging existing ones to enable them to cook, bathe, sleep, work, and relax, or else breaking through narrow doorways or carports or jack-hammering public sidewalks in order to make inhospitable spaces livable and visitable.

The devices or habits cultivated by the people whom Lifchez studied or observed or interviewed came from their own needs, and their perception of what would enable them to accomplish the tasks that they needed to do, either at home or in the workplace. As architectural historian Ignacio Galán has described in great detail, Lifchez and his research team observed a world of sustained ingenuity, motivated by necessity and survival rather than by design for design's sake.[7] In working with members of the disability community in Berkeley, Lifchez helped establish what would become known, in 1972, as the Center for Independent Living, originally housed in a battered former car dealership on Telegraph Avenue in downtown Berkeley just a few blocks from the university campus—and significantly, at the intersection of Telegraph and Blake, the site of the first curb cut made by local disability rights activists.[8] In books like *Design for Independent Living* (1979, coauthored with Barbara Winslow) and *Rethinking Architecture* (1986), Lifchez used these examples as the basis for challenging the potential of architecture to be either built from scratch or else infinitely adjustable to accommodate people whose bodily needs are rarely if ever accounted for in design practice, especially as it is taught at architecture schools and other schools of design. In later years, Lifchez endowed a design competition called the Berkeley Prize for undergraduates who are working on projects organized around using architecture and design for social justice. Lifchez spent the rest of his career, until his death in 2023 at the age of ninety, teaching students how to be better attuned to what people with disabilities and members of other populations, such as survivors of natural disasters and government inaction, need materially to fulfill their social and political potential.

In 2016, I interviewed Lifchez and asked him how he came up with the idea of asking people with disabilities how they worked with or around architecture to get through the day. His answer was that it simply "made sense" to him.[9] He wasn't thinking about methodology or history. It seemed like the most obvious thing in the world to want to know how people who live in environments not made for them change those environments—sometimes subtly, sometimes radically; sometimes with a piece of string, sometimes with a sledgehammer—in order to embody fully the spaces they occupy. What Lifchez helped to do was to disaggregate the difference between architectural and spatial interventions made by nondisabled architects who were professionally tasked with providing access and accommodation, and architectural and spatial interventions made by disabled nonarchitects: people who found improvisation and living creatively the means to survive in a world not built for them, precisely the kinds of experiences characterized by many of the stories found throughout this book.

∵

One of the brighter, if often neglected, moments during the *annus horriblis* of 1968 took place not in the lecture halls of elite universities or the august chambers of Supreme Court justices but as a document brought to the desk of President Lyndon Johnson for his signature. On August 6, Congress passed the Architectural Barriers Act (ABA), a legal mandate that required all institutions that received federal funding to remove barriers to access and to ensure architecture to be fully accessible to all citizens. The spaces mandated by the ABA included federal office buildings, courthouses, federal prisons, and post offices, as well as national parks and nongovernment facilities that received federal funding, such as public universities and schools, public housing, and mass transit systems. In addition, the ABA initiated and maintained standards of access, with detailed specifications for ramps, parking, doors, elevators, restrooms, assistive listening systems, fire alarms, and signs.

The ABA is not generally included in the list of civil rights triumphs typically associated with the Kennedy-Johnson era. This may be the result of the way that the ABA is overshadowed by all the other events of the *annus horribilis*. Both the ABA and its immediate forerunner, the Fair Employment and Housing Act, were passed in the weeks following national tragedy: the assassinations of Rev. Martin Luther King Jr. in April, and Robert Kennedy in June. But it may also be the result of the way that some might regard the ABA as addressing only a minority set of interests—a narrow vision of what the ABA not only materially effectuated but what it symbolized in the moment. The ABA grew directly out of the civil rights era's insistence that access to physical spaces was essential to recalibrating forms of inclusive citizenship. It proposed that architects treat accessibility as more than an afterthought. Wheelchair ramps, wide doorways and broad interior vestibules, chirping elevators or crosswalks, Braille labels, teletypewriter (TTY) devices in constructed commercial spaces like airports and shopping malls, and support bars for toilets, bathtubs, and showers could be reimagined not only as technologies of access but also as technologies of autonomy that made it possible for both people with disabilities and people with a spectrum of body types and individual needs to move through space. Indeed, one could argue that the ABA built upon the desegregation of classrooms, train stations, public toilets, and water fountains to take the civil rights focus on public access to its next logical step.

[In March 1968, Stevie Wonder was completing his high school diploma at the Michigan School for the Blind in Lansing; his worldwide 1969 hit "My Cherie Amour" was based on a melody he had written at the school while a student there.[10] Pedagogy for students at the school embraced making music and art, learning Braille, and listening to the library's huge selection of Talking Books, the last of which inspired the title of one of Wonder's sonic masterpieces. But tactile models, the type produced by WPA workers for Michigan's Museum Extension Project discussed in chapter 3, were rarely, if ever, still used in classrooms in the late 1960s, often regarded as outmoded technology and out of step with contemporary needs. Katherine Ott, senior curator at the National Museum of American History in Washington, DC, rescued many of the surviving models for the Smithsonian's collections after the Michigan School closed its doors in 1995.]

Any person who either lived through or who studies the late 1960s and early 1970s cannot help but notice a crushing irony to all of this optimism. The moral imperative to design, a lingering legacy of modernism, was profoundly shaped by those who regarded architecture not only as a medium for resolving soc moral imperatives, such as the utopian qualities of inclusion and access one might want to attribute to the ABA, took place in a period that saw the expansion of large-scale urban renewal programs (often called "Negro removal" by critics) alongside the misadventures of jingoistic nationalism in Vietnam, Cambodia, and Laos. Throughout the decade, great public debates took shape among architects and their critics, and routinely questioned the profession's moral compass and profit motive while sacrificing the role of urban planning as a public good. Jane Jacobs's *The Death and Life of Great American Cities* (1961) was required reading for critics of the urban renewal impulse gone awry, alongside Paul and Percival Goodman's *Communitas* (1947), and Michael Harrington's *The Other America* and Rachel Carson's *Silent Spring* (both 1962). By the end of the 1960s, radical experiments with an anti-urban focus, often on communes, retreats, and farms, were flourishing across the United States at precisely the same time when many young architects and designers were exploring radical experiments in urban form: from practitioner-theorists like Victor Papanek and Paolo Soleri to art collectives in France like the Situationist International (which we saw in chapter 2) and in the United Kingdom, such as Archigram and Ant Farm. Meanwhile, the vilification of modernism and the rise of postmodernism (which we saw in chapter 4) was played out in corporate and commercial designs offered by architects like Philip Johnson, Robert Venturi, Aldo Rossi, Peter Eisenman, Frank Gehry, and Moshe Safdie. By the time an architect like Stanley Tigerman was completing his design for the Illinois Regional Library for the Blind and Physically Handicapped in the mid-1970s, the divisions between those who believed in the power of architecture as a way to build a moral universe and those who believed that "architecture" was a concept to deconstruct could not have been more stark.

To speak of architecture in relation to a "moral universe" of 1968 is to acknowledge that the phrase itself is associated with one of the most quoted civil rights speeches of the era. In his commencement address at Wesleyan University in 1964, Reverend Martin Luther King Jr. spoke both to the occasion of the moment and to the larger civil rights struggle he had helped to galvanize nearly a decade earlier when he said, "the arc of the moral universe is long, but it bends toward justice." These words did not originate with King; they came from the pen of Reverend Theodore Parker, a Unitarian minister and staunch supporter of the abolitionist movement, who declared in 1852: "I do not pretend to understand the moral universe, the arc is a long one, my eye reaches but little ways. I cannot calculate the curve and complete the figure by the experience of sight; I can divine it by conscience. But from what I see I am sure it bends towards justice."[11]

King's use of the phrase "moral universe" brought the concept to an exponentially larger audience, which helped to turn it into a famous soundbite. But as all soundbites tend to do, the phrase simplifies the sentiment of Parker's original, which brings together an understanding of a moral universe driven as much by questions of social injustice as by questions of sensory comprehension. Parker argues that the moral universe cannot be seen. Guided by intuition and faith, morality is nonrational. It cannot be arrived at by ordinary means or through typical channels of cognition reserved for law. And, importantly, it is *spatial* though not dependent on sight. And while it cannot be seen, it can be felt. The moral universe is one that may be arrived at collectively but is necessarily experienced subjectively. Like prayer, it does not depend upon the tacit knowledge of the empirically knowable universe. But unlike prayer, its long-term effects can be adjudicated in a court of law. The original context of Reverend Parker's words remind us that the universe may have infinite dimension, but for humans the moral universe is bounded by the particularities of the spaces we provide for people other than ourselves.

∵

On the first day of June 1968, Helen Keller died at her home in Easton, Connecticut, at the age of eighty-seven. The author, political activist, and disability rights advocate was found in the bedroom of Arcan Ridge, the house that had been designed for her exactly thirty years earlier. Keller was interred in the Chapel of St. Joseph of Arimathea in the crypt of the Washington National Cathedral in Washington, DC, in a ceremony on June 5, the same day that Robert F. Kennedy was shot at the Ambassador Hotel in Los Angeles. Keller's cremated remains were placed in the same columbarium where her beloved teacher, Anne Sullivan Macy, had been interred in 1936—the tomb that Anne and Helen will share for eternity (see figure E.3).

In late March 2023, my husband Brian and I boarded a train in New York City bound for Washington, DC. We had decided to visit the Washington National Cathedral for two reasons: for one, neither of us had ever seen Keller and Sullivan Macy's tomb before; for another, we wanted to pay our respects to Matthew Shepard. Shepard was the young gay college student who had been tortured and murdered by a pair of homophobic killers in Laramie, Wyoming, in 1998. Two decades later, in 2018, Shepard's family arranged with the cathedral's administration for their son's final resting place to be in the Chapel of St. Joseph of Arimathea, less than a hundred feet from Keller and Sullivan Macy. Brian and I were living in Washington, DC, in 1998 when news of Shepard's murder struck grief and anger around the

FIGURE E.3. Photograph of the plaque, with information in both embossed
text and Braille, affixed to the columbarium containing the remains of Helen
Keller and Anne Sullivan Macy in the Chapel of St. Joseph of Arimathea, located
in the crypt (the structural heart) of the Washington National Cathedral,
Washington, DC. The area surrounding and including the Braille text is bright
due to the number of visitors who have used their fingers to read or touch or rub
the plaque. The cathedral maintains an archive of all of the plaques touched by
previous generations of visitors to the crypt. Photograph c. 1990s. Reprinted with
permission of imageBROKER.com. GmbH & Co. KG / Alamy Stock Photo.

world. We left our apartment on East Capitol Street and joined a march pro-
testing violence against lesbians and gay men, already in progress, that was
heading northwest on Pennsylvania Avenue, and would end at the doors
of the Lambda Rising bookstore on Connecticut Avenue in Dupont Circle
(lamentably closed since 2010). Now, a quarter of a century later, we were
returning to the District on a beautiful cloudless and cold spring afternoon.

That Helen Keller and Matthew Shepard are honored in the Washington National Cathedral *because* of who they are, and not *despite* who they
are is not an insignificant detail in recounting the stories of their respective lives. Not so long ago, people like Keller and Shepard would have been
written out of the national narrative—literally and figuratively erased—and
excluded from a hallowed space like a cathedral, let alone one named for
the nation. For much of the twentieth century, people with significant physical or sensory or cognitive disabilities, people who were gender or sexual nonconforming, and anyone deemed to present moral and economic
challenges to the perceived "health" of the state were the chosen targets

of eugenicists, social reformers, surgical specialists in sterilization and lobotomies, hormonal specialists in chemical castration, and religious hysterics who believed that they could miraculously cure the deformed and the deviant through the power of science or prayer (or both). Within the Chapel of St. Joseph of Arimathea, Keller's and Shepard's tombs line up on either side of giant arches that support the entire cathedral complex. Matching plaques (printed in both embossed text and Braille) are attached to the fronts of Keller's and Shepard's respective columbaria, which can be read or touched. Shepard's parents deliberately chose the crypt of the Washington National Cathedral for Matthew's burial site because of the values of an open and accessible world that Keller helped to launch across the span of her lifetime, values that both she and Shephard continue to embody in the early decades of our own century. But for those visitors who are mobility impaired, the Chapel of St. Joseph of Arimathea remains inaccessible. One can take an elevator down to the doors leading to the chapel—and must then descend a dramatic set of wide steps once inside (see figure E.4).

While the profound importance and symbolism of their columbaria in the heart of the nation's cathedral does not depend upon ever physically visiting the site itself, what does it mean that almost six decades after the passage of the ABA—and nearly three and half decades after the passage of the ADA—we maintain architecture in the nation's capital that for some people remains difficult to navigate, touch, and experience? Of course, one must make a necessary distinction between older buildings like the Washington National Cathedral, for which retrofitting options would be difficult if not impossible to implement without damaging the building's structure, and new buildings that require compliance with accessibility laws. At the same time, one cannot *touch* Keller and Sullivan Macy's and Shepard's tombs without physical access if one wants to be sensorially present in the chapel. A sighted person in a wheelchair can observe the space of the Chapel of St. Joseph of Arimathea from outside its doors, and a hearing person in a wheelchair can access the sound of the chapel through an audio recording. But short of being carried down the steps, no person who wants to engage the chapel through the modalities of touch or smell or vibration as constituent parts of their subjective experience of the world can do so without full physical access. To convene a haptic conversation with the physical space; to read the wall plaques in the language of Braille; to smell the chapel's mix of stone, paint, incense, dust, metal, and fabric; to confer with the dead through the medium of touch—access, in this context, is a means to a very specific end.

No person's status as a citizen will ever depend on visiting where Helen Keller and Matthew Shepard are interred; the fight for disability rights or

FIGURE E.4. Photograph of a bald white man with glasses wearing a dark sweater standing beneath a giant chandelier at the intersection of three enormous arches. On the far left and far right sides of the photograph are stairs with landings and hand rails. This is the author standing in the Chapel of St. Joseph of Arimathea, located in the crypt (the structural heart) of the Washington National Cathedral in Washington, DC. The spot where the author stands is the midway point between the shared tomb of Helen Keller and Anne Sullivan Macy (the dark rectangle on the left; see figure E.3) and the tomb of Matthew Shepard (the dark rectangle on the right) Photograph taken March 30, 2023, by Brian Selznick and reprinted with his permission.

LGBTQ+ rights did not begin, nor will it end, with having access to their tombs. But making evident the dichotomy between the symbolic presence of Keller, Sullivan Macy, and Shepard in the Washington National Cathedral and the material absence of access to their tombs parallels what I have tried to make evident throughout this book. Many of the physical and sensorial encounters with architecture and space explored in these chapters have nothing to do with meeting legal or social mandates for inclusion, nothing to do with complying with local, state, or federal codes. But in showcasing the many possible ways in which architectural and spatial encounters have taken shape in the historical past, I hope this book has provided more than a few examples for thinking about how sensory encounters with architecture and space can be used to build the kind of world—and the kind of moral universe—that we want to inhabit. After all, what we have inherited from

Jean-Julien Lemordant and Joseph Merrick and Helen Keller and Sargent Johnson and Stanley Tigerman and Matthew Shepard are strategies for surviving modernity; strategies that imagine a world that not only strives for openness and equality and access but also honors subjective bodily differences and multimodal pleasures. To paraphrase the title of one of Keller's early publications, this is the world that we live in—a world not just for *those* people, but for all of us.

Acknowledgments

This book began about fifteen years ago, as a conversation with the late Doug Mitchell, my beloved friend and former editor at the University of Chicago Press. Doug and I were having dinner, and I showed him a photograph I'd discovered of Helen Keller window shopping in Paris. We spent the rest of the evening sharing stories about our lives as queer men living with assorted physical impairments who carefully navigated our way through urban spaces. We talked about all of the people who identified as queer and/or disabled that we knew, all the ones who came before us, who had developed strategies of survival for living in a world not made for us—indeed, a world made to keep us in our place. Even then, Doug intuited what this book could be. That was his particular genius.

Before his untimely death, in 2019, Doug made sure to introduce me to his colleague at the press Kyle Wagner, who has been the very definition of a heroic editor. Kyle not only helped me bring this project to fruition but encouraged me to expand or contract as needed at every step along the way with clarity, compassion, and good humor. Thank you, Kyle, for everything you've done to bring the spark of that original conversation with Doug to a satisfying and meaningful conclusion. Enormous thanks as well to Daniel Goldberg, Nathan Petrie, Kristin Rawlings, Stephen Twilley, Lys Weiss, and Glenn Westrom for all of their fantastic work throughout the book's production and design process. And to my dear friend Catherine Opie for taking my author photo: thank you for seeing me.

In addition to Doug, Rosemarie Garland-Thomson, *mia bella amica*, has also played a pivotal role in the development of this book. Over a thirty-year friendship, Rosemarie has always challenged me to think about what disability makes possible, not what it forecloses. Her insights took on a profound significance for me after I sustained a traumatic head injury, in 2010. I have learned new strategies for researching, writing, and editing that are not tied to the solitary neurotypical practices expected of academic professionals. The chapters in this book were composed and edited over many

years through a variety of modalities, including voice-activated compos-
ing software and the efforts of indefatigable human transcribers and no-
tetakers, particularly the efforts of my husband, Brian Selznick. Disability
is what has made this book possible, and it is through my disability that I
share this book with you, no matter the format or mode through which you
encounter these words.

Many institutions supported this work during the *longue durée* of its
creation. Fellowships or research grants from the American Philosophical Society, the Getty Foundation, the Graham Foundation for Advanced
Studies in the Fine Arts, and the National Science Foundation provided
much-needed financial support while enabling much-needed intellectual
and creative freedom. An early draft of chapter 1 took shape while I was
a Fellow in Architectural Criticism at the MacDowell Colony, where for
seven weeks I wrote about Joseph Merrick while tending to a fire in a cabin
in the New Hampshire woods; it was a gift of unbounded time I will never
forget. A significant portion of the introduction was written at the American Academy in Rome after I was awarded the Rome Prize in Architecture.
Brian and I lived in Rome during the first eight months of 2021, at the very
height of the global pandemic. Our time there, challenging as it was, gave
me an opportunity to think about how humans have survived for millennia
in urban environments that have rarely been hospitable to them. I remain
eternally grateful to the Academy for our time in the Eternal City.

I am indebted to the many librarians, archivists, visual and material
culture experts, researchers, and colleagues whose knowledge helped me
track down and locate objects in every conceivable medium.

For the book's introduction, thanks to Michael Miller at the American
Philosophical Society Library for access to vital documentation of the Kansas Free Fair. *Merci beaucoup* to Bernard Chevojon for generously permit-
ting me to reprint a Studio Chevojon photograph of chez Lemordant. And
grazie mille to Susanna Soglia for her superb work translating the words of a
1930s French journalist into a recognizable contemporary voice.

For chapter 1, thanks to Kate Jarman of the Barts Health NHS Trust Archives for permission to reprint photographs of Joseph Merrick, and also
a belated thanks to Jonathan Evans, formerly of the Royal London Hospital Archives, when it was still located in the crypt of St. Philip's Church,
for providing me access to Merrick's model of the Mainz Cathedral. For
archival images of Leicester, including aerial images of the London Union
Workhouse, I thank Graham Deacon at the Historic England Archive and
Adam Goodwin of the Record Office of Leicestershire, Leicester, and Rutland. For archival images of London, I thank the helpful staff members at
the Wellcome Collection and the Bishopsgate Institute. Finally, thanks to

Sherri Middleton and Morgan Potts at Bonhams auction house for providing images from the auction of Merrick's armchair.

For chapter 2, I was fortunate to rekindle a grad school connection with *another* amazing Helen, the ever-ebullient Helen Selsdon, formerly the archivist for the American Foundation for the Blind. Helen S. is the person who launched the AFB's Helen Keller Digitization Project, a treasure trove of materials accessible to users all over the world. For help with access to the astonishing collection of tactile maps and objects at the Perkins School for the Blind, thanks to Susanna Coit at the Perkins School Archives. For help with materials related to Nancy Hamilton's 1954 documentary, *The Unconquered: Helen Keller in Her Story*, I thank Kate Long at the Sophia Smith Library at Smith College, the repository of Hamilton's papers, and Hailey Linville at the American Foundation for the Blind. Finally, *les plus chaleureux remerciements* to Silvia Radelli for allowing me to reproduce her extraordinary *Métroféminin* project. A very early version of chapter 2 was published as "Disabling the *Flâneur*," in the *Journal of Visual Culture* 5, no. 2 (August 2006): 193–208.

Chapter 3 began years ago, when the amazing Cathy Kudlick, now professor emerita at San Francisco State University, told me about *Des clés pour bâtir*, a book that uses Braille and embossed printing to teach readers with visual impairments about French architecture. Around the same time, Katherine Ott, senior curator at the National Museum of American History and life-changing superhero to many (including me), introduced me to a group of tactile models made in the late 1930s for students at the Michigan School for the Blind that she had recently absorbed into the collections of the Smithsonian. At that moment, the possibility of engaging methodologically with tactile objects, and with tactility itself, set me on a journey of discovery. Thank you to CK and KO for putting these objects into my hands.

For providing access to many other archival treasures used in chapter 3, thanks to Tom Baione and Mai Reitmeyer of the Gottesman Research Library at the American Museum of Natural History; Josué Hurtado at the Special Collections Research Center, Temple University Libraries; Kellen Cutsforth and Heidi Young of the Denver Public Library; Cynthia Tovar and Jean Patterson of the Huntington Library and Museum; Emily Smith of the Library Company of Philadelphia; Ashely Rodriguez and Jenni Salamon of the Ohio History Connection; and Lillian Perricone, formerly with the Dianne and Michael Bienes Special Collection and Rare Book Library in Fort Lauderdale, who connected me with a thriving subculture of collectors. Special thanks to Barbara Berstein and Harvey Smith of the Living New Deal project (https://livingnewdeal.org/) for providing access to Harvey's excellent photographs of the proscenium Sargent Johnson made in 1937 for the auditorium of the California School for the Blind. A short, exploratory version of chapter 3 was published as "Learning at Your Fingertips," in *Cabinet* 39 (Fall 2010): 70–73, while another version of chapter 3 (with many more images than I could include in this book) was adapted for the *Places Journal* (placesjournal.org), in May 2024. I dedicate chapter 3 to the memory and example of Eve Kosofsky Sedgwick, whose gentle and loving encouragement to think about the sensuality and queerness of objects still resonates with me and everyone who knew her and loved her.

For chapter 4, I am deeply grateful to Margaret McCurry for conversations about materials related to the design of the Illinois Regional Library for the Blind and Physically Handicapped and to David Hofer for locating and reproducing those materials from the Tigerman McCurry Archive in the Ryerson and Burnham Art and Architecture Archives at the Art Institute of Chicago. I also thank Katie Zimmerman of MIT Libraries for help with Tigerman photographs from the G. E. Kidder Smith Collection; Jill Vuchetich of the Walker Arts Center, Minneapolis, and George Smart of USModernist / Modernist Archive (https://usmodernist.org/) for help with vintage US architecture magazines; and Douglas Steiner, whose online archive (http://www.steinerag.com/flw/index.htm) is an extraordinary resource for anyone doing research on Frank Lloyd Wright. An early version of chapter 4 was published as "Banking on Postmodernism: Saving Stanley Tigerman's Illinois Regional Library for the Blind and Physically Handicapped," in *Future Anterior* 16, no. 1 (Summer 2019): 86–108; thank you to David Gissen and Jorge Otero-Pailos for helping to shape that early version. I dedicate chapter 4 to Stanley Tigerman, architect and force of nature, who generously granted me an interview and shared much with me about the library project during the research process.

Finally, for the epilogue, I thank Jocelyn Wilk of the Columbia University Archives for archival images of the proposed gym at Columbia, and Patrick Smith of the Washington National Cathedral for his insights about the Keller and Shepard columbaria. I dedicate the epilogue to Raymond Lifchez (1932–2023), one of the gentlest and kindest souls I have ever met; someone whose humility, empathy, and generosity will continue to shape scholars, activists, and practitioners for many generations to come.

During the process of working on this book, I was honored to receive invitations to present portions of the book as work in progress. Early versions of what became the introduction were presented for the Arcus Endowment Lecture series at the College of Environmental Design at UC Berkeley; the Altman Endowed Lecture series at Miami University; Kellogg College at the University of Oxford; the Princeton-Mellon Research Forum on Architecture, Urbanism, and the Humanities at Princeton University; the Carpenter

Center for the Visual Arts at Harvard University; the Department of American Studies at the University of Kansas; the Department of English at the University at Buffalo; and the Center for Disability Studies at New York University. Early versions of chapter 1 were presented for the Mellon Sawyer Seminar on Homosexualities from Antiquity to the Present at UCLA and for the School of Architecture and the Built Environment at the University of Westminster. Early iterations of what became chapter 2 were presented for the Department of Architecture at Pennsylvania State University, the PhD Program in the History of Art at Bryn Mawr College, and the Architectural History MA Program at the Bartlett School of Architecture at University College London. Lisa Cartwright and Elspeth Brown, extraordinary colleagues and friends, invited me to share my work in progress about Helen Keller's 1952 trip to Paris at the "Feeling Photography" workshop they co-organized at UC San Diego. For great comments on early versions of chapter 3, I thank audiences at the Program in History of Science at Princeton University, the Department of the History and Philosophy of Science at the University of Cambridge, the Center for the Study of Social Difference at Columbia University, the Science in Society Program at Wesleyan University, the Department of Disability Studies at the University of Toledo, the Disability Research Centre at Goldsmiths, University of London, and the Braille Institute of San Diego. Finally, for their responses to early versions of the epilogue, I thank audiences at the Third Biennial Disability Symposium at the University of Virginia, the Yale School of Architecture, and the Sciame Lecture Series at the Spitzer School of Architecture at the City University of New York.

All work is relational and context specific, and I know that this book would not exist, *could* not exist, if I were not a member of the Department of Communication at UC San Diego. Twenty years ago, I arrived as a cultural historian, confident that I knew everything I needed to know to complete my next big project. Little did I realize that I would be joining a community of scholars, thinkers, and media producers that would challenge everything I knew, simultaneously expanding my horizons while also disorienting my senses in the most productive ways imaginable. Two decades later, I remain proud to call this island of misfit toys my institutional home. For their continued support and inspiration, I thank so many colleagues, past as well as current: Patty Ahn, Morana Alač, Patrick Anderson, Boatema Boateng, Angela Booker, Lisa Cartwright, Matilde Córdoba Azcárate, Zeinabu Davis, Andrew DeWaard, Fernando Domínguez Rubio, Alex Fattal, Gary Fields, Kelly Gates, Stuart Geiger, Brian Goldfarb, Dan Hallin, Anthony Harb, Erin Hill, Robert Horwitz, Tom Humphries, Lilly Irani, Caroline Jack, Shawna Kidman, Dan Martinico, Chandra Mukerji, Carol Padden, Thomas

Schmidt, Christo Sims, Stefan Tanaka, Lillian Walkover, and Elana Zilberg. I also thank the Academic Senate at UC San Diego for its unwavering commitment to this book project through multiple research grants and a publication grant to assist with the acquisition of images. These funds helped me engage the ingenuity and resourcefulness of many fabulous research assistants over the years, including Kate Clark, Thomas Conner, Rachel Fox, Jacob Hellman, Poyao Huang, Julia Kott, Marion "Googie" Puuvadi-Daniels, and Lore Silva.

Many fellow crips, queers, and confederates gave me encouragement (and the occasional gentle nudge) to finish this book, and I could not have done so without their support. Thanks to Rachel Adams, Jos Boys, Elspeth Brown, Susan Burch, Amy Chazkel, Paloma Checa-Gismero, Cathy Davidson, Cathy Gere, Aimi Hamraie, Louise Hickman, Adria Imada, Rob Imrie, Lochlann Jain, Georgina Kleege, Wanda Katja Liebermann, Laura Mauldin, Mara Mills, Natalia Molina, Kevin P. Murphy, Kim Nielsen, Katherine Ott, Andrew Parker, Graham Pullin, Ben Reiss, Rachely Rotem, Jason Ruiz, Joel Sanders, Sue Schweik, Hal Sedgwick, Nayan Shah, Marquard Smith, Shawn Michelle Smith, Jonathan Sterne, Jennifer Tucker, Bess Williamson, Mabel Wilson, and Ken Wissoker.

During the long process of completing this book, I also received copious love and care from friends near and far, including Syd Atlas, Katy Barkan, Aaron Belkin, Lisa Cartwright, Deborah De Furia, Robyn Dutra, Marie Edesses, Brian Goldfarb, Jessica Griffin, Sara Harrison, Dan Hurlin, Nina Katchadourian, Rebecca Levitan, David Levithan, Tanya Melich, Cathy Opie, Pam Muñoz Ryan, Sina Najafi, Frances Richard, Noel Silverman, and Cathy St. Germans. I also thank Mary Walters, who has been for fifteen years the safest of ports in the heaviest of storms. I am profoundly grateful and humbled to have people in my life like Sasha Archibald, Michael Davidson, Fernando Domínguez Rubio, David Gissen, Rob Goldberg, Elizabeth Guffey, Sara Hendren, Joe Masco, Barbara Penner, and Danny Smith, who read multiple iterations of these chapters with patience, intelligence, and insight, and helped me understand what this book was about.

To my extended family all over the world, which includes not only varieties of Serlins but also Selznicks and Spectors and Levine/Inouyes: thank you for your love and encouragement and for always asking good questions. Roslyn Selznick is simply the best mother-in-law anyone could ever ask for, and I thank her for her unending kindness and generosity.

For nearly fifteen years, my mother, Renee Levine Serlin, would ask me one simple question every time we spoke on the phone: "How's Helen?" My mother was interested in the whole book, of course, but she expressed a special kinship with Keller; my mother worked in midtown Manhattan in the early 1950s, and I often imagine her and Helen brushing past each other while window shopping along Fifth Avenue. My mother never stopped encouraging me to finish this book. So, in answer to your question, Mom: Helen is doing well. Thank you for asking.

When I first began thinking about this project, my then boyfriend, Brian Selznick, and I had just celebrated our twelfth anniversary together. We have now been together for twenty-seven years and, of those, married for ten. There isn't a thing in this book that hasn't been part of a conversation, an experience, a place, or an object that we've introduced to or shared with each other. When it was too difficult for me to work, Brian not only took care of me but acted as my amanuensis, translating my dictated thoughts into the words you are reading or listening to right now. Thank you for loving me so much, Brian, and for everything you do to honor and protect this little world. After nearly three decades, you continue to amaze me. It's to you, and to the memory of Doug Mitchell, that I dedicate this book.

Notes

INTRODUCTION

1. Antony Goissaud, "A Town House for a Painter-Artist," *La Construction moderne* (October 4, 1931), 18–28; translation by Susanne Soglia.

2. For an incisive discussion see Jan Kenneth Birksted, "'Beyond the Clichés of the Hand-Book': Le Corbusier's Architectural Promenade," *Journal of Architecture* 11, no. 1 (2006): 55–132.

3. *La Cité & tekhne* 10, no. 6 (June 1932): 37.

4. See, for example, Roxanne Panchasi, *Future Tense: The Culture of Anticipation between the Wars* (Ithaca, NY: Cornell University Press, 2009); and Rebecca Scales, *Radio and the Politics of Sound in Interwar France, 1921–1939* (New York: Cambridge University Press, 2016).

5. Sarah F. Rose, *No Right to Be Idle: The Invention of Disability, 1840s–1930s* (Chapel Hill: University of North Carolina Press, 2017), 225–26. See also Louis Bertrand, Vincent Caradec, and Jean-Sébastién Eideliman, "Situating Disability: The Recognition of 'Disabled Workers' in France," *Alter* 8, no. 4 (October–December 2014), 269–81.

6. See Jos Boys, ed., *Disability, Space, Architecture: A Reader* (Routledge, 2017); David Gissen, *The Architecture of Disability: Buildings, Cities, and Landscapes beyond Access* (Minneapolis: University of Minnesota Press, 2023); Elizabeth Guffey, *Designing Disability: Symbols, Space, and Society* (New York: Routledge, 2015); Aimi Hamraie, *Building Access: Universal Design and the Politics of Disability* (Minneapolis: University of Minnesota Press, 2017); Wanda Katja Liebermann, "Humanizing Modernism? Jaap Bakema's Het Dorp, a Village for Disabled Citizens," *Journal of the Society of Architectural Historians* 75, no. 2 (June 2016), 158–81; and Bess Williamson, *Accessible America* (New York: NYU Press, 2017).

7. See Elizabeth Ellcessor, *Restricted Access: Media, Disability, and the Politics of Participation* (New York: NYU Press, 2016); Gerard Goggin and Christopher Newell, *Digital Disability: The Social Construction of Disability in New Media* (Lanham, MD: Rowman & Littlefield, 2002); Mara Mills and Jonathan Sterne, "Aural Speed-Reading: Some Historical Bookmarks," *Proceedings of the Modern Language Association* 135, no. 2 (2020): 401–11; and Jaipreet Virdi, "Materializing User Identities through Disability Technologies," in *Making Disability Modern: Design Histories*, ed. Bess Williamson and Elizabeth Guffey (London: Bloomsbury, 2020), 225–41.

8. Throughout this book, I will use the word "nondisabled" to refer to people who are often identified with the word "able-bodied." Sue Schweik has succinctly captured the distinction between "able-bodied" and "nondisabled" in *The Ugly Laws: Disability in Public* (New York: NYU Press, 2009) and the reason why there is a case for privileging the latter term over the former: as she writes, "there is no such thing as an entirely, unalterably able body and since 'nondisabled,' refreshingly, places the 'disabled' subject at the center, it relegates others to the zone of the prefix" (11).

9. See, for example, Beatriz Colomina, *X-Ray Architecture* (Zürich: Lars Müller, 2019), 62–65, 69–73, 74–80, 98–100. Some have made the argument that the Villa Savoye's ramp is an example of "disability-friendly" architecture, which I personally find unconvincing; see Beth Tauke and Korydon Smith, "Crossing the Threshold: Disability and Modernist Housing," in *Disabling Domesticity*, ed. Michael Rembis (New York: Palgrave Macmillan, 2018), 49–66.

10. R. O. Hughes, *Civic Training*, 8th ed. (New York: Allyn & Bacon, 1936), 205.

11. Margaret Campbell, "What Tuberculosis Did for Modernism: The Influence of a Curative Environment on Modernist Design and Architecture," *Medical History* 49, no. 4 (October 2005): 478.

12. The Architectural Barriers Act of 1968 was first piece of federal legislation in the world that prioritized access in the design process. See "Architectural Barriers Act (ABA)," enacted August 1968; published on the website of the US Department of Labor: https://www.dol.gov/agencies/oasam/centers-offices/civil-rights-center/dlms2-0600#603.

13. Kahn's original quotation is: "Even a brick wants to be something. A brick wants to be something. It aspires. Even a common, ordinary brick . . . wants to be something more than it is. It wants to be something better than it is." Cited in Wendy Lesser, *You Say to Brick: The Life of Louis Kahn* (New York: Farrar, Straus & Giroux, 2017), 11.

14. Tschapeller, quoted in Audrey Wachs, "At Cornell's New Fine Arts Library, the Book Sets the Standard," *Metropolis* (November 1, 2019).

15. See Kathryn Stamm, "Design over People? New Fine Arts Library Critiqued for See-Through, Grated Floors," *Cornell Daily Sun* (November 17, 2019).

16. See Aimi Hamraie, "Universal Design Research as a New Materialist Practice," *Disability Studies Quarterly* 32, no. 4 (2012).

17. See Wanda Katja Liebermann, "Teaching Embodiment: Disability, Subjectivity, and Architectural Education," *Journal of Architecture* 24, no. 6 (2019): 803–28; and Liebermann, *Architecture's Problem with Disability* (New York: Routledge, 2024).

18. Rob Imrie, quoted in interview with Eva Egermann, "Buildings That Fit Society," in *Transcultural Modernisms*, ed. Model House Research Group (Berlin: Sternberg Press, 2013), 216.

19. Jos Boys, *Doing Disability Differently: An Alternative Handbook on Architecture, Dis/Ability and Designing for Everyday Life* (London: Routledge, 2014), 25.

20. Catherine Ingraham, *Architecture, Animal, Human: The Asymmetrical Condition* (New York: Routledge, 2006), 5, emphasis mine.

21. David Gissen, *The Architecture of Disability: Buildings, Cities, and Landscapes beyond Access* (Minneapolis: University of Minnesota Press, 2022), 89.

22. Marcel Proust, "Combray," in Proust, *Swann's Way*, trans. C. K. Scott Moncrieff (New York: Modern Library, 1956 [1928]), 105–6. Thanks to Brian for leading me back to Proust.

23. Simi Linton, *Claiming Disability: Knowledge and Identity* (New York: NYU Press, 1998), 140.

24. Schweik, *The Ugly Laws.*

25. Williamson, *Accessible America.*

26. Donna Haraway, "Situated Knowledges: The Science Question in Feminism and the Privilege of Partial Perspectives," *Feminist Studies* 14, no. 3 (Autumn 1988): 575–99.

27. Kimberley Dovey, *Framing Places: Mediating Power in Built Form*, 2nd ed. (London: Routledge, 2008 [1998]); and Karen A. Franck and Bianca Lepori, *Architecture from the Inside Out: From the Body, the Senses, the Site and the Community*, 2nd ed. (Chichester: Wiley-Academy, 2007).

28. See David Serlin, "Disabling the *Flâneur*," *Journal of Visual Culture* 5, no. 2 (2006): 193–208.

29. See Kevin Hetherington's discussion of the subject and object in sensory modalities like touch in "Spatial Textures: Place, Touch, and Praesentia," *Environment and Planning A* 35 (2003): 1933–44.

30. François Laplantine, *The Life of the Senses: Introduction to a Modal Anthropology*, trans. James Furniss (London: Bloomsbury, 2015), 83, emphasis in original.

31. H-Dirksen L. Bauman and Joseph J. Murray, eds., *Deaf Gain: Raising the Stakes for Human Diversity* (Minneapolis: University of Minnesota Press, 2014); and Rosemarie Garland-Thomson, "The Case for Conserving Disability," *Journal of Bioethical Inquiry* 9 (2012): 339–55.

32. Michel de Certeau, "The Black Sun of Language: Michel Foucault (1973)," in *Heterologies: Discourse on the Other*, trans. Brian Massumi (Minneapolis: University of Minnesota Press, 1986), 177.

33. Elizabeth Mock, *Built in USA 1932–1944* (New York: Simon & Schuster, 1944).

34. Elizabeth Guffey and Bess Williamson, eds., *Making Disability Modern* (London: Bloomsbury, 2021). See also Sven-Olov Wallenstein, *Biopolitics and the Emergence of Modern Architecture* (New York: Buell Center / FORuM Project and Princeton Architectural Press, 2008), especially 36–39, 42.

35. Anne Anlin Cheng, *Second Skin: Josephine Baker and the Modern Surface* (New York: Oxford University Press, 2013), 19; and Adrienne Brown, *The Black Skyscraper: Architecture and the Perception of Race* (Baltimore: Johns Hopkins University Press, 2019), 16–17, 30–33.

36. Christina Cogdell, *Eugenic Design: Streamlining America in the 1930s* (Philadelphia: University of Pennsylvania Press, 2004).

37. Joy Monice Malnar and Frank Vodvarka, *Sensory Design* (Minneapolis: University of Minnesota Press, 2004), 39.

38. Kenny Cuppers, *Use Matters: An Alternative History of Architecture* (London: Routledge, 2013).

39. Hamraie, quoted in Mara Mills and Rebecca Sanchez, introduction to *Crip Authorship: Disability as Method* (New York: NYU Press, 2023), 9, my emphasis.

40. Adria Imada, *An Archive of Skin, an Archive of Kin: Disability and Life-Making during Medical Incarceration* (Berkeley: University of California Press, 2022), 31.

41. For an excellent examination of these questions, see for example Ilsa Barbash, Molly Rogers, and Deborah Willis, eds., *To Make Their Own Way in the World: The Enduring Legacy of the Zealy Daguerreotypes* (New York: Aperture/Peabody Museum Press, 2020).

42. Imada, *An Archive of Skin, an Archive of Kin*, 31, emphasis mine.

CHAPTER ONE

1. Chronology of the museum's receipt of the Mainz Cathedral model provided by Jonathan Evans, Trust Archivist for the Royal London Hospital Museum and Archives (communication with author, February 21, 2005) and Madge Kendal, letter, March 14, 1917, in Barts Health NHS Trust.

2. Many scholars in Victorian literary and cultural studies have situated Merrick's story within late nineteenth-century reforms to ameliorate urban poverty. Historian Seth Koven, for example, has argued that, as someone rescued from "the streets," Merrick became associated with the homeless and destitute street urchins of London's East End. This capacious category of impoverishment inserted Merrick within the available social scripts of the day that offered reform to young nondisabled men and boys who worked in dangerous, marginal, and often disreputable occupations, as well as those who relied on petty larceny as means of survival. See Koven, *Slumming: Sexual and Social Politics in Victorian London* (Princeton, NJ: Princeton University Press, 2006), 62–63.

3. According to Evans, the model was insured for £10,000 (communication with author, July 3, 2007), or about £21,000 in 2024 currency.

4. Michael Howell and Peter Ford, *The True History of the Elephant Man* (London: Allison & Busby, 1980); Peter W. Graham and Fritz H. Oehlschlaeger, *Articulating the Elephant Man: Joseph Merrick and His Critics* (Baltimore: Johns Hopkins University Press, 1992).

5. See Bernard Pomerance, *The Elephant Man: A Play* (New York: Grove Press, 1979); *The Elephant Man*, dir. David Lynch (Paramount, 1980). For a useful comparative reading of these two fictional depictions of Merrick's life, see William Holladay and Stephen Watt, "Viewing the Elephant Man," *PMLA* 104, no. 5 (October 1989): 868–81.

6. Ian Hodder, *Entangled: An Archaeology of the Relationships between Humans and Things* (Malden, MA: Wiley-Blackwell, 2012), 89.

7. See Katherine Ott, "Disability Things," in *Disability Histories*, edited by Susan Burch and Michael Rembis (Urbana: University of Illinois Press, 2014), 119–35.

8. William A. Cohen, *Embodied: Victorian Literature and the Senses* (Minneapolis: University of Minnesota Press, 2009), 136.

9. Aimi Hamraie and Kelly Fritsch, "Crip Technoscience Manifesto," *Catalyst: Feminism, Theory, Technoscience* 5, no. 1 (2019): 1–34.

10. There is a robust cottage industry of works of research about Merrick by academic and independent scholars and writers alike. The latter group includes Jeanette Sitton and Mae Siu-Wai Stroshane, *Measured by Soul: The Life of Joseph Carey Merrick*

(Also Known as 'The Elephant Man') (self-published, Lulu.com, 2012); and Joanne Vigor-Mungovin, *Joseph: The Life, Times and Places of The Elephant Man* (London: Mango Books, 2016).

11. BBC documentary *Two Town Mad* (first broadcast February 28, 1964), available on YouTube.

12. *St George's Cultural Quarter Action Plan, 2016–2020* (Mayor's Office, City of Leicester, 2016), 7. https://www.leicester.gov.uk/media/183943/st-georges-cultural -quarter-action-plan.pdf.

13. See *Indices of Deprivation 2019: Briefing on Implications for Leicester* (Division of Public Health, Leicester City Council, 2019). https://www.leicester.gov.uk/media /x33jvoab/indices-of-deprivation-in-leicester-briefing-on-implications-2019.pdf.

14. Howell and Ford, *The True History of the Elephant Man*, 48.

15. Mark Mitcheley, *William Flint: Leicester's Classical Architect* (Market Harborough, UK: Fuzzy Flamingo, 2019), 83.

16. See Kate Thompson, "The Building of the Leicester Union Workhouse 1836– 1839," in *The Adaptation of Change: Essays upon the History of Nineteenth-Century Leicester and Leicestershire*, ed. Daniel Williams, (Leicester: Leicestershire Museums, 1980).

17. "1881 Census Listing" for Leicester Union Workhouse. https://www.storyof leicester.info/a-working-town/leicester-union-workhouse/.

18. From the *Report from His Majesty's Commissioners for inquiring into the Administration and Practical Operation of the Poor Laws* (London, 1834), 306.

19. For a further elaboration of this distinction, see Nadia Durbach, "Monstrosity, Masculinity and Medicine: Re-Examining 'the Elephant Man,'" *Cultural and Social History* 4, no. 2 (2007): 202–5.

20. Felix Driver, *Power and Pauperism: The Workhouse System, 1834–1884* (New York: Cambridge University Press, 1993), 13–14; see also James Schmeichen, "The Victorians, the Historians, and the Idea of Modernism," *American Historical Review* 93, no. 2 (April 1988): 287–316.

21. See, for example, Barry Edginton, "Moral Architecture: The Influence of the York Retreat on Asylum Design," *Health & Place* 3, no. 2 (1997): 91–99.

22. H. Austin, *Report on Plans of the Proposed Lodging House at Huddersfield* (May 17, 1853), 95, in General Board of Health Correspondence, Ministry of Health Papers, Public Records Office, UK.

23. See Frederick Treves, "A Case of Congenital Deformity," *Transactions of the Pathological Society of London* 36 (March 1885): 494–98. See also Andrew Smith, "Pathologising the Gothic: The Elephant Man, the Neurotic and the Doctor," *Gothic Studies* 2, no. 3 (2000): 292–304, especially 294–96.

24. Photographs, not published during Merrick's lifetime, taken at the Pathological Society of London ca. 1884, which became the basis for the drawings published in Treves, "A Case of Congenital Deformity," now part of the Royal London Hospital Archive collection, Barts Health NHS Trust, provided to the author in digitized form courtesy of Jonathan Evans. Readers can find my own beliefs about the ethics of reprinting these photographs in the introduction, 27–28.

25. See Ilisa Barbash, Molly Rogers, and Deborah Willis, eds., *To Make Their Own Way in the World: The Enduring Legacy of the Zealy Daguerreotypes*, illustrated edition (Cambridge, MA: Aperture, 2020).

26. Kevin Hetherington, "Spatial Textures: Place, Touch, and Praesentia," *Environment and Planning A* 35 (2003): 1935.

27. Merrick's sentiments conveyed in F. C. Carr Gomm, "The Elephant Man," *The Times* (London), December 4, 1886.

28. For more about the economic history of rehabilitation projects developed for the blind, see Edwin C. Vaughan, *Social and Cultural Perspectives on Blindness* (Springfield, IL: Charles C. Thomas, 1998).

29. See Carole Rawcliffe, *Leprosy in Medieval England* (Rochester, NY: Boydell Press, 2006).

30. See Christine Stevenson, *Medicine and Magnificence: British Hospital and Asylum Architecture, 1660–1815* (New Haven, CT: Yale University Press, 2000), 62, 144–46.

31. Stevenson, *Medicine and Magnificence*, 144–46.

32. See Dana Arnold, "The Country House: Form, Function and Meaning" (1998), reprinted in *Architecture and Design in Europe and America, 1750 to 2000*, ed. Abigail Harrison-Moore and Dorothy C. Rowe (Malden, MA: Blackwell, 2006), 59–72. See also Robert Adam and James Adam, "Plans and Elevations for the Villa of Lord Mansfield at Kenwood (1822)," and John Summerson, "Palladian Permeation: The Villa (1953)," both in *Architecture and Design in Europe and America, 1750–2000*, 50–54 and 74–75, respectively.

33. See Michael Baxandall, *Painting and Experience in Fifteenth-Century Italy* (New York: Oxford University Press, 1988).

34. Arnold, "The Country House: Form, Function and Meaning," 68.

35. Arnold, "The Country House: Form, Function and Meaning," 71.

36. Mainwaring's original plan can be viewed in prints published in the early 1750s to entice investors and subscribers.

37. Irene Cheng, Mabel Wilson, and Charles Davis, *Race and Modern Architecture: A Critical History from the Enlightenment to the Present* (Pittsburgh: University of Pittsburgh Press, 2020). See also Charles Davis, *Building Character: The Racial Politics of Modern Architectural Style* (Pittsburgh: University of Pittsburgh, 2019).

38. Merrick (emphasis mine) wrote this as part of an addendum for *The Elephant Man* (London: John Bale & Sons, 1888), a published pamphlet that was an expanded version of "The 'Elephant Man,'" an article that originally appeared in the *British Medical Journal* 2 (December 11, 1886): 1188–89.

39. "The 'Elephant Man,'" 1188.

40. Martha Stoddard Holmes, *Fictions of Affliction: Physical Disability in Victorian Culture* (Ann Arbor: University of Michigan Press, 2004), 14.

41. Maria Frawley, *Invalidism and Identity in Nineteenth-Century Britain* (Chicago: University of Chicago Press, 2004), 207.

42. Howell and Ford, *The True History of the Elephant Man*, 119.

43. See, for example, John Potvin, *Bachelors of a Different Sort: Queer Aesthetics, Material Culture and the Modern Interior in Britain* (Manchester: Manchester University Press, 2015).

44. See William Rutherford Hayes Trowbridge, *Queen Alexandra: A Study in Royalty* (London: T. Fisher Unwin Ltd., 1921), 200–201.

45. John E. Crowley, *The Invention of Comfort: Sensibilities and Design in Early Modern Britain and Early America* (Baltimore: Johns Hopkins University Press, 2001), 142–43.

46. George R. Sims, *How the Poor Live* (London, 1883), 14, emphasis mine.

47. Howell and Ford, *The True History of the Elephant Man*, 89.

48. Michael Davitt (1885) quoted in Philip Priestley, *Victorian Prison Lives: English Prison Biography, 1830–1914* (London: Pimlico, 1985), 44–45.

49. "Improved Dwellings for the Poor," *Jewish Chronicle* (London), March 13, 1885, 6. For more about the creation of Jewish ventures for improved housing in the East End, see Lloyd P. Gartner, *The Jewish Immigrant in England, 1870–1914* (Detroit: Wayne State University Press, 1960).

50. *Jewish Chronicle* (London), December 10, 1886, 8.

51. For more about the development of Victorian plumbing and toilet technology, see Judith Flanders, *Inside the Victorian Home: A Portrait of Domestic Life in Victorian England* (New York: W. W. Norton, 2004), 326–32.

52. William J. Fishman, *East End 1888* (1893; reprint, Nottingham, UK: Five Leaves Publishing, 2005), 56.

53. Communication from Queen Victoria to the Marquis of Salisbury, dated November 10, 1888, in *The Letters of Queen Victoria*, 3rd ser., vol. 1, 1886–90 (London, 1930). According to Fishman in *East End 1888*, "The Whitechapel Board of Works were debating the extension of gas lamps into the dimly-lit alleys and culs-de-sac of Spitalfields on [August 5, 1888,] the eve of the Ripper's first attack!" (259).

54. Report by the Sanitary Committee of the Mile End District quoted in "Night Shelters for Outcasts—A Bad State of Affairs," *East London Advertiser*, October 27, 1888, 2.

55. *Bayswater Chronicle* (London), June 10, 1899, quoted in Rappaport, *Shopping for Pleasure*, 84–85.

56. Kevin Hetherington, "Spatial Textures: Place, Touch, and Praesentia," *Environment and Planning A* 35 (2003): 1933–44.

57. Sara Ahmed, *Queer Phenomenology: Orientations, Objects, Others* (Durham, NC: Duke University Press, 2006), 86, emphasis mine.

58. Michael Howell and Peter Ford, the predominant biographers of Merrick, make only a few cursory references to his relation to toy models, including the Mainz Cathedral model; see *The True History of the Elephant Man*, especially 95, 112, 169.

59. Jon McKenzie, "Telepathy, the Elephant Man, Monstration," *Journal of Popular Culture* 28, no. 4 (Spring 1995): 20.

60. Fernando Domínguez Rubio, *Still Life: Ecologies of the Modern Imagination at the Art Museum* (Chicago: University of Chicago Press, 2020).

61. See Vigor-Mungovin's appeal at https://www.gofundme.com. For further information see also "Elephant Man: Leicester Council Backs Statue Plan," *BBC News*, May 11, 2019. Vigor-Mungovin established a reputation as a leading advocate for Merrick as an author but also after she announced in early 2019 that she had discovered records confirming that Merrick's nonskeletal remains were buried in the City of London Cemetery and Crematorium in a "common grave" for the dead without any identifying markers. After a campaign for its recognition, the physical site of Merrick's burial now features a simple blue and gold marker that reads, "In Memoriam Joseph Merrick 1862–1890." See "Elephant Man: Joseph Merrick's Grave 'Found' by Author," *BBC News*, May 5, 2019.

62. Danyal Hussein, "Plans for a £100,000 Statue of Elephant Man Joseph Merrick Sparks Row in His Hometown of Leicester as Locals Call Him a 'Freak of Nature' Who Doesn't Deserve a Memorial," *Daily Mail*, January 20, 2021.

63. For an analysis of Quin's sculpture, see my essay, "On Walkers and Wheelchairs: Disabling the Narratives of Urban Modernity," *Radical History Review* 114 (2012): 19–28.

64. Fiona Candlin, *Art, Museums and Touch* (Manchester: Manchester University Press, 2010).

65. Greig Watson, "Leicester: Elephant Man Statue Plan Shelved as Appeal Falls Short," *BBC News*, July 27, 2023.

CHAPTER TWO

1. Abby McIntyre, "If Women Ruled the World, Paris Metro Map Edition," *Slate* (March 19, 2014).

2. See "The Dinner Party (1974–79)," https://judychicago.com/gallery/the-dinner -party/dp-artwork/.

3. Rebecca Solnit and Joshua Jelly-Schapiro, *Nonstop Metropolis: A New York Atlas* (Berkeley: University of California Press, 2016).

4. See, for instance, Sara Ahmed, *Queer Phenomenology: Orientations, Objects, Others* (Durham, NC: Duke University Press, 2006).

5. See, for example, Patrick Devlieger, Frank Renders, Hubert Froyen, and Kristel Wildiers, eds., *Blindness and the Multi-Sensorial City* (Antwerp: Garant, 2006); and Victoria Henshaw, *Urban Smellscapes: Understanding and Designing City Smell Environments* (New York: Routledge, 2014).

6. See David Gissen, *The Architecture of Disability: Buildings, Cities, and Landscapes beyond Access* (Minneapolis: University of Minnesota Press, 2023), 45.

7. Helen Keller, *Midstream: My Later Life* (Garden City, NY: Doubleday Doran & Co., 1929), 198–99.

8. See Kim Nielsen, *The Radical Lives of Helen Keller* (New York: NYU Press, 2004); and Georgina Kleege, *Blind Rage: Letters to Helen Keller* (Washington, DC: Gallaudet University Press, 2005).

9. Keller, *The Story of My Life* (Garden City, NY: Doubleday, Liveright & Co., 1904), 108.

10. Kim Nielsen, "Helen Keller and the Politics of Civic Fitness," in *The New Disability History*, ed. Paul Longmore and Laurie Umansky (New York: NYU Press,

2002), 268–90. The lingering effects of "fitness," fearful of both disability and political radicalism, may explain why retellings of Keller's life story continue to represent her as a child at the water pump; as disability scholar Andrew Marcum has argued, as recently as 2004 the state of Alabama chose Keller to represent its history in the US Capitol's rotunda, but presented her as the little girl at the water pump rather than as the adult woman. See Marcum, "Material Embodiments, Queer Visualities: Presenting Disability in American Public History," PhD diss., University of New Mexico, 2014, chap. 1.

11. See Nielsen, *The Radical Lives of Helen Keller*; see also Kleege, *Blind Rage*.

12. Marie Dominique Garnier, "En Route: Helen Keller's Travels," *Studies in Travel Writing* 24, no. 3 (2020): 226.

13. Peter Stallybrass and Allon White, *The Politics and Poetics of Transgression* (Ithaca, NY: Cornell University Press, 1986), 135.

14. See Patrick Joyce, *The Rule of Freedom: Liberalism and the Modern City* (New York: Verso Books, 2003), especially 149–57 and 164.

15. See Chandra Mukerji, *Territorial Ambitions and the Gardens of Versailles* (New York: Cambridge University Press, 1997); and Dell Upton, *Another City: Urban Life and Urban Spaces in the New American Republic* (New Haven, CT: Yale University Press, 2008).

16. Carol A. Breckenridge and Candace Vogler, "The Critical Limits of Embodiment: Disability's Criticism," *Public Culture* 13 (2001): 350, emphasis in original.

17. Anne Friedberg, *Window Shopping: Cinema and the Postmodern* (Berkeley: University of California Press, 1994).

18. In contemporary urban discourse, people with disabilities are rarely, if ever, included in discussions of public space. Policies that promote the "walkable city" (for example, to combat climate change through fewer vehicles and more bike lanes, or greater density and less sprawl) are rarely attuned to the needs of people with disabilities who depend on infrastructures that can only be provided and maintained by state or municipal governments. In New York City, the bike lane program inaugurated in 2014 by ineffectual former mayor Bill De Blasio is still called "Vision Zero," which is intended to produce "zero" bike fatalities but which sounds like a eugenics program directed at people with visual impairments concocted by scientists from the dystopian science fiction film *Alphaville* (dir. Jean-Luc Godard, 1965).

19. Robert McRuer and Merri Lisa Johnson, "Proliferating Cripistemologies: A Virtual Roundtable," *Journal of Literary and Cultural Disability Studies* 8, no. 2 (2014): 149–69. In the interest of full disclosure, I was a participant in this roundtable.

20. See, for example, Joseph P. Shapiro, *No Pity: People with Disabilities Forging a New Civil Rights Movement* (New York: Three Rivers Press, 1993); and Doris Zames Fleischer and Frieda Zames, *The Disability Rights Movement: From Charity to Confrontation* (Philadelphia: Temple University Press, 2001), 68.

21. For an excellent application of the principles of cripistemology in the context of design politics, see Aimi Hamraie and Kelly Fritsch, "Crip Technoscience Manifesto," *Catalyst: Feminism, Theory, Technoscience* 5, no. 1 (2019): 1–34.

22. Georgina Kleege, "Helen Keller and the 'Empire of the Normal,'" *American Quarterly* 52, no. 2 (June 2000): 324.

23. Keller, *The Story of My Life*, 117.

24. "Helen Keller's Twenty-Mile Ride," *Boston Evening Transcript*, May 5, 1899, 7.

25. The large, five-bedroom house designed in the American Queen Anne style where Keller, Sullivan Macy, and Macy lived for more than two decades (1917–38) no longer exists; the site is now occupied by the Reform Temple of Forest Hills. The site's proximity to the Continental Avenue (now 71st Avenue) station of the Long Island Railroad, which opened in 1936, made it possible for Keller to travel to and from Queens by train. In May 2019, a mural featuring Keller opened inside the Ascan Avenue underpass of the Long Island Railroad near the 71st Avenue Station; see Michael Perlman, "Coming Attractions: Helen Keller Mural in Forest Hills," *Rego-Forest Preservation Council Newsletter* (March 6, 2021), available at https://regoforestpreservation.blogspot.com /2019/03/Helen-Keller-Mural-Coming-To-Forest-Hills.html.

26. See Richard Martin, "J. C. Leyendecker and the Homoerotic Invention of Men's Fashion Icons, 1910–1930," *Prospects* 21 (October 1996): 453–70.

27. Charles Leerhsen, *Blood and Smoke: A True Tale of Mystery, Mayhem, and the Birth of the Indy 500* (New York: Simon & Schuster, 2012), 170.

28. Keller, "I Go Adventuring," reprinted in her collection *Midstream: My Later Life* (Garden City, NY: Doubleday, Doran & Co., 1929), 117.

29. Erica Fretwell, *Sensory Experiments: Psychophysics, Race, and the Aesthetics of Feeling* (Durham, NC: Duke University Press, 2020); and Zeynep Çelik Alexander, *Kinaesthetic Knowing: Aesthetics, Epistemology, Modern Design* (Chicago: University of Chicago Press, 2017).

30. "Size of Music Hall Amazes Miss Keller," *New York Times*, February 2, 1933, 21.

31. "'Eyes' for the Blind Listener!" *Stand By*, January 15, 1938, 3.

32. "Miss Keller Told Height: Blind and Deaf, She Had Plane's Altitude Estimated Correctly," *New York Times*, June 18, 1939, 3.

33. Between 1920 and 1922, motivated by economic necessity, Keller and Anne Sullivan Macy appeared on the vaudeville circuit (including an enviously long stint at the Palace Theatre at Broadway and Forty-Seventh Street in midtown Manhattan), with Keller presenting her life story for twenty minutes followed by a question-and-answer segment from the audience, all interpreted live by Sullivan Macy through her voice (but not through sign language), thus making the performances accessible for members of the audience who may have been visually impaired but not hearing-impaired. A diagram intended for stage managers used during an appearance in Buffalo in April 1920, preserved in the Keller Archives, shows a set decorated like a drawing room—with potted palms, a baby grand piano, a sofa in the background—as if you had been invited into their living room for an intimate conversation. When the curtain rises, Keller and Sullivan Macy are sitting in adjacent reading chairs, facing the audience. See "Vaudeville stage plans for Helen Keller, April 16, 1920, Buffalo, N.Y.," available at https://www .afb.org/HelenKellerArchive?a=d&d=A-HK03-FF1-D2-F01-198.1.1.

34. Justin Lieber, "Helen Keller as Cognitive Scientist," *Philosophical Psychology* 9, no. 4 (1996): 435.

35. Letter from Helen Keller to John H. Finley, dated 13 January 1932, in the collections of the Helen Keller Archives, American Foundation for the Blind.

36. "HOOVER WILL OPEN EMPIRE STATE TODAY; President Will Press a Key in Washington Turning on Lights in Building's Lobby; EX-GOV. SMITH TO PRE-

SIDE; 2,000 Persons Invited to the Various Ceremonies, Which Will Continue Until Midnight," *New York Times*, May 1, 1931, 15.

37. Keller, quoted in "Symbol of Faith," *Sunday Times* (Chicago), February 23, 1941, 17M.

38. Helen Keller, "No Word Lovelier Than Home," *Perfect Home* (April 1951), 3. *Perfect Home* was a magazine affiliated with the National Association of Real Estate Boards published in individual real estate markets and sponsored by local businesses in the real estate industry.

39. Diana Fuss, *The Sense of an Interior: Four Writers and the Rooms That Shaped Them* (New York: Routledge, 2004), 141. See Also Erica Fretwell, "Stillness Is a Move: Helen Keller and the Kinaesthetics of Autobiography," *American Literary History* 25, no. 3 (Fall 2013): 563–87.

40. Letter from Cameron Clark to Helen Keller, dated 20 November 1939, in the collections of the Helen Keller Archives, American Foundation for the Blind.

41. Ruth Gordon, "Devotedly, Helen Keller," *New York Times*, August 10, 1969, D1.

42. Gordon, "Devotedly Helen Keller," D1.

43. "Aveugle, sourde et muette Helen Kelen connait huit langues[,] écrit des livres [,] étudie la botanique [,] danse, nage [,] et monte à cheval" ("Blind, deaf, and mute Helen Kelen [*sic*] knows eight languages, writes books, studies botany, dances, swims, and rides a horse"), *Paris-soir*, January 31, 1937.

44. Helen Keller, *Helen Keller's Journal* (London: Michael Joseph, 1938), 164.

45. Keller, *Helen Keller's Journal*, 169.

46. See, for instance, Ian Walker, *City Gorged with Dreams: Surrealism and Documentary Photography in Interwar Paris* (Manchester: Manchester University Press, 2002).

47. This episode recounted in Antonine Prost, *In the Wake of War: "Les Anciens Combattants" and French Society* (Providence, RI: Berg, 1992), 30.

48. Rebecca Scales, *Radio and the Politics of Sound in Interwar France, 1921–1939* (New York: Cambridge University Press, 2016), 71, original emphasis.

49. Susan Buck-Morss, "The Flaneur, the Sandwichman and the Whore: The Politics of Loitering," *New German Critique* 39 (1985): 105.

50. Priscilla Parkhurst Ferguson, "The Flâneur On and Off the Streets of Paris," in *The Flâneur*, ed. Keith Tester (London: Routledge, 1994), 26.

51. See, for example, Deborah Parsons, *Streetwalking the Metropolis: Women, the City, and Modernity* (New York: Oxford University Press, 2000); Griselda Pollock, *Vision and Difference: Femininity, Feminism, and Histories of Art* (New York: Routledge, 1988); Elizabeth Wilson, *The Contradictions of Culture: Cities, Culture, Women* (Thousand Oaks, CA: Sage, 2001); and Janet Wolff, "The Invisible Flâneuse: Women and the Literature of Modernity," *Theory, Culture & Society* 2, no. 3 (1985): 37–46.

52. Keller, *Helen Keller's Journal*, 169.

53. Victor Burgin, *In/Different Spaces: Place and Memory in Visual Culture* (Berkeley: University of California Press, 1996), 145.

54. Walter Benjamin, "The Return of the Flâneur (1929)," in *Selected Writings*, vol. 1, part 1, *1927–1930*, ed. Michael W. Jennings, Howard Eiland, and Gary Smith, trans. Rodney Livingstone (Cambridge, MA: Belknap Press of Harvard University Press, 2005), 37.

55. Walter Benjamin, "The Work of Art in the Age of Its Technological Reproducibility," in *Selected Writings*, vol. 3, *1935–1938*, ed. Howard Eiland and Michael W. Jennings, trans. Edmund Jephcott (Cambridge, MA: Belknap Press of Harvard University Press, 2006), 119–20. All quotations taken from this early (c. early 1936), unpublished, and arguably more developed iteration of Benjamin's core ideas than the version with the better known title.

56. Benjamin, "The Work of Art in the Age of Its Technological Reproducibility," 120.

57. Michael Taussig, "Tactility and Distraction," in *Beyond the Body Proper: Reading the Anthropology of Material Life*, ed. Margaret M. Lock and Judith Farquhar (Durham, NC: Duke University Press, 2007 [1992]), 136.

58. See Abbie Garrington, *Haptic Modernism: Touch and the Tactile in Modernist Writing* (Edinburgh: Edinburgh University Press, 2013); Sara Danius, *The Senses of Modernism: Technology, Perception, and Aesthetics* (Ithaca, NY: Cornell University Press, 2002); Michael Davidson, *Invalid Modernism: Disability and the Missing Body of the Aesthetic* (New York: Oxford University Press, 2019); and Fretwell, *Sensory Experiments*.

59. Letter from Nancy Hamilton to Polly Thomson, dated 11 June 1952, in the collections of the Helen Keller Archives, American Foundation for the Blind.

60. A brief overview of Letellier's oeuvre can be found at https://en.unifrance.org /directories/person/377753/jacques-letellier. For more about the history of *Cahiers du cinéma*, see Emily Bickerton, *A Short History of "Cahiers du Cinéma"* (New York: Verso Books, 2014).

61. See, for instance, *Pathway into Light*, dir. Terry Ashwood (London: Associated British Pathé, Ltd./National Institute for the Blind, 1952), archived on YouTube at https://www.youtube.com/watch?v=k3jDNoNEl0o.

62. One might recall here Frank O'Hara's poem "The Day Lady Died" (1964), which includes the lines, "I walk up the muggy street beginning to sun / and have a hamburger and a malted and buy / an ugly NEW WORLD WRITING to see what the poets / in Ghana are doing these days." From *The Collected Poems of Frank O'Hara*, ed. Donald Allen (Berkeley: University of California Press, 1995 [1971]), 325.

63. See Roland Barthes, *Mythologies* (Paris: Éditions du Seuil, 1957). See also Kristin Ross, *Fast Cars, Clean Bodies: Decolonization and the Reordering of French Culture* (Cambridge, MA: MIT Press, 1996).

64. Kevin Hetherington, "Spatial Textures: Place, Touch, and Praesentia," *Environment and Planning A* 35 (2003): 1941.

65. Adam Philips, *On Kissing, Tickling, and Being Bored: Psychoanalytic Essays on the Unexamined Life* (Cambridge, MA: Harvard University Press, 1998), 9–11.

66. Elspeth Brown, *Work! A Queer History of Modeling* (Durham, NC: Duke University Press, 2019).

67. For a broad overview of the Situationists' techniques, see Carl Lavery, "Rethinking the *Dérive:* Drifting and Theatricality in Theatre and Performance Studies," *Performance Research* 23, no. 7 (2018), 1–15.

68. Simon Sadler, *The Situationist City* (Cambridge, MA: MIT Press, 1998), 56.

69. Guy Debord, *The Society of the Spectacle* (Paris: Buchet-Chastel, 1967).

70. Gissen, *The Architecture of Disability*, 116.

71. Mac E. Barrick, "The Helen Keller Joke Cycle," *Journal of American Folklore* 93, no. 370 (October–December 1980): 441–49.

72. Anthony Vidler, *The Architectural Uncanny: Essays in the Modern Unhomely* (Cambridge, MA: MIT Press, 1992).

73. Keller's accomplishments have been the source of conspiracy theories on contemporary social media sites like TikTok, where some users have accused Keller of being a fraud, a deceitful invention of earlier generations. See Rebecca Onion, "Did Helen Keller Really 'Do All That'?" *Slate* (February 26, 2021), available at https://slate.com /human-interest/2021/02/helen-keller-tiktok-conspiracy.html.

CHAPTER THREE

1. William Leuchtenberg, *Franklin D. Roosevelt and the New Deal, 1932–40* (New York: Harper Torchbooks, 1963), 126.

2. See Alfred Gus Karger, *Longview: An Ohio State Hospital in Cincinnati for the Mentally Ill* (Cincinnati: Longview, 1937).

3. For instance, although there is substantial scholarship related to the ways in which the WPA was associated with the economic liberalism of the 1930s, only a handful of scholars have put modern definitions of disability into alignment with modern definitions of work. See, for example, Sarah F. Rose, *No Right to Be Idle: The Invention of Disability, 1840s–1930s* (Chapel Hill: University of North Carolina Press, 2017).

4. Historian Cheryl Lynn Greenberg has successfully shown that some 400,000 African American workers were part of the WPA, albeit under segregated conditions and locations, such as at historically black colleges, public schools, libraries, and so forth. See Greenberg, *To Ask for an Equal Chance: African Americans and the Great Depression* (Rowman & Littlefield, 2009). Greenberg argues that the number of Black workers does not diminish the impact of structural racism on the history of the WPA, but it does challenge the charge that the WPA was a singularly racist agency that excluded people of color from all forms of work. This is a good example of the interpretive struggle of assessing twentieth-century modernisms: federal and state governments bend just enough to employ those who endure segregation in the private sector, but oppose any legislation that would seek to overturn the conditions that produce that segregation in the first place.

5. See, for example, John Louis Recchiuti, *Civic Engagement: Social Science and Progressive-Era Reform in New York City* (Philadelphia: University of Pennsylvania Press, 2007).

6. Fred Turner, *The Democratic Surround: Multimedia and American Liberalism from World War II to the Psychedelic Sixties* (Chicago: University of Chicago Press, 2013), 78.

7. Turner, *The Democratic Surround*, 81.

8. For more about professional approaches to the concept of "self" in this period, see Pamela Haag, "In Search of 'The Real Thing': Ideologies of Love, Modern Romance, and Women's Sexual Subjectivity in the United States, 1920–40," in *American Sexual Politics: Sex, Gender, and Race Since the Civil War*, ed. John C. Fout and Maura Shaw Tantillo (Chicago: University of Chicago Press, 1993), 161–92; Elizabeth Lunbeck, *The Psychiatric Persuasion: Knowledge, Gender, and Power in Modern America*

(Princeton, NJ: Princeton University Press, 1994); Joel Pfister, "Glamorizing the Psychological: The Politics of the Performances of Modern Psychological Identities," in *Inventing the Psychological: Toward a Cultural History of Emotional Life in America*, ed. Joel Pfister and Nancy Schnog (New Haven, CT: Yale University Press, 1997), 167–213; and Jonathan Metzl, *Prozac on the Couch: Prescribing Gender in the Era of Wonder Drugs* (Durham, NC: Duke University Press, 2003). See also David Serlin, "Carney Landis and the Psychosexual Landscape of Touch in Mid-20th Century America," *History of Psychology* 15, no. 3 (2012): 209–16.

9. Barbara Melosh, *Engendering Culture: Manhood and Womanhood in New Deal Public Art and Theater* (Washington, DC: Smithsonian Scholarly Press, 1991); and the groundbreaking volume by A. Joan Saab, *For the Millions: American Art and Culture between the Wars* (Philadelphia: University of Pennsylvania Press, 2009).

10. Frances A. Koestler, *The Unseen Minority: A Social History of Blindness in America* (New York: D. McKay Co., 1976), 193.

11. See Beatriz Colomina, *X-Ray Architecture* (Zürich: Lars Müller Publishers, 2019); and Juliet Kinchin, ed., *Century of the Child: Growing by Design, 1900–2000* (New York: Museum of Modern Art, 2012).

12. Duiker, quoted in Kinchin, "The New School," in *Century of the Child*, ed. Kinchin, 102.

13. "Sickly child," quoted in Kinchin, "The New School," in *Century of the Child*, ed. Kinchin, 99.

14. Johnson (1932), quoted in Aidan O'Connor, "'A Setting for Childlife': The New School in the United States," in *Century of the Child*, ed. Kinchin, 105.

15. Farnsworth Crowder, "The House of Magic," *Hygeia* (May 1941), 386–92, 424.

16. Kinchin, *Century of the Child*, 89.

17. Kinchin, *Century of the Child*, 99.

18. David Mitchell and Sharon Snyder, *Cultural Locations of Disability* (Chicago: University of Chicago Press, 2006).

19. Patrick White, "Sex Education; or, How the Blind Became Heterosexual," *GLQ* 9, no. 1–2 (2003): 133–47.

20. Rachel Elder, "Safe Seizures, Schoolyard Stoics, and the Making of Contained Citizens at Detroit's School for Epileptic Children, 1935–1956," *Journal of the History of Childhood and Youth* 7, no. 3 (2014): 435.

21. See, for example, Sven-Olav Wallenstein, *Biopolitics and the Emergence of Modern Architecture* (New York: Buell Center / FORuM Project and Princeton Architectural Press, 2008), especially 36–39, 42.

22. Charles Wilkins Short and Rudolph Stanley-Brown, *Public Buildings: A Survey of Architecture of Projects Constructed by Federal and Other Governmental Bodies between the Years 1933 and 1939 with the Assistance of the Public Works Administration* (Washington, DC: GPO, 1939), 185, my emphasis.

23. See, for instance, David Brody, *Visualizing American Empire: Orientalism and Imperialism in the Philippines* (Chicago: University of Chicago Press, 2010).

24. Newspaper clipping, "Los Angeles Pool for Crippled Tots Dedicated," April 5, 1934, unknown source, author's collection, my emphasis.

25. *Twelfth Report of the West Virginia Board of Control for the Period of July 1, 1936 to June 30, 1939* (Wheeling, WV: GPO), 122, my emphasis.

26. Elizabeth Mock, ed., *Built in USA: 1932–1944* (New York: Museum of Modern Art, 1944).

27. See Margret A. Winzer, *The History of Special Education: From Isolation to Integration* (Washington, DC: Gallaudet University Press, 1993).

28. See Roger G. Kennedy, *When Art Worked: The New Deal, Art, and Democracy* (New York: Rizzoli, 2009).

29. See "School for Crippled Children Denver, Colo," *Architectural Forum* (November 1937), 114–18; and "Education: Cripples' School," *Time*, September 6, 1940.

30. Commentary, author and source unknown, supplementing the circulation of a photograph of the Boettcher School, January 10, 1943, author's collection.

31. See, for example, Ira Katznelson, *Fear Itself: The New Deal and the Origins of Our Time* (New York: W. W. Norton, 2013).

32. See Rose, *No Right to Be Idle;* and Kim Nielsen, "Incompetent and Insane: Labor, Ability, and Citizenship in Nineteenth- and Early-Twentieth-Century United States," *Rethinking History* 23, no. 2 (2019).

33. Paul Longmore and David Goldberger, "The League of the Physically Handicapped and the Great Depression: A Case Study in the New Disability History," *Journal of American History* 87, no. 3 (December 2000): 888–922.

34. See Greenberg, *To Ask for an Equal Chance.*

35. Algernon Austin, "When the WPA Created Over 400,000 Jobs for Black Workers," Center for Economic and Policy Research (February 9, 2023).

36. Greenberg, *To Ask for an Equal Chance*, 119.

37. See Kim Nielsen, "Memorializing FDR," *OAH Magazine of History* 27, no. 1 (January 2013): 23–26; Daniel J. Wilson, "Passing in the Shadow of FDR: Polio Survivors, Passing, and the Negotiations of Disability," in *Disability and Passing: Blurring the Lines of Identity*, ed. Jeffrey A. Brune and Daniel J. Wilson (Philadelphia: Temple University Press, 2013), 13–25; and the pioneering study by Hugh Gallagher, *FDR's Splendid Deception* (New York: Dodd, Mead, 1985).

38. See Matthew Rubery, *The Untold Story of the Talking Book* (Cambridge, MA: Harvard University Press, 2016); and Elizabeth Ellcessor, *Restricted Access: Media, Disability, and the Politics of Participation* (New York: NYU Press, 2016). For an excellent overview of the development of Talking Books, see also Mara Mills and Jonathan Sterne, "Aural Speed-Reading: Some Historical Bookmarks," *Proceedings of the Modern Language Association* 135, no. 2 (2020): 401–11.

39. Corinne Frazier Gillett, "The WPA and the Blind," *Outlook for the Blind* 35, no. 3 (1941).

40. Gillett, "The WPA and the Blind." See also Jen Hale, "WPA Projects at the Howe Press," blog post, Perkins Archives Blog, Perkins School for the Blind, January 13, 2021, https://www.perkins.org/wpa-projects-howe-press/.

41. Interview with Bernard DiMarco (originally published 1939), featured in David Shannon, *The Great Depression* (Englewood Cliffs, NJ: Prentice Hall, 1960), 163–71.

42. David B. Danbom, *Going It Alone: Fargo Grapples with the Great Depression* (St. Paul: Minnesota Historical Society Press, 2005), 89.

43. *Wisconsin Works Progress Administration 1939* (Milwaukee: WPA, 1939), 55–56. For further insight see Lois M. Quinn, "Replacing Welfare with Work in the WPA: The Handicraft Project That Made Milwaukee Famous," 28th Annual Morris Fromkin Memorial Lecture, University of Wisconsin-Milwaukee, October 30, 1997, author's collection.

44. Mary Kellogg Rice, *Useful Work for Unskilled Women: A Unique Milwaukee WPA Project* (Milwaukee: Milwaukee County Historical Society, 2003), 3, 13.

45. Federal Art Project, file on the Carrie Tingley School for Crippled Children, Archives of American Art, Smithsonian Institution.

46. Photograph of the Salem Federal Arts Center in the collections of the National Archives and Records Administration.

47. All references to *Work Pays America* (Washington, DC: Works Progress Administration, 1937), available at the Internet Archive, https://archive.org/details/WorkPays1937.

48. "Blind Man Directs 38 Eyes in Braille Transcription," *Baltimore Sun*, June 13, 1938.

49. See, for instance, Richard D. McKinzie, *The New Deal for Artists* (Princeton, NJ: Princeton University Press, 1973).

50. For a complete recounting of this episode, see Carol Pogash, "Berkeley's Artwork Loss is a Museum's Gain," *New York Times*, February 20, 2012.

51. Very little scholarship exists about the Museum Extension Projects; see James A. Findlay and Lillian Perricone, *WPA Museum Extension Project 1935–1943: Government Created Visual Aids for the Children from the Collections of the Museum of the Modern Book* (Fort Lauderdale: Bienes Museum of the Modern Book, 2009).

52. Federal Works Agency, *Final Report on the WPA Program, 1935–43* (Washington, DC: US Government Printing Office, 1947), 63.

53. Findlay and Perricone, *WPA Museum Extension Project 1935–1943*, 36.

54. Document from the Connecticut Work Projects Administration, Professional & Service Division (New Haven, CT: Work Projects Administration, 1937[?]), iii. In the collections of the Bienes Museum of the Modern Book, Fort Lauderdale, Florida.

55. Nicole Belolan, "An 'Effort to Bring This Little Handicapped Army in Personal Touch with Beauty': Democratizing Art for Crippled Children at the Metropolitan Museum of Art, 1919–1934," *New York History* 96, no. 1 (Winter 2015): 46.

56. Belolan, "An 'Effort to Bring This Little Handicapped Army in Personal Touch with Beauty,'" 50. For a broader history of museum education in the period just before the WPA, see Jeffrey Trask, *Things American: Art Museums and Civic Culture in the Progressive Era* (Philadelphia: University of Pennsylvania Press, 2012). Art historian Steve Conn has dated the suspension of object-based learning sessions in museum settings to 1926, when, he argues, the use of physical objects declined in favor of text- and visual-based learning. See Conn, *Museums and American Intellectual Life, 1876–1926* (Chicago: University of Chicago Press, 1998).

57. Koestler, *The Unseen Minority*, 422.

58. Brad Byrom, "The Progressive Movement and the Child with Physical Disabilities," in *Children with Disabilities in America: A Historical Handbook and Guide*, ed. Philip L. Safford and Elizabeth J. Safford (Westport, CT: Greenwood Press, 2006), 59.

59. In a contemporary review of Cutsforth's book, distinguished educational psychologist Rudolph Pintner argued that "all of the author's criticisms may be true, although there is little evidence for some of them, and many of his generalizations are far too sweeping. The trouble lies just there. The book will create an antagonistic feeling among educators of the blind and fail to have that influence which it deserves to have because of the many important questions which it raises." See Pintner's review in *Psychological Bulletin* 32, no. 1 (1935): 106–8. In his own work, Pintner was among a number of well-regarded contemporary psychological researchers who appeared to believe in a strong correlation between physical disability and neurotic behavior: see Rudolph Pintner, Jon Eisenson, and Mildred Stanton, *The Psychology of the Physically Handicapped* (New York: F. S. Crofts, 1941).

60. Thomas D. Cutsforth, *The Blind in School and Society: A Psychological Study* (New York: D. Appleton, 1933), 58.

61. See Mabel Wilson, *Negro Building: Black Americans in the World of Fairs and Museums* (Berkeley: University of California Press, 2012); and Carol Duncan, *Civilizing Rituals: Inside Public Art Museums* (New York: Routledge, 1995).

62. *Models for the Blind* (Columbus: Ohio Museum Extension Project/Works Progress Administration of Ohio, 1941). In the collections of the Bienes Museum of the Modern Book, Fort Lauderdale, Florida.

63. Yvonne Eriksson, *Tactile Pictures: Pictorial Representations for the Blind, 1784–1940* (Gothenburg, Sweden: Acta Universitatis Gothoburgensis, 1998), 148–53.

64. For more about the collections of the Blinden-Museum an der Johann-August-Zeune-Schule Berlin, see the website: https://www.zeune-schule.de/.

65. Susan Stewart, *On Longing: Narratives of the Miniature, the Gigantic, the Souvenir, the Collection* (Durham, NC: Duke University Press, 1992); and Margaret Gibson, "Melancholy Objects," *Mortality* 9, no. 4 (November 2004): 285–99.

66. A photograph of *Chronic Illness* (c. 1937) found in the files of the Archives of American Art, Smithsonian Institution, is reproduced in Richard D. McKinzie's classic text, *A New Deal for Artists* (New York: Princeton Architectural Press, 1973), 133.

67. For an insightful analysis of the visual rhetoric attached to social workers during this period, see Shawn Michelle Smith's chapter, "Nursing the Nation: The 1930s Public Health Nurse as Image and Icon," in *Imagining Illness: Public Health and Visual Culture*, ed. David Serlin (Minneapolis: University of Minnesota Press, 2010). For more about the evolution of social workers during this period, see Daniel J. Walkowitz, *Working with Class* (Chapel Hill: University of North Carolina Press, 2000).

68. Martin Jay, *Downcast Eyes: The Denigration of Vision in Twentieth-Century French Thought* (Berkeley: University of California Press, 1993), 160.

69. Caro Verbeek, "Prière de toucher: Tactilism in Early Modern and Contemporary Art," *Senses & Society* 7, no. 2 (2012): 227.

70. Filippo Tommaso Marinetti, "Manifesto of Tactilism," first published January 1921.

71. F. T. Marinetti, "Le tavole tattili costruite da Benedetta sulla spiaggia di Antignano," in *La grande Milano tradizionale e futurista*, ed. L. De Maria (Milan: Mondadori, 1969), 263–67. For further interpretation of the *tavola tattile*, see Verbeek, "Prière de toucher," 227–29.

72. Devon Stillwell, "Eugenics Visualized: The Exhibit of the Third International Congress of Eugenics, 1932," *Bulletin of the History of Medicine* 86, no. 2 (Summer 2012): 205–36.

73. Karen Barad, *Meeting the Universe Halfway: Quantum Physics and the Entanglement of Matter and Meaning* (Durham, NC: Duke University Press, 2007).

74. See, for instance, Lara U. Marks, *Touch: Sensuous Theory and Multisensory Media* (Minneapolis: University of Minnesota Press, 2002).

75. Vivan Bozalek et al, "Touching Matters: Affective Entanglements in Coronatime," *Qualitative Inquiry* 27, no. 7 (2021): 844–52.

76. See, for instance, Karen Barad, "After the End of the World: Entangled Nuclear Colonialisms, Matters of Force, and the Material Force of Justice," *Theory & Event* 22, no. 3 (2019): 524–50.

CHAPTER FOUR

1. Philip Johnson, "The Seven Crutches of Modern Architecture," in John M. Jacobus, *Philip Johnson* (New York, George Braziller, 1961), 113–18. Originally published in *Perspecta* 3 (1955): 41–44.

2. "New Look in Hospitals: New Orleans Crippled Children's Hospital," *Life*, June 11, 1955.

3. David Mitchell and Sharon Snyder, *Narrative Prosthesis Disability and the Dependencies of Discourse* (Ann Arbor. University of Michigan Press, 2000).

4. Sarah Williams Goldhagen and Réjean Legault, eds., *Anxious Modernisms: Experimentation in Postwar Architectural Culture* (Cambridge, MA: MIT Press, 2000).

5. Monica Penick, *Tastemaker: Elizabeth Gordon, House Beautiful, and the Postwar American Home* (New Haven, CT: Yale University Press, 2017).

6. Robert Imrie, *Disability and the City: International Perspectives* (New York: St. Martin's, 1996), 80.

7. Geoffrey Scott, *The Architecture of Humanism: A Study in the History of Taste* (New York: W. W. Norton, 1999), 110.

8. Wanda Katja Liebermann, *Architecture's Disability Problem* (New York: Routledge, 2024), especially chap. 2.

9. See, for example, Jorge Oteros-Pailos, *Architecture's Historical Turn: Phenomenology and the Rise of the Postmodern* (Minneapolis: University of Minnesota Press, 2010), especially 100–145.

10. See Frederic Jameson, *A Singular Modernity* (New York: Verso, 2002), 23–30. See also Reinhold Martin, *Utopia's Ghost: Architecture and Postmodernism, Again* (Minneapolis: University of Minnesota, 2010).

11. Nathan Brown, "Postmodernity, Not Yet: Toward a New Periodisation," *Radical Philosophy* 201 (February 2018): 11.

12. See, for instance, Paul Goldberger's glowing review, "Library for the Blind an Architectural Triumph," *New York Times*, August 9, 1978.

13. "Eleven Works by Stanley Tigerman," *A+U* 67 (July 1976): 72–120.

14. Although the two-car garage does not survive, a pristine cardboard maquette made by Tigerman was donated by the architect to the collections of the Art Institute of Chicago. See https://www.artic.edu/artworks/214954/two-car-garage-regional -library-for-the-blind-chicago-illinois-model.

15. Barbara Penner, "From Ergonomics to Empathy: Herman Miller and Meta-Form," in *The Routledge Companion to Design Studies*, ed. Penny Sparke and Fiona Fisher (New York: Routledge, 2016), 279.

16. Goldberger, "Library for the Blind an Architectural Triumph."

17. For a good background on Netsch's approach to the University of Illinois at Chicago's "Circle Campus," see the online history exhibit at https://uicarchives.library .uic.edu/circle-campus/.

18. Martin, *Utopia's Ghost*, especially 29–48.

19. Mara Mills, "The Co-Construction of Blindness and Reading," in *Disability Trouble*, ed. Ulrike Bergermann (Berlin: B Books, 2013), 195–204.

20. Aimi Hamraie, *Building Access: Universal Design and the Politics of Disability* (Minneapolis: University of Minnesota Press, 2017), 107–12.

21. Tigerman, "Library for the Blind," *Design Quarterly* (1978): 31.

22. Tigerman, quoted in Diana Bitting, "Giving Back," *Modern Luxury* (October 4, 2013).

23. See Sara Hendren's portfolio of design projects: https://sarahendren.com/about/. See also Graham Pullin, *Design Meets Disability* (Cambridge, MA: MIT Press, 2011).

24. Pierre Bourdieu, "Structure, Habitus, Practice," in *Outline of a Theory of Practice* (New York: Cambridge University Press, 1977), 78–86.

25. Bess Williamson, *Accessible America: A History of Disability and Design* (New York: NYU Press, 2019), especially 69–95.

26. Hamraie, *Building Access*, 120–25.

27. Michael A. Jones and John Caitlin, "Design for Access," *Progressive Architecture* (April 1978): 70.

28. Felicity Scott, *Architecture or Techno-Utopia: Politics after Modernism* (Cambridge, MA: MIT Press, 2007), 130.

29. David Gissen, "Disability as Architectural Criticism," *HTC Experiments*, October 3, 2008. See https://htcexperiments.org/2008/10/03/disability-as-architectural -criticism-yale-1996/.

30. For a particularly acrid interpretation of architectural modernism, see Sven-Olav Wallenstein, *Biopolitics and the Emergence of Modern Architecture* (New York: Temple Hoyne Buell Center for the Study of American Architecture/Princeton Architectural Press, 2010).

31. Magali Sarfatti Larson, *Behind the Postmodern Façade: Architectural Change in Late Twentieth-Century America* (Berkeley: University of California Press, 1993), 176.

32. In 2016, Dutch architect Jurgen Bey unveiled his design for a meeting space for the European Council in Brussels, which was reminiscent of Tigerman's design for preschool children. It consisted of "28 interlocking furniture pieces representing the EU's 28 member states, echoing the motto of the European Union 'united in diversity.'" https://www.creativeholland.com/en/new-interior-european-council-brussels-dutch -designers.

33. "Lakeside Bank," Pappageorge Haymes Partners' description of project, available at http://www.pappageorgehaymes.com/projects/lakeside-bank.

34. Tigerman, "Library for the Blind," 24.

35. Lee Bey, "St. Ignatius Acquires Architecturally Significant Bank Building," *Chicago Sun-Times*, July 29, 2023.

EPILOGUE

1. Quentin Crisp (transcribed by author) in an interview with Bernard Braden, 1968. The interview was broadcast two years later as part of "Seven Men," an episode of the Granada Television series *World in Action* (London, 1970); see segment with Crisp, available on YouTube.

2. See Thomas Frank, *The Conquest of Cool* (Chicago: University of Chicago Press, 1998).

3. See Elizabeth Guffey, *Designing Disability* (New York: Routledge, 2015).

4. For an extended account of this shameful episode in Columbia University's history, see Sharon Sutton, *When Ivory Towers Were Black* (New York: Fordham University Press, 2017). See also Stefan M. Bradley, *Harlem vs. Columbia University: Black Student Power in the Late 1960s* (Champaign: University of Illinois Press, 2009).

5. See Todd Gitlin, *The Sixties: Years of Hope, Days of Rage* (New York: Bantam, 1987).

6. Ray Lifchez, interview with author, August 10, 2016.

7. Ignacio Galán, "Unlearning Ableism: Design Knowledge, Contested Models, and the Experience of Disability in 1970s Berkeley," *Journal of Design History* 36, no. 1 (2022): 73–92. See also Bess Williamson, *Accessible America* (New York: NYU Press, 2017).

8. See Bess Williamson, "The People's Sidewalks: Designing Berkeley's Wheelchair Route, 1970–1974," *Boom: A Journal of California* 2, no. 1 (Spring 2012): 49–52. See also, in the same issue, David Serlin, "Architecture and Social Justice: Independent Living on Campus," 53–54.

9. Ray Lifchez, interview with author, August 10, 2016.

10. Carl Wilson, "The Sunshine of Our Lives," *Slate*, December 18, 2016.

11. Theodore Parker, "Of Justice and the Conscience" (1852), in *Ten Sermons of Religion* (Boston: Crosby, Nichols & Co., 1853), 84–85.

Bibliography

Abram, David. *The Spell of the Sensuous: Perception and Language in a More-Than-Human World*. New York: Vintage Books, 2017.

Adam, Robert, and James Adam. "Plans and Elevations for the Villa of Lord Mansfield at Kenwood (1822)." In *Architecture and Design in Europe and America, 1750–2000*, edited by Abigail Harrison-Moore and Dorothy Rowe. Malden, MA: Blackwell, 2006.

Adams, Annmarie. *Medicine by Design: The Architect and the Modern Hospital, 1893–1943*. Minneapolis: University of Minnesota Press, 2007.

Adams, James Eli. *Dandies and Desert Saints: Styles of Victorian Masculinity*. Ithaca, NY: Cornell University Press, 1995.

After Dark. "Daredevil." October 1980.

Agamben, Giorgio. *The Signature of All Things: On Method*. Translated by Luca di Santo and Kevin Attell. New York: Zone Books, 2009.

Aggregate (Group). *Governing by Design: Architecture, Economy, and Politics in the Twentieth Century*. Pittsburgh: University of Pittsburgh Press, 2012.

Agrest, Diana. "The Return of the Repressed: Nature." In *The Sex of Architecture*, edited by Diana Agrest, Patricia Conway, and Leslie Kanes Weisman. New York: Harry N. Abrams, 1996.

Agrest, Diana, and Mario Gandelsonas. "Semiotics and the Limits of Architecture." *Architecture and Urbanism (A+u)* 67 (July 1976).

Ahmed, Sara. *Queer Phenomenology: Orientations, Objects, Others*. Durham, NC: Duke University Press, 2006.

Alexander, Michael. *Medievalism: The Middle Ages in Modern England*. New Haven, CT: Yale University Press, 2017.

Allan, John. *Berthold Lubetkin: Architecture and the Tradition of Progress*. London: RIBA Publications, 1992.

Arboleda, Molly. *Educating Young Children in WPA Nursery Schools: Federally-Funded Early Childhood Education from 1933–1943*. New York: Routledge, 2018.

Armstrong, Tim. *Modernism, Technology, and the Body: A Cultural Study*. Cambridge: Cambridge University Press, 1998.

Arnheim, Rudolf. "Beginning with the Child." In *Discovering Child Art: Essays on Childhood, Primitivism, and Modernism*, edited by Jonathan David Fineberg, 15–26. Princeton, NJ: Princeton University Press, 1998.

Arnold, Dana. "The Country House: Form, Function and Meaning (1998)." In *Archi-

tecture and Design in Europe and America, 1750–2000, edited by Abigail Harrison-Moore and Dorothy Rowe. Malden, MA: Blackwell, 2006.

Arnold, Dana, and Joanna Sofaer Derevenski. *Biographies and Space: Placing the Subject in Art and Architecture*. New York: Routledge, 2008.

Arts and the Handicapped: An Issue of Access. New York: Educational Facilities Laboratories and the National Endowment for the Arts, 1975.

Augé, Marc. *In the Metro*. Translated by Tom Conley. Minneapolis: University of Minnesota Press, 2002.

Aureli, Pier Vittorio. *The Project of Autonomy: Politics and Architecture within and against Capitalism*. New York: Buell Center for the Study of American Architecture / FORuM Project and Princeton Architectural Press, 2008.

Awan, Nishat, Tatjana Schneider, and Jeremy Till. *Spatial Agency: Other Ways of Doing Architecture*. New York: Routledge, 2011.

Azoulay, Ariella. *The Civil Contract of Photography*. Translated by Rela Mazali and Ruvik Danieli. Princeton, NJ: Zone Books, 2012.

Bachelard, Gaston. *The Poetics of Space*. Translated by Maria Jolas. 1964. Reprint, Boston: Beacon Press, 1994.

Bahr, Ehrhard. *Weimar on the Pacific: German Exile Culture in Los Angeles and the Crisis of Modernism*. Berkeley: University of California Press, 2007.

Baird, George. *The Space of Appearance*. Cambridge, MA: MIT Press, 1995.

Banham, Reyner. *Theory and Design in the First Machine Age*. 2nd ed. 1960. Reprint, Cambridge, MA: MIT Press, 1980.

Barbara, Anna, and Anthony Perliss. *Invisible Architecture: Experiencing Places through the Sense of Smell*. Milan: Skira, 2006.

Barbash, Ilisa, Molly Rogers, and Deborah Willis, eds. *To Make Their Own Way in the World: The Enduring Legacy of the Zealy Daguerreotypes*. Illustrated edition. Cambridge, MA: Aperture, 2020.

Barker, Jennifer M. *The Tactile Eye: Touch and the Cinematic Experience*. Berkeley: University of California Press, 2009.

"Barrier Free Design." *Progressive Architecture*, April 1978.

Barthes, Roland. "Garbo's Face (1957)." In *Mythologies: The Complete Edition, in a New Translation*, translated by Richard Howard and Annette Lavers. New York: Hill & Wang, 2013.

———. "Martians (1957)." In *Mythologies: The Complete Edition, in a New Translation*, translated by Richard Howard and Annette Lavers. New York: Hill & Wang, 2013.

———. "Power and 'Cool' (1957)." In *Mythologies: The Complete Edition, in a New Translation*, translated by Richard Howard and Annette Lavers. New York: Hill & Wang, 2013.

———. "Toys (1957)." In *Mythologies: The Complete Edition, in a New Translation*, translated by Richard Howard and Annette Lavers. New York: Hill & Wang, 2013.

Bauman, Zygmunt. *The Individualized Society*. Cambridge: Polity Press, 2001.

———. *Liquid Modernity*. Cambridge: Polity Press, 2000.

Bayes, Kenneth, and Sandra Franklin, eds. *Designing for the Handicapped: The Mentally Retarded, the Mentally Ill, the Maladjusted, the Blind, the Deaf, Those with Learning Difficulties, the Gifted or Exceptional Child*. London: George Godwin Ltd., 1971.

Bell, Christopher M., ed. *Blackness and Disability: Critical Examinations and Cultural Interventions*. East Lansing: Michigan State University Press, 2011.

Bell, Nicholas R. "Designing for Wonder: Losing Your Self at the Museum." In *De-*

signing for Empathy: Perspectives on the Museum Experience, edited by Elif M. Gökçiğdem. Lanham, MD: American Alliance of Museums (AAM) and Rowman & Littlefield, 2019.

Benhabib, Seyla. *Another Cosmopolitanism*. Edited by Robert Post. New York: Oxford University Press, 2006.

Benjamin, Walter. "The Return of the Flâneur (1929)." In *Selected Writings*. Vol. 2, part 1, *1927–1930*, edited by Michael W. Jennings, Howard Eiland, and Gary Smith, translated by Rodney Livingstone. Cambridge, MA: Belknap Press of Harvard University Press, 2005.

———. "The Work of Art in the Age of Its Technological Reproducibility (circa Early 1936, Unpublished Version)." In *Selected Writings*. Vol. 3, *1935–1938*, edited by Howard Eiland and Michael W. Jennings, translated by Edmund Jephcott. Cambridge, MA: Belknap Press of Harvard University Press, 2006.

Berger, Martin A. *Sight Unseen: Whiteness and American Visual Culture*. Berkeley: University of California Press, 2005.

Berk, Louis, and Rachel Kolsky. *Secret Whitechapel*. Gloucestershire: Amberley Publishing Ltd., 2017.

———. *Whitechapel in 50 Buildings*. Gloucestershire: Amberley Publishing Ltd., 2016.

Berlant, Lauren Gail, ed. *Compassion: The Culture and Politics of an Emotion*. New York: Routledge, 2004.

Biraghi, Marco. *Project of Crisis: Manfredo Tafuri and Contemporary Architecture*. Cambridge, MA: MIT Press, 2013.

Bivona, Daniel, and Roger B. Henkle. *The Imagination of Class: Masculinity and the Victorian Urban Poor*. Columbus: Ohio State University Press, 2006.

Blackmore, Lisa. *Spectacular Modernity: Dictatorship, Space and Visuality in Venezuela, 1948–1958*. Pittsburgh: University of Pittsburgh Press, 2017.

Blumin, Stuart M. *The Encompassing City: Streetscapes in Early Modern Art and Culture*. Manchester: Manchester University Press, 2008.

Borja-Villel, Manuel, and Thomas Keenan. *The End(s) of the Museum: Els límits del museu*. Barcelona: Fundació Antoni Tàpies, 1995.

Bouvet, Vincent, and Gerard Durozoi. *Paris between the Wars 1919–1939: Art, Life, and Culture*. London: Vendome Press, 2010.

Bowe, Frank. *Handicapping America: Barriers to Disabled People*. New York: Harper & Row, 1978.

Boys, Jos, ed. *Disability, Space, Architecture: A Reader*. New York: Routledge, 2017.

———. *Doing Disability Differently: An Alternative Handbook on Architecture, Dis/Ability and Designing for Everyday Life*. London: Routledge, 2014.

Brennan, Teresa. *The Transmission of Affect*. Ithaca, NY: Cornell University Press, 2004.

Brooks, Michael W. *John Ruskin and Victorian Architecture*. London: Thames & Hudson, 1989.

Brown, Adrienne. *The Black Skyscraper*. Baltimore: Johns Hopkins University Press, 2019.

Brown, Bill. *A Sense of Things: The Object Matter of American Literature*. Chicago: University of Chicago Press, 2003.

———, ed. *Things*. Chicago: University of Chicago Press, 2004.

Brückner, Martin. *The Geographic Revolution in Early America: Maps, Literacy, and National Identity*. Chapel Hill: Published for the Omohundro Institute of Early American History and Culture by University of North Carolina Press, 2006.

Bruggeman, Seth C., ed. *Born in the U.S.A.: Birth, Commemoration, and American Public Memory*. Amherst: University of Massachusetts Press, 2012.

Bruno, Giuliana. *Atlas of Emotion: Journeys in Art, Architecture, and Film*. New York: Verso, 2018.

———. *Streetwalking on a Ruined Map: Cultural Theory and the City Films of Elvira Notari*. Princeton, NJ: Princeton University Press, 1993.

Buckley, Cheryl. *Designing Modern Britain*. Chicago: Reaktion Books, 2007.

Bunzl, Matti. *Symptoms of Modernity: Jews and Queers in Late-Twentieth-Century Vienna*. Berkeley: University of California Press, 2004.

Burch, Susan, and Hannah Joyner. *Unspeakable: The Story of Junius Wilson*. Chapel Hill: University of North Carolina Press, 2007.

Burgin, Victor. *In/Different Spaces: Place and Memory in Visual Culture*. Berkeley: University of California Press, 1996.

Busbea, Larry. *Topologies: The Urban Utopia in France, 1960–1970*. Cambridge, MA: MIT Press, 2007.

Calcatinge, Alexandru. *Visions of the Real: An Architect's Approach on Cultural Landscape Studies*. Berlin: LIT Verlag, 2011.

Candlin, Fiona. *Art, Museums and Touch*. Illustrated edition. Manchester: Manchester University Press, 2010.

Candlin, Fiona, and Raiford Guins, eds. *The Object Reader*. New York: Routledge, 2009.

Cartwright, Lisa. *Moral Spectatorship: Technologies of Voice and Affect in Postwar Representations of the Child*. Durham, NC: Duke University Press, 2008.

Castiglia, Christopher. *Interior States: Institutional Consciousness and the Inner Life of Democracy in the Antebellum United States*. Durham, NC: Duke University Press, 2008.

Castronovo, Russ. *Necro Citizenship: Death, Eroticism, and the Public Sphere in the Nineteenth-Century United States*. Durham, NC: Duke University Press, 2001.

Cavell, Richard. *McLuhan in Space: A Cultural Geography*. 2002. Reprint, Toronto: University of Toronto Press, 2003.

Chakrabarty, Dipesh. *Habitations of Modernity: Essays in the Wake of Subaltern Studies*. Chicago: University of Chicago Press, 2002.

Cheah, Pheng, and Bruce Robbins, eds. *Cosmopolitics: Thinking and Feeling beyond the Nation*. Minneapolis: University of Minnesota Press, 1998.

Cheng, Anne Anlin. *Second Skin: Josephine Baker and the Modern Surface*. New York: Oxford University Press, 2013.

Chivers, Sally, and Nicole Markotić, eds. *The Problem Body: Projecting Disability on Film*. Columbus: Ohio State University Press, 2010.

Clark, T. J., and Anne M. Wagner. *Lowry and the Painting of Modern Life*. New York: Tate, 2014.

Classen, Constance. *The Deepest Sense: A Cultural History of Touch*. Urbana: University of Illinois Press, 2012.

Cockayne, Emily. *Hubbub: Filth, Noise, and Stench in England, 1600–1770*. New Haven, CT: Yale University Press, 2021.

Cohen, Lizabeth. *Making a New Deal: Industrial Workers in Chicago, 1919–1939*. 2nd ed. New York: Cambridge University Press, 2008.

Cohen, William A. *Embodied: Victorian Literature and the Senses*. Minneapolis: University of Minnesota Press, 2009.

Colomina, Beatriz. *Privacy and Publicity: Modern Architecture as Mass Media*. Cambridge, MA: MIT Press, 1996.

———. *X-Ray Architecture*. Zürich: Lars Müller, 2019.

Colomina, Beatriz, and Mark Wigley. *Are We Human? Notes on an Archaeology of Design*. Zürich: Lars Müller, 2016.

Conway, Hazel, and Rowan Roenisch. *Understanding Architecture: An Introduction to Architecture and Architectural History*. 2nd ed. New York: Routledge, 2005.

Cook, Matt. *London and the Culture of Homosexuality, 1885–1914*. New York: Cambridge University Press, 2003.

Copeland, Roger. *Merce Cunningham: The Modernizing of Modern Dance*. New York: Routledge, 2004.

Corbin, Alain. *The Foul and the Fragrant: Odor and the French Social Imagination*. Cambridge, MA: Harvard University Press, 1986.

Costanza-Chock, Sasha. *Design Justice: Community-Led Practices to Build the Worlds We Need*. Cambridge, MA: MIT Press, 2020.

Crary, Jonathan. *Suspensions of Perception: Attention, Spectacle, and Modern Culture*. Cambridge, MA: MIT Press, 1999.

———. *Techniques of the Observer: On Vision and Modernity in the Nineteenth Century*. Cambridge, MA: MIT Press, 1990.

Crawford, Lucas. *Transgender Architectonics: The Shape of Change in Modernist Space*. New York: Routledge, 2016.

Crinson, Mark. "Architecture and 'National Projection' between the Wars." In *Cultural Identities and the Aesthetics of Britishness*, edited by Dana Arnold. Manchester: Manchester University Press, 2004.

Crosby, Christina. *A Body, Undone: Living On after Great Pain*. New York: New York University Press, 2017.

Cupers, Kenny, ed. *Use Matters: An Alternative History of Architecture*. New York: Routledge, 2013.

Curtis, William J. R. *Modern Architecture since 1900*. 3rd ed. London: Phaidon, 1996.

Dagdelen Ast, Gunduz. *Architectural Barriers and the Handicapped: An Urban Center Case Study*. Chicago: Rehabilitation Institute of Chicago, 1976.

Danius, Sara. *The Senses of Modernism: Technology, Perception, and Aesthetics*. Ithaca, NY: Cornell University Press, 2002.

Darke, Paul Anthony. "The Changing Face of Representations of Disability in the Media (1993)." In *Disabling Barriers: Enabling Environments*, edited by John Swain, Sally French, Colin Barnes, and Carol Thomas. 2nd ed. London: SAGE Publications, 2004.

Davidson, Michael. *Distressing Language: Disability and the Poetics of Error*. New York: New York University Press, 2022.

———. *Invalid Modernism: Disability and the Missing Body of the Aesthetic*. New York: Oxford University Press, 2019.

Davis, Lennard J., ed. *The Disability Studies Reader*. 5th ed. New York: Routledge, Taylor & Francis Group, 2017.

———. *The End of Normal: Identity in a Biocultural Era*. Ann Arbor: University of Michigan Press, 2013.

Day, Joe. *Corrections and Collections: Architectures for Art and Crime*. New York: Routledge, 2013.

De Certeau, Michel. "The Black Sun of Language: Foucault" (1973). In *Heterologies:*

Discourse on the Other, translated by Brian Massumi. Minneapolis: University of Minnesota Press, 1986.

———. "Walking in the City (1984)." In *Beyond the Body Proper: Reading the Anthropology of Material Life*, edited by Margaret M. Lock and Judith Farquhar. Durham, NC: Duke University Press, 2007.

Dennett, Andrea Stulman. *Weird and Wonderful: The Dime Museum in America*. New York: NYU Press, 1997.

Dennis, Richard. *Cities in Modernity: Representations and Productions of Metropolitan Space, 1840–1930*. New York: Cambridge University Press, 2008.

Derrida, Jacques. "No (Point of) Madness—Maintaining Architecture" (1986). In *Psyche: Inventions of the Other*, edited by Peggy Kamuf and Elizabeth G. Rottenberg. Stanford: Stanford University Press, 2008.

Deslandes, Paul R. *Oxbridge Men: British Masculinity and the Undergraduate Experience, 1850–1920*. Bloomington: Indiana University Press, 2005.

Devlieger, Patrick, Frank Renders, Hubert Froyen, and Kristel Wildiers, eds. *Blindness and the Multi-Sensorial City*. Antwerp: Garant, 2006.

Diffrient, Niels, Alvin R. Tilley, and Joan C. Bardagjy. *Humanscale 1/2/3*. Cambridge, MA: MIT Press, 1974.

"Disorienting Phenomenology." *Log* 42 (2018).

Doane, Mary Ann. *The Emergence of Cinematic Time: Modernity, Contingency, the Archive*. Cambridge, MA: Harvard University Press, 2002.

Dolmage, Jay. *Academic Ableism: Disability and Higher Education*. Ann Arbor: University of Michigan Press, 2017.

Dovey, Kim. *Becoming Places: Urbanism/Architecture/Identity/Power*. New York: Routledge, 2010.

———. *Framing Places: Mediating Power in Built Form*. 2nd ed. 1999. Reprint, London: Routledge, 2008.

———. "The Silent Complicity of Architecture." In *Habitus: A Sense of Place*, edited by Emma Rooksby and Jean Hillier. 2nd ed. London: Routledge, 2005.

Driver, Felix. *Power and Pauperism: The Workhouse System, 1834–1884*. New York: Cambridge University Press, 1993.

Dubin, Steven C. *Displays of Power: Memory and Amnesia in the American Museum*. New York: NYU Press, 1999.

Duncan, Carol. *Civilizing Rituals: Inside Public Art Museums*. New York: Routledge, 1995.

Ebersberger, Eva, Daniela Zyman, and Thyssen-Bornemisza Art Contemporary, eds. *Jorge Otero-Pailos: The Ethics of Dust*. Vienna: Walther König, 2009.

Egan, Kieran. *Getting It Wrong from the Beginning: Our Progressivist Inheritance from Herbert Spencer, John Dewey and Jean Piaget*. New Haven, CT: Yale University Press, 2004.

The Elephant Man. Feature film. Paramount Pictures, 1980.

Ellis, Katie, Rosemarie Garland-Thomson, Mike Kent, and Rachel Robertson, eds. *Interdisciplinary Approaches to Disability: Looking towards the Future*. New York: Routledge, 2019.

Ellis, Russell, and Dana Cuff, eds. *Architects' People*. New York: Oxford University Press, 1989.

Emmons, Paul, John Shannon Hendrix, and Jane Lomholt, eds. *The Cultural Role of Architecture: Contemporary and Historical Perspectives*. London: Routledge, 2012.

Eriksson, Yvonne. *Tactile Pictures: Pictorial Representations for the Blind, 1784–1940*. Gothenburg, Sweden: Acta Universitatis Gothoburgensis, 1998.

Esperdy, Gabrielle M. *Modernizing Main Street: Architecture and Consumer Culture in the New Deal*. Chicago: University of Chicago Press, 2008.

Faherty, Duncan. *Remodeling the Nation: The Architecture of American Identity, 1776–1858*. Durham: University of New Hampshire Press, 2009.

Findlay, James A., and Margaret Bing. *The WPA: An Exhibition of Works Progress Administration (WPA) Literature and Art from the Collections of the Bienes Center for the Literary Arts*. Fort Lauderdale, FL: Bienes Center, 1998.

Findlay, James A., and Lillian Perricone. *WPA Museum Extension Project, 1935–1943: Government Created Visual Aids for Children from the Collections of the Bienes Museum of the Modern Book*. Fort Lauderdale, FL: Bienes Museum of the Modern Book, 2009.

Fishman, William J. *East End 1888*. 1893. Reprint, Nottingham, UK: Five Leaves Publishing, 2005.

Fiss, Karen. *Grand Illusion: The Third Reich, the Paris Exposition, and the Cultural Seduction of France*. Chicago: University of Chicago Press, 2010.

Flanders, Judith. *Inside the Victorian Home: A Portrait of Domestic Life in Victorian England*. New York: W. W. Norton, 2003.

Fletcher, Geoffrey, and Dan Cruickshank. *The London Nobody Knows*. 1962. Reprint, Stroud, UK: History Press, 2011.

Fraiman, Susan. *Extreme Domesticity: A View from the Margins*. New York: Columbia University Press, 2017.

Frampton, Kenneth. *Modern Architecture: A Critical History*. 4th ed. 1980. Reprint, New York: Thames & Hudson, 2007.

Franck, Karen A., and R. Bianca Lepori. *Architecture from the Inside Out: From the Body, the Senses, the Site and the Community*. 2nd ed. Chichester: Wiley-Academy, 2007.

Frawley, Maria H. *Invalidism and Identity in Nineteenth-Century Britain*. Chicago: University of Chicago Press, 2010.

Freedman, Russell. *Martha Graham: A Dancer's Life*. New York: Houghton Mifflin Harcourt, 1998.

Friedberg, Anne. *Window Shopping: Cinema and the Postmodern*. Berkeley: University of California Press, 1994.

Frost, Samantha. *Biocultural Creatures: Toward a New Theory of the Human*. Durham, NC: Duke University Press, 2018.

Früchtl, Josef. *The Impertinent Self: A Heroic History of Modernity*. Translated by Sarah L. Kirkby. Stanford: Stanford University Press, 2009.

Fry, Tony. *Design as Politics*. New York: Berg, 2010.

Fumerton, Patricia. *Unsettled: The Culture of Mobility and the Working Poor in Early Modern England*. Chicago: University of Chicago Press, 2006.

Fuss, Diana. *The Sense of an Interior: Four Rooms and the Writers That Shaped Them*. New York: Routledge, 2004.

Gagnier, Regenia. *Individualism, Decadence and Globalization: On the Relationship of Part to Whole, 1859–1920*. New York: Palgrave Macmillan, 2010.

———. *Subjectivities: A History of Self-Representation in Britain, 1832–1920*. New York: Oxford University Press, 1991.

Gane, Nicholas. *The Future of Social Theory*. New York: Continuum, 2004.

Garb, Tamar. *Bodies of Modernity: Figure and Flesh in Fin-de-Siècle France*. New York: Thames & Hudson, 1998.

Garrington, Abbie. *Haptic Modernism: Touch and the Tactile in Modernist Writing*. Edinburgh: Edinburgh University Press, 2013.

Gay, Peter. *Modernism: The Lure of Heresy*. New York: W. W. Norton, 2010.

Gere, Cathy. *Pain, Pleasure, and the Greater Good: From the Panopticon to the Skinner Box and Beyond*. Chicago: University of Chicago Press, 2017.

Gibson, James Jerome. *The Senses Considered as Perceptual Systems*. New York: Bloomsbury Academic, 1966.

Giedion, Sigfried. *Space, Time and Architecture: The Growth of a New Tradition*. 5th ed., revised and enlarged. Cambridge, MA: Harvard University Press, 2009.

Giffney, Noreen, and Myra Hird, eds. *Queering the Non/Human*. 2008. Reprint, New York: Routledge, 2016.

Gilbert, Pamela K. *Mapping the Victorian Social Body*. Albany: State University of New York Press, 2004.

Gins, Madeline. *Helen Keller or Arakawa*. Oakland, CA: Burning Books, 1994.

Gins, Madeline, and Arakawa. *Architecture: Sites of Reversible Destiny—Architectural Experiments after Auschwitz-Hiroshima*. London: Academy Editions, 1994.

Gissen, David. *The Architecture of Disability: Buildings, Cities, and Landscapes beyond Access*. Minneapolis: University of Minnesota Press, 2022.

———. *Subnature: Architecture's Other Environments*. New York: Princeton Architectural Press, 2009.

Gitelman, Lisa, and Geoffrey B. Pingree. "Introduction: What's New about New Media?" In *New Media, 1740–1915*. Cambridge, MA: MIT Press, 2004.

Glinert, Ed. *East End Chronicles*. London: Penguin, 2006.

Gökçiğdem, Elif M. *Designing for Empathy: Perspectives on the Museum Experience*. Lanham, MD: American Alliance of Museums (AAM) and Rowman & Littlefield, 2019.

Goldhagen, Sarah Williams, and Réjean Legault, eds. *Anxious Modernisms: Experimentation in Postwar Architectural Culture*. Cambridge, MA: MIT Press, 2000.

Goldsmith, Selwyn. *Designing for the Disabled: The New Paradigm*. 1963. Reprint, Oxford: Architectural Press, 1997.

Gordon, Avery. *Ghostly Matters: Haunting and the Sociological Imagination*. Minneapolis: University of Minnesota Press, 2008.

Gordon, Tammy S. *Private History in Public: Exhibition and the Settings of Everyday Life*. Lanham, MD: Rowman & Littlefield, 2010.

Gorman-Murray, Andrew, and Matt Cook, eds. *Queering the Interior*. London: Routledge, 2020.

Graham, Peter W., and Fritz H. Oehlschlaeger. *Articulating the Elephant Man: Joseph Merrick and His Interpreters*. Baltimore: Johns Hopkins University Press, 1992.

Grieve, Victoria. *The Federal Art Project and the Creation of Middlebrow Culture*. Urbana: University of Illinois Press, 2009.

Griffin, Roger. *Modernism and Fascism: The Sense of a Beginning under Mussolini and Hitler*. Basingstoke: Palgrave Macmillan, 2007.

Gringeri-Brown, Michelle. *Atomic Ranch: Midcentury Interiors*. Layton, UT: Gibbs Smith, 2012.

Grospierre, Nicolas. *Modern Forms: A Subjective Atlas of 20th-Century Architecture*. Edited by Alona Pardo and Elias Redstone. Munich: Prestel, 2018.

Guffey, Elizabeth. *Designing Disability: Symbols, Space and Society*. New York: Bloomsbury Academic, 2017.

———, ed. *After Universal Design: The Disability Design Revolution*. London: Bloomsbury Visual Arts, 2023.

Gunn, Simon. *The Public Culture of the Victorian Middle Class: Ritual and Authority in the English Industrial City 1840–1914*. Manchester: Manchester University Press, 2008.

Gunn, Simon, and James Vernon, eds. *The Peculiarities of Liberal Modernity in Imperial Britain*. Berkeley: University of California Press, 2011.

Hamraie, Aimi. *Building Access: Universal Design and the Politics of Disability*. Minneapolis: University of Minnesota Press, 2017.

———. "Mapping Access: Digital Humanities, Disability Justice, and Sociospatial Practice." *American Quarterly* 70, no. 3 (2018): 455–82.

Harkness, Sarah P., and James N. Groom. *Building without Barriers for the Disabled*. New York: Watson-Guptill Publications for Whitney Library of Design, 1976.

Harris, Jonathan. *Federal Art and National Culture: The Politics of Identity in New Deal America*. New York: Cambridge University Press, 1995.

Harrity, Richard, and Ralph G. Martin. *The Three Lives of Helen Keller*. New York: Doubleday, 1962.

Harvard Architecture Review. "Beyond the Modern Movement, Editorial." In *Rehabilitation: The Legacy of the Modern Movement*, edited by Dirk Snauwaert, Christophe Van Gerrewey, and Elena Filipovic. 1980. Reprint, Wiels and MER Paper Kunsthalle, 2010.

Harvey, Elizabeth D., ed. *Sensible Flesh: On Touch in Early Modern Culture*. Philadelphia: University of Pennsylvania Press, 2003.

Hawes, Joseph M., and N. Ray Hiner, eds. *American Childhood: A Research Guide and Historical Handbook*. Westport, CT: Greenwood Press, 1985.

———, eds. *Children between the Wars: American Childhood 1920–1940*. New York: Twayne, 1997.

Hawkins, Hildi, and Danielle Olsen, eds. *The Phantom Museum and Henry Wellcome's Collection of Medical Curiosities*. London: Profile, 2003.

Hays, K. Michael. *Architecture's Desire: Reading the Late Avant-Garde*. Cambridge, MA: MIT Press, 2010.

Heller-Roazen, Daniel. *The Inner Touch: Archaeology of a Sensation*. New York: Zone Books, 2007.

Hendren, Sara. *What Can a Body Do? How We Meet the Built World*. New York: Riverhead Books, 2020.

Henshaw, Victoria. *Urban Smellscapes: Understanding and Designing City Smell Environments*. New York: Routledge, 2014.

Herman, Bernard L. *Town House: Architecture and Material Life in the Early American City, 1780–1830*. Chapel Hill: Omohundro Institute of Early American History and Culture and University of North Carolina Press, 2005.

Herrmann, Dorothy. *Helen Keller: A Life*. Chicago: University of Chicago Press, 1999.

Hetherington, Kevin. *Capitalism's Eye: Cultural Spaces of the Commodity*. New York: Routledge, 2007.

Heumann, Judith E. *Being Heumann: An Unrepentant Memoir of a Disability Rights Activist*. Boston: Beacon Press, 2020.

Heynen, Hilde. *Architecture and Modernity: A Critique*. Cambridge, MA: MIT Press, 1999.

Hill, John. *Sex, Class and Realism: British Cinema 1956–1963*. London: British Film Institute, 1986.

Hodder, Ian. *Entangled: An Archaeology of the Relationships between Humans and Things*. Malden, MA: Wiley-Blackwell, 2012.

Holmes, Kat. *Mismatch: How Inclusion Shapes Design*. Cambridge, MA: MIT Press, 2018.

Horton, James Oliver, and Lois E. Horton, eds. *Slavery and Public History: The Tough Stuff of American Memory*. Chapel Hill: University of North Carolina Press, 2009.

Houlbrook, Matt. *Queer London: Perils and Pleasures in the Sexual Metropolis, 1918–1957*. Chicago: University of Chicago Press, 2006.

Howell, Michael, and Peter Ford. *The True History of the Elephant Man*. London: Allison & Busby, 1980.

Howes, David. "Hyperaesthesia, or, The Sensual Logic of Late Capitalism." In *Empire of the Senses: The Sensual Culture Reader*, edited by David Howes. New York: Berg, 2005.

Hughes, R. O. *Civic Training*. Boston: Allyn & Bacon, 1946.

Huhtamo, Erkki, and Jussi Parikka, eds. *Media Archaeology: Approaches, Applications, and Implications*. Berkeley: University of California Press, 2011.

Huyssen, Andreas. *Miniature Metropolis: Literature in an Age of Photography and Film*. Cambridge, MA: Harvard University Press, 2015.

Imrie, Robert. *Accessible Housing: Quality, Disability and Design*. New York: Routledge, 2005.

———. "From Universal to Inclusive Design in the Built Environment (1993)." In *Disabling Barriers: Enabling Environments*, edited by John Swain, Sally French, Colin Barnes, and Carol Thomas. 2nd ed. London: SAGE Publications, 2004.

Imrie, Robert, and Eva Egermann. "Buildings That Fit Society." In *Transcultural Modernisms*, edited by Model House Research Group. Berlin: Sternberg Press, 2013.

Jackson-Perry, David, Hannah Bertilsdotter Rosqvist, Marianthi Kourti, and Jenn Layton Annable. "Sensory Stranger: Travels in Normate Sensory Worlds." In *Neurodiversity Studies: A New Critical Paradigm*, edited by Hanna Bertilsdotter Rosqvist, Nick Chown, and Anna Stenning. Abingdon: Routledge, 2020.

Jacobs, Frank. *Strange Maps: An Atlas of Cartographic Curiosities*. New York: Penguin, 2009.

Jaffe, Aaron. *The Way Things Go: An Essay on the Matter of Second Modernism*. Minneapolis: University of Minnesota Press, 2014.

Jameson, Fredric. *A Singular Modernity*. 2002. Reprint, London: Verso, 2012.

Jaskot, Paul B. *The Nazi Perpetrator: Postwar German Art and the Politics of the Right*. Minneapolis: University of Minnesota Press, 2012.

Jencks, Charles. "The Death of Modern Architecture." In *Rehabilitation: The Legacy of the Modern Movement*, edited by Dirk Snauwaert, Christophe Van Gerrewey, and Elena Filipovic. 1977. Reprint, Wiels and MER Paper Kunsthalle, 2010.

Jencks, Charles, and Karl Kropf, eds. *Theories and Manifestoes of Contemporary Architecture*. 2nd ed. Chichester: Wiley-Academy, 2006.

Joyce, Patrick. *The Rule of Freedom: Liberalism and the Modern City*. London: Verso, 2003.

Kallipoliti, Lydia. *The Architecture of Closed Worlds: Or, What Is the Power of Shit?* Zürich: Lars Müller, 2018.

Kaplan, Alice. *Dreaming in French: The Paris Years of Jacqueline Bouvier Kennedy, Susan Sontag, and Angela Davis*. Chicago: University of Chicago Press, 2012.

Karp, Ivan, Corinne A. Kratz, Lynn Szwaja, and Tomas Ybarra-Frausto, eds. *Museum Frictions: Public Cultures/Global Transformations*. Durham, NC: Duke University Press, 2006.

Karp, Ivan, and Steven D. Lavine, eds. *Exhibiting Cultures: The Poetics and Politics of Museum Display*. Washington, DC: Smithsonian Books, 1991.

Keller, Helen. *Helen Keller: Selected Writings*. Edited by Kim E. Nielsen. New York: New York University Press, 2005.

———. *Helen Keller's Journal*. London: Michael Joseph Ltd., 1938.

Kinchin, Juliet, Aidan O'Connor, and Tanya Harrod. *Century of the Child: Growing by Design, 1900–2000*. New York: Museum of Modern Art, 2012.

Kingwell, Mark. *Concrete Reveries: Consciousness and the City*. New York: Viking, 2008.

Kleege, Georgina. *Blind Rage: Letters to Helen Keller*. Washington, DC: Gallaudet University Press, 2006.

———. *More Than Meets the Eye: What Blindness Brings to Art*. Oxford: Oxford University Press, 2017.

Kliment, Stephen A. "Into the Mainstream: A Syllabus for a Barrier-Free Environment." American Institute of Architects by the Rehabilitation Services Administration of the US Department of Health, Education, and Welfare, 1975.

Knoblauch, Joy. *The Architecture of Good Behavior: Psychology and Modern Institutional Design in Postwar America*. Pittsburgh: University of Pittsburgh Press, 2020.

Koestler, Frances A. *The Unseen Minority: A Social History of Blindness in America*. New York: D. McKay Co., 1976.

Koven, Seth. *Slumming: Sexual and Social Politics in Victorian London*. Princeton, NJ: Princeton University Press, 2006.

Krasner, James. *Home Bodies: Tactile Experience in Domestic Space*. Columbus: Ohio State University Press, 2010.

Lamster, Mark. *The Man in the Glass House: Philip Johnson, Architect of the Modern Century*. Boston: Little, Brown, 2018.

Laplantine, François. *The Life of the Senses: Introduction to a Modal Anthropology*. Translated by Jamie Furniss. New York: Routledge, 2020.

Latham, Alan, Derek McCormack, Kim McNamara, and Donald McNeill. *Key Concepts in Urban Geography*. London: SAGE Publications, 2009.

Latour, Bruno, ed. *Reset Modernity!* Cambridge, MA: MIT Press, 2016.

———. *We Have Never Been Modern*. Translated by Catherine Porter. Cambridge, MA: Harvard University Press, 1993.

Lay, Samantha. *British Social Realism: From Documentary to Brit Grit*. New York: Wallflower Press, 2019.

Lears, T. J. Jackson. *No Place of Grace: Antimodernism and the Transformation of American Culture, 1880–1920*. Chicago: University of Chicago Press, 1994.

Lefebvre, Henri. *Toward an Architecture of Enjoyment*. Edited by Lucasz Stanek. Translated by Robert Bononno. Minneapolis: University of Minnesota Press, 2014.

Leon, Warren, and Roy Rosenzweig, eds. *History Museums in the United States: A Critical Assessment*. Urbana: University of Illinois Press, 1989.

Leuchtenburg, William E. *Franklin D. Roosevelt and the New Deal: 1932–1940*. New York: Harper & Row, 1998.

Levenson, Michael H. *Modernism*. New Haven, CT: Yale University Press, 2011.

Levent, Nina, and Alvaro Pascual-Leone. *The Multisensory Museum: Cross-Disciplinary Perspectives on Touch, Sound, Smell, Memory, and Space.* Lanham, MD: Rowman & Littlefield, 2014.

Lichtenstein, Rachel. *On Brick Lane.* London: Hamish Hamilton, 2007.

Lifchez, Raymond. *Rethinking Architecture: Design Students and Physically Disabled People.* 1987. Reprint, Berkeley: University of California Press, 2022.

Lifchez, Raymond, and Barbara Winslow. *Design for Independent Living: The Environment and Physically Disabled People.* 1979. Reprint, Berkeley: University of California Press, 1981.

Looby, Christopher. "The Roots of the Orchis, the Iuli of Chesnuts: The Odor of Male Solitude." In *The Smell Culture Reader*, edited by Jim Drobnick. New York: Berg, 2006.

López-Durán, Fabiola. *Eugenics in the Garden: Transatlantic Architecture and the Crafting of Modernity.* Austin: University of Texas Press, 2018.

Love, Heather. *Feeling Backward: Loss and the Politics of Queer History.* Cambridge, MA: Harvard University Press, 2009.

Lowenstein, Otto. *The Senses.* London: Pelican Original/Penguin, 1966.

Ludington, Townsend, ed. *A Modern Mosaic: Art and Modernism in the United States.* Chapel Hill: University of North Carolina Press, 2000.

Luke, Timothy W. *Museum Politics: Power Plays at the Exhibition.* Minneapolis: University of Minnesota Press, 2002.

Lupton, Ellen. *Beautiful Users: Designing for People.* New York: Princeton Architectural Press in association with Cooper-Hewitt, Smithsonian Design Museum, 2014.

Lusseyran, Jacques. *Against the Pollution of the I: Selected Writings of Jacques Lusseyran.* Sandpoint, ID: Morning Light Press, 2006.

MacKian, Sara. "Touched by Spirit: Sensing the Material Impacts of Intangible Encounters." In *Touching Space, Placing Touch*, edited by Mark Paterson and Martin Dodge. London: Routledge, 2016.

Manning, Erin. *Politics of Touch: Sense, Movement, Sovereignty.* Minneapolis: University of Minnesota Press, 2007.

Markus, Thomas A. *Buildings and Power: Freedom and Control in the Origin of Modern Building Types.* New York: Routledge, 1993.

Marshall, Daniel, Kevin P. Murphy, and Zeb Tortorici, eds. "Queering Archives: Intimate Tracings." *Radical History Review* 15, no. 122 (May 2015).

Marshall, Kate. *Corridor: Media Architectures in American Fiction.* Minneapolis: University of Minnesota Press, 2013.

Mathews, Stanley. *From Agit Prop to Free Space: The Architecture of Cedric Price.* London: Black Dog Architecture, 2007.

McBrinn, Joseph. "Refashioning Disability: The Case of Painted Fabrics Ltd, 1915–1959." In *The Routledge Companion to Design Studies*, edited by Penny Sparke and Fiona Fisher. London: Routledge, 2016.

McElvaine, Robert S., ed. *Down and Out in the Great Depression: Letters from the Forgotten Man.* Chapel Hill: University of North Carolina Press, 1983.

McKinzie, Richard D. *The New Deal for Artists.* Princeton, NJ: Princeton University Press, 1973.

McRuer, Robert, and Merri Lisa Johnson. "Proliferating Cripistemologies: A Virtual Roundtable." *Journal of Literary & Cultural Disability Studies* 8, no. 2 (2014): 149–69.

Melosh, Barbara. *Engendering Culture: Manhood and Womanhood in New Deal Public Art and Theater*. Washington, DC: Smithsonian Institution Press, 1991.

Meringolo, Denise D. *Museums, Monuments, and National Parks: Toward a New Genealogy of Public History*. Amherst: University of Massachusetts Press, 2012.

Mertins, Detlef. *Modernity Unbound*. London: Architectural Association Publications, 2011.

Miller, Nory. "Fanciful and Functional." *Progressive Architecture*, April 1978.

Millett-Gallant, Ann. *The Disabled Body in Contemporary Art*. New York: Palgrave Macmillan, 2010.

The Miracle Worker. Feature film. United Artists, 1962.

Mirzoeff, Nicholas. *Bodyscape: Art, Modernity, and the Ideal Figure*. New York: Routledge, 1995.

Mitchell, David T., and Sharon L. Snyder. *The Biopolitics of Disability*. Ann Arbor: University of Michigan Press, 2015.

Mladenov, Teodor. *Critical Theory and Disability: A Phenomenological Approach*. London: Bloomsbury, 2016.

Model House Research Group, ed. *Transcultural Modernisms*. Berlin: Sternberg Press, 2013.

Mon Oncle. Feature film. Dir. Jacques Tati. 1958.

Montagu, Ashley. *The Elephant Man: A Study in Human Dignity*. 1971. Reprint, Lafayette, LA: Acadian House, 2001.

———. *Touching: The Human Significance of the Skin*. New York: William Morrow, 1986.

Morris, William. "Architecture and History (1884)." In *Art and Architecture: Essays 1870–1884*. Holicong, PA: Wildside Press, 2003.

———. "The Prospects of Architecture in Civilization (1881)." In *William Morris on Art and Socialism*, edited by Norman Kelvin. Mineola, NY: Dover, 1999.

Mount, Toni. *Everyday Life in Medieval London: From the Anglo-Saxons to the Tudors*. Gloucestershire: Amberley Publishing Ltd., 2014.

Mullin, Amy. *Reconceiving Pregnancy and Childcare: Ethics, Experience, and Reproductive Labor*. Cambridge: Cambridge University Press, 2005.

Murphy, Robert. *The British Cinema Book*. London: British Film Institute, 2005.

Neiswander, Judith A. *The Cosmopolitan Interior: Liberalism and the British Home 1870–1914*. New Haven, CT: Yale University Press for the Paul Mellon Centre for Studies in British Art, 2008.

Nelson, George. *Building a New Europe: Portraits of Modern Architects*. New Haven, CT: Yale University Press, 2007.

Nielsen, Kim E. *The Radical Lives of Helen Keller*. New York: New York University Press, 2004.

Nord, Philip G. *France's New Deal: From the Thirties to the Postwar Era*. Princeton, NJ: Princeton University Press, 2010.

Oberlander, H. Peter, and Eva M. Newbrun. *Houser: The Life and Work of Catherine Bauer, 1905–64*. 1999. Reprint, Vancouver: University of British Columbia Press, 2000.

O'Brien, Ruth. *Bodies in Revolt: Gender, Disability, and a Workplace Ethic of Care*. New York: Routledge, 2005.

O'Connor, Erin. *Raw Material: Producing Pathology in Victorian Culture*. Durham, NC: Duke University Press, 2000.

Ogborn, Miles. *Spaces of Modernity: London's Geographies, 1680–1780*. New York: Guilford Press, 1998.

O'Rourke, Kathryn E. *Modern Architecture in Mexico City: History, Representation, and the Shaping of a Capital*. Pittsburgh: University of Pittsburgh Press, 2016.

O'Toole, Tina. "The New Woman Flaneuse or Streetwalker." In *Reconnecting Aestheticism and Modernism: Continuities, Revisions, Speculations*, edited by Bénédicte Coste, Catherine Delyfer, and Christine Reynier. New York: Routledge, 2016.

Otter, Chris. *The Victorian Eye: A Political History of Light and Vision in Britain, 1800–1910*. Chicago: University of Chicago Press, 2008.

Ovenden, Mark. *Paris Underground: The Maps, Stations, and Design of the Metro*. Edited by Julian Pepinster and Peter B. Lloyd. 2nd ed. New York: Penguin, 2009.

Pallasmaa, Juhani. *The Eyes of the Skin: Architecture and the Senses*. 3rd ed. 1996. Reprint, Chichester: Wiley, 2012.

Panero, Julius, and Martin Zelnik. *Human Dimension and Interior Space: A Source Book of Design Reference Standards*. New York: Whitney Library of Design, 1979.

Parikka, Jussi. *What Is Media Archaeology?* Cambridge: Polity Press, 2012.

Paterson, Mark. *The Senses of Touch: Haptics, Affects, and Technologies*. New York: Berg, 2007.

Patten, Robert. "From House to Square to Street: Narrative Traversals." In *Nineteenth-Century Geographies: The Transformation of Space from the Victorian Age to the American Century*, edited by Helena Michie and Ronald R. Thomas. New Brunswick, NJ: Rutgers University Press, 2003.

Pearlman, Jill E. *Inventing American Modernism: Joseph Hudnut, Walter Gropius, and the Bauhaus Legacy at Harvard*. Charlottesville: University of Virginia Press, 2007.

Pearse, Innes Hope, and Lucy H. Crocker. *The Peckham Experiment: A Study of the Living Structure of Society*. 1943. Reprint, Abingdon: Routledge, 2007.

Penner, Barbara. "From Ergonomics to Empathy: Herman Miller and MetaForm." In *The Routledge Companion to Design Studies*, edited by Penny Sparke and Fiona Fisher. New York: Routledge, Taylor & Francis Group, 2016.

Pérez, David M. Callejo, Steve Fain, and Judith J. Slater, eds. *Pedagogy of Place: Seeing Space as Cultural Education*. New York: Peter Lang Inc., International Academic Publishers, 2003.

Phillips, Ruth B. "Performing the Native Woman: Primitivism and Mimicry in Early Twentieth-Century Visual Culture." In *Antimodernism and Artistic Experience: Policing the Boundaries of Modernity*, edited by Lynda Jesseup. Toronto: University of Toronto Press, 2001.

Phillips, Sarah D. *Disability and Mobile Citizenship in Postsocialist Ukraine*. Bloomington: Indiana University Press, 2010.

Pile, Steve. *The Body and the City: Psychoanalysis, Space, and Subjectivity*. New York: Routledge, 1996.

Pink, Sarah. *Doing Sensory Ethnography*. 2nd ed. London: SAGE Publications, 2015.

———. *The Future of Visual Anthropology: Engaging the Senses*. New York: Routledge, 2006.

———. *Home Truths: Gender, Domestic Objects and Everyday Life*. Abingdon: Routledge, 2004.

Platt, Lucinda. "Exploring Social Spaces of Muslims." In *Muslims in Britain: Making Social and Political Space*, edited by W. I. U. Ahmad and Ziauddin Sardar. New York: Routledge, 2012.

Poirier, Agnès. *Left Bank: Art, Passion, and the Rebirth of Paris, 1940–50*. New York: Henry Holt, 2018.

Potvin, John. *Bachelors of a Different Sort: Queer Aesthetics, Material Culture and the Modern Interior in Britain*. Manchester: Manchester University Press, 2015.

Program for Bernard Pomerance's "The Elephant Man." Theater of St. Peter's Church, New York, January 1979.

Rabinowitz, Paula. "Social Representations within American Modernism." In *The Cambridge Companion to American Modernism*, edited by Walter B. Kalaidjian. New York: Cambridge University Press, 2005.

Raizman, David. *History of Modern Design: Graphics and Products since the Industrial Revolution*. London: Laurence King Publishing, 2003.

Rand, Erica. *The Ellis Island Snow Globe*. Durham, NC: Duke University Press, 2005.

Reed, Peter. *Alvar Aalto: Between Humanism and Materialism*. New York: Museum of Modern Art, 1998.

Reisley, Roland. *Usonia, New York: Building a Community with Frank Lloyd Wright*. New York: Princeton Architectural Press, 2001.

Rice, Charles. *The Emergence of the Interior: Architecture, Modernity, Domesticity*. London: Routledge, 2007.

———. "'So the Flâneur Goes for a Walk in His Room': Interior, Arcade, Cinema, Metropolis." In *Intimate Metropolis: Urban Subjects in the Modern City*, edited by Vittoria Di Palma, Diana Periton, and Marina Lathouri. New York: Routledge, 2009.

Rice, Mary Kellogg. *Useful Work for Unskilled Women: A Unique Milwaukee WPA Project*. Milwaukee, WI: Milwaukee County Historical Society, 2003.

Richter, Amy G., ed. *At Home in Nineteenth-Century America: A Documentary History*. New York: New York University Press, 2015.

Riley, Denise. *Impersonal Passion: Language as Affect*. Durham, NC: Duke University Press, 2005.

Roberts, Perri Lee. *Modern Living: Gio Ponti and the Twentieth-Century Aesthetics of Design*. Athens, GA: Georgia Museum of Art, University of Georgia, 2017.

Rodaway, Paul. *Sensuous Geographies: Body, Sense and Place*. New York: Routledge, 1994.

Rodgers, Daniel T. *Age of Fracture*. Cambridge, MA.: Harvard University Press, 2012.

———. *Atlantic Crossings: Social Politics in a Progressive Age*. Cambridge, MA: Belknap Press of Harvard University Press, 2000.

Rose, Sarah F. *No Right to Be Idle: The Invention of Disability, 1840s–1930s*. Chapel Hill: University of North Carolina Press, 2017.

Rosenfeld, Gavriel David. *Building after Auschwitz: Jewish Architecture and the Memory of the Holocaust*. New Haven, CT: Yale University Press, 2011.

Ross, Ellen, ed. *Slum Travelers: Ladies and London Poverty, 1860–1920*. Berkeley: University of California Press, 2007.

Rottman, André. "Reflexive Systems of Reference: Approximations to 'Referentialism' in Contemporary Art." In *Rehabilitation: The Legacy of the Modern Movement*, edited by Dirk Snauwaert, Christophe Van Gerrewey, and Elena Filipovic. 2008. Reprint, Wiels and MER Paper Kunsthalle, 2010.

Rowe, Colin. "Introduction to Five Architects." In *Rehabilitation: The Legacy of the Modern Movement*, edited by Dirk Snauwaert, Christophe Van Gerrewey, and Elena Filipovic. 1975. Reprint, Wiels and MER Paper Kunsthalle, 2010.

Rubenhold, Hallie. *The Five: The Untold Lives of the Women Killed by Jack the Ripper*. Boston: Houghton Mifflin Harcourt, 2019.

Rule, Fiona. *The Worst Street in London*. 2008. Reprint, Gloucestershire: History Press, 2018.

Rusk, Howard A., and Eugene J. Taylor, eds. *Living with a Disability*. New York: Blakiston Company, 1953.

Russell, Marta. *Beyond Ramps: Disability at the End of the Social Contract*. Monroe, ME: Common Courage Press, 1998.

Sanchez, Rebecca. *Deafening Modernism: Embodied Language and Visual Poetics in American Literature*. New York: New York University Press, 2015.

Sandell, Richard. *Museums, Prejudice, and the Reframing of Difference*. London: Routledge, 2007.

Sandell, Richard, Jocelyn Dodd, and Rosemarie Garland-Thomson, eds. *Re-Presenting Disability: Activism and Agency in the Museum*. London: Routledge, 2010.

Sapio, Joseph De. *Modernity and Meaning in Victorian London: Tourist Views of the Imperial Capital*. New York: Palgrave Macmillan, 2014.

Scales, Rebecca P. *Radio and the Politics of Sound in Interwar France, 1921–1939*. New York: Cambridge University Press, 2016.

Scandura, Jani. *Down in the Dumps: Place, Modernity, American Depression*. Durham, NC: Duke University Press, 2008.

Scandura, Jani, and Michael Thurston, eds. *Modernism, Inc.: Body, Memory, Capital*. New York: New York University Press, 2001.

Schillmeier, Michael. *Rethinking Disability: Bodies, Senses, and Things*. New York: Routledge, Taylor & Francis Group, 2012.

Schillmeier, Michael W. J., and Miquel Domenech, eds. *New Technologies and Emerging Spaces of Care*. Surrey: Ashgate, 2010.

Schivelbusch, Wolfgang. *Three New Deals. Reflections on Roosevelt's America, Mussolini's Italy, and Hitler's Germany, 1933–1939*. New York: Picador, 2006.

Schwartz, Vanessa R. *Spectacular Realities: Early Mass Culture in Fin-de-Siècle Paris*. Berkeley: University of California Press, 2001.

Schwenger, Peter. *The Tears of Things: Melancholy and Physical Objects*. Minneapolis: University of Minnesota Press, 2006.

Scully, Vincent. *Modern Architecture and Other Essays*. Edited by Neil Levine. Princeton, NJ: Princeton University Press, 2005.

Sedgwick, Eve Kosofsky. *Between Men*. New York: Columbia University Press, 1986.

———. *Touching Feeling: Affect, Pedagogy, Performativity*. Durham, NC: Duke University Press, 2003.

Sedgwick, Eve Kosofsky, and Adam Frank, eds. *Shame and Its Sisters: A Silvan Tomkins Reader*. Durham, NC: Duke University Press, 1995.

Seremetakis, Constantina Nadia, ed. *The Senses Still: Perception and Memory as Material Culture in Modernity*. Chicago: University of Chicago Press, 1996.

Serlin, David. "Banking on Postmodernism: Saving Stanley Tigerman's Illinois Library for the Blind and Physically Handicapped (1978)." *Future Anterior* 16, no. 1 (Summer 2019): 86–108.

———. "Constructing Autonomy: Smart Homes for Disabled Veterans and the Politics of Normative Citizenship." *Critical Military Studies* 1, no. 1 (February 2015): 38–46.

———. "Disabling the *Flâneur*." *Journal of Visual Culture* 5, no. 2 (2006): 193–208.

———. "On Walkers and Wheelchairs: Disabling the Narratives of Urban Modernity." *Radical History Review* 114 (Fall 2012): 19–28.

———. "Pissing Without Pity: Disability, Gender, and the Public Toilet." In *Toilet: Public Restrooms and the Politics of Sharing,* edited by Harvey Molotch and Laura Norén (New York: New York University Press, 2010), 167–85.

Severs, Dennis. *18 Folgate Street: The Tale of a House in Spitalfields.* New York: Vintage, 2002.

Sharr, Adam, ed. *Reading Architecture and Culture: Researching Buildings, Spaces, and Documents.* New York: Routledge, 2012.

Short, C. W., and R. Stanley-Brown. *Public Buildings: Architecture under the Public Works Administration, 1933–39.* New York: Da Capo Press, 1986.

Siebers, Tobin. *Disability Aesthetics.* Ann Arbor: University of Michigan Press, 2010.

Sitton, Jeanette, and Mae Siu-Wai Stroshane. *Measured by Soul: The Life of Joseph Carey Merrick (Also Known as 'The Elephant Man').* Self-published, Lulu.com, 2012.

Smith, Andrew. *Victorian Demons: Medicine, Masculinity, and the Gothic at the Fin-de-Siècle.* Manchester: Manchester University Press, 2004.

Smith, Mark M. *Sensing the Past: Seeing, Hearing, Smelling, Tasting, and Touching in History.* Berkeley: University of California Press, 2008.

Snauwaert, Dirk, Christophe Van Gerrewey, and Elena Filipovic, eds. *Rehabilitation: The Legacy of the Modern Movement.* Wiels and MER Paper Kunsthalle, 2010.

Soane, John. "Lecture V: From the Royal Academy Lectures on Architecture" (1813). In *Architecture and Design in Europe and America, 1750–2000,* edited by Abigail Harrison-Moore and Dorothy Rowe. Malden, MA: Blackwell, 2006.

Spieker, Sven. *The Big Archive: Art from Bureaucracy.* Cambridge, MA: MIT Press, 2008.

Spurr, David. *Architecture and Modern Literature.* Ann Arbor: University of Michigan Press, 2012.

Stallybrass, Peter, and Allon White. "Bourgeois Perception." In *The Book of Touch,* edited by Constance Classen. New York: Berg, 2005.

———. "The City: The Sewer, the Gaze, and the Contaminating Touch (1986)." In *Beyond the Body Proper: Reading the Anthropology of Material Life,* edited by Margaret M. Lock and Judith Farquhar. Durham, NC: Duke University Press, 2007.

Stanley, Adam C. *Modernizing Tradition: Gender and Consumerism in Interwar France and Germany.* Baton Rouge: Louisiana State University Press, 2008.

Sterne, Jonathan. *The Audible Past: Cultural Origins of Sound Reproduction.* Durham, NC: Duke University Press, 2003.

Stevenson, Christine. *Medicine and Magnificence: British Hospital and Asylum Architecture, 1660–1815.* New Haven, CT: Yale University Press, 2000.

Stewart, John. "Housing and Independent Living (1993)." In *Disabling Barriers: Enabling Environments,* edited by John Swain, Sally French, Colin Barnes, and Carol Thomas. 2nd ed. London: SAGE Publications, 2004.

Stewart, Kathleen. *Ordinary Affects.* Durham, NC: Duke University Press, 2007.

Stewart, Susan. *The Ruins Lesson: Meaning and Material in Western Culture.* Chicago: University of Chicago Press, 2020.

Stoler, Ann Laura, ed. *Imperial Debris: On Ruins and Ruination.* Durham, NC: Duke University Press, 2013.

Stoller, Paul. *Sensuous Scholarship.* Philadelphia: University of Pennsylvania Press, 1997.

Sullivan, George. *Helen Keller: Her Life in Pictures*. New York: Scholastic Nonfiction, 2007.

Summerson, John. "Palladian Permeation: The Villa (1953)." In *Architecture and Design in Europe and America, 1750–2000*, edited by Abigail Harrison-Moore and Dorothy Rowe. Malden, MA: Blackwell, 2006.

Taussig, Michael. "Tactility and Distraction (1992)." In *Beyond the Body Proper: Reading the Anthropology of Material Life*, edited by Margaret M. Lock and Judith Farquhar. Durham, NC: Duke University Press, 2007.

Taylor, Charles. *Modern Social Imaginaries*. Durham, NC: Duke University Press, 2003.

Tester, Keith, ed. *The Flâneur*. New York: Routledge, 1994.

Thompson, Kate. "The Building of the Leicester Union Workhouse 1836–1839." In *The Adaptation of Change: Essays upon the History of Nineteenth-Century Leicester and Leicestershire*, edited by Daniel Williams. Leicester: Leicestershire Museums, 1980.

Thomson, John. *Victorian London Street Life in Historic Photographs*. New York: Dover, 1994.

Tigerman, Stanley. "Library for the Blind." *Design Quarterly* (1978).

———. "The Sinking of the Titanic. Letter to Mies." In *Rehabilitation: The Legacy of the Modern Movement*, edited by Dirk Snauwaert, Christophe Van Gerrewey, and Elena Filipovic. 1982. Reprint, Wiels and MER Paper Kunsthalle, 2010.

Titchkosky, Tanya. *The Question of Access: Disability, Space, Meaning*. Toronto: University of Toronto Press, 2011.

Tuan, Yi-Fu. "The Pleasures of Touch." In *The Book of Touch*, edited by Constance Classen. New York: Berg, 2005.

Turner, Fred. *The Democratic Surround: Multimedia and American Liberalism from World War II to the Psychedelic Sixties*. Chicago: University of Chicago Press, 2013.

Twin Cities GLBT Oral History Project (MN). *Queer Twin Cities*. Edited by Kevin P. Murphy, Jennifer L. Pierce, and Larry Knopp. Minneapolis: University of Minnesota Press, 2010.

Vadillo, Ana. "Poetics on the Line: The Effect of Mass Transport in Urban Culture." In *Nineteenth-Century Geographies: The Transformation of Space from the Victorian Age to the American Century*, edited by Helena Michie and Ronald R. Thomas. New Brunswick, NJ: Rutgers University Press, 2003.

Van P, Denis. *Joseph Carey Merrick*. Sandawe, 2015.

Verderber, Stephen, and David J. Fine. *Healthcare Architecture in an Era of Radical Transformation*. New Haven, CT: Yale University Press, 2000.

Vernon, James. *Distant Strangers: How Britain Became Modern*. Berkeley: University of California Press, 2014.

Vidler, Anthony. *Histories of the Immediate Present: Inventing Architectural Modernism*. Cambridge, MA: MIT Press, 2008.

———. *Warped Space: Art, Architecture, and Anxiety in Modern Culture*. Cambridge, MA: MIT Press, 2002.

Vigor-Mungovin, Joanne. *Joseph: The Life, Times and Places of the Elephant Man*. London: Mango Books, 2016.

Virdi, Jaipreet. *Hearing Happiness: Deafness Cures in History*. Chicago: University of Chicago Press, 2020.

"Visual Archives of Sex." *Radical History Review* 2022, no. 142 (January 1, 2022).

Volvey, Anne. "Field Work: How to Get In to Touch." In *Touching Space, Placing Touch*, edited by Mark Paterson and Martin Dodge. New York: Routledge, 2016.

Wailoo, Keith. *Pain: A Political History*. Baltimore: Johns Hopkins University Press, 2014.

Walkowitz, Rebecca L. *Cosmopolitan Style: Modernism beyond the Nation*. New York: Columbia University Press, 2006.

Wallach, Alan. *Exhibiting Contradiction: Essays on the Art Museum in the United States*. Amherst: University of Massachusetts Press, 1998.

Wallenstein, Sven-Olov. *Biopolitics and the Emergence of Modern Architecture*. New York: Buell Center / FORuM Project and Princeton Architectural Press, 2008.

Wallis, Brian, ed. *Art after Modernism*. Boston: David R. Godine, 1992.

Widenheim, Cecilia, and Eva Rudberg, eds. *Utopia and Reality: Modernity in Sweden 1900–1960*. New Haven, CT: Yale University Press, 2002.

Williams, Daniel, ed. *The Adaptation of Change: Essays upon the History of Nineteenth-Century Leicester and Leicestershire*. Leicester: Leicestershire Museums, 1980.

Williamson, Bess, and Elizabeth E. Guffey, eds. *Making Disability Modern: Design Histories*. London: Bloomsbury Visual Arts, 2020.

Wilson, Kristina. *Livable Modernism: Interior Decorating and Design during the Great Depression*. New Haven, CT: Yale University Press, in association with Yale University Art Gallery, 2004.

Wittich, John. *Discovering London Street Names*. 3rd ed. 1977. Reprint, London: Shire Publications, 1996.

Wolf-Meyer, Matthew J. *Unraveling: Remaking Personhood in a Neurodiverse Age*. Minneapolis: University of Minnesota Press, 2020.

Woolgar, C. M. *The Senses in Late Medieval England*. New Haven, CT: Yale University Press, 2006.

Wright, Alexa. *Monstrosity: The Human Monster in Visual Culture*. London: I. B. Tauris, 2013.

Yanni, Carla. *Nature's Museums: Victorian Science and the Architecture of Display*. New York: Princeton Architectural Press, 2005.

Zegher, M. Catherine de, and Mark Wigley, eds. *The Activist Drawing: Retracing Situationist Architectures from Constant's New Babylon to Beyond*. Cambridge, MA: MIT Press, 2001.

Zielinski, Siegfried. *Deep Time of the Media: Toward an Archaeology of Hearing and Seeing by Technical Means*. Cambridge, MA: MIT Press, 2006.

Index